Thinking Through the Past

A CRITICAL THINKING APPROACH TO U.S. HISTORY

VOLUME I: TO 1877

JOHN HOLLITZ

COMMUNITY COLLEGE OF SOUTHERN NEVADA

HOUGHTON MIFFLIN COMPANY   Boston   New York

Editor-in-Chief: Jean L. Woy
Associate Editor: Leah Strauss
Associate Project Editor: Heather Hubbard
Production/Design Coordinator: Jodi O'Rourke
Senior Manufacturing Coordinator: Sally Culler

Cover design: Sandra Burch, NYC.

Cover image: Division of Political History, National Museum of American History, Smithsonian Institution.

Printed in the U.S.A.

Library of Congress Catalog Card Number: 00-104719

ISBN: 0-618-04668-2

5 6 7 8 9-EB-04 03 02

CONTENTS

3

EVALUATING PRIMARY SOURCES: WAS PENNSYLVANIA "THE BEST POOR MAN'S COUNTRY?"

4

EVALUATING ONE HISTORIAN'S ARGUMENT: LOYALISTS AND THE MEANING OF THE REVOLUTION

5

MOTIVATION IN HISTORY: CHARLES BEARD AND THE FOUNDING FATHERS

6

IDEAS IN HISTORY: RACE IN JEFFERSON'S REPUBLIC   96

7

THE PROBLEM OF HISTORICAL CAUSATION:
THE SECOND GREAT AWAKENING   125

8

GRAND THEORY AND HISTORY: DEMOCRACY AND THE FRONTIER

11

THE EMERGENCE OF AN IDEOLOGY:
ANTISLAVERY AND THE BOUNDS OF WOMANHOOD   **229**

12

GRAND THEORY, GREAT BATTLES, AND HISTORICAL CAUSES: WHY SECESSION FAILED

13

THE IMPORTANCE OF HISTORICAL INTERPRETATION: THE MEANING OF RECONSTRUCTION

PREFACE

The encouraging response to the first edition from students and instructors has prompted me to create a second edition of *Thinking Through the Past*. As before, this book is inspired by the idea that interpretation is at the heart of history. That is why learning about the past involves more than mastering facts and dates, and why historians often disagree. As teachers, we know the limitations of the deadly dates-and-facts approach to the past. We also know that encouraging students to think critically about historical sources and historians' arguments is a good way to create excitement about history and to impart understanding of what historians do. The purpose of *Thinking Through the Past*, therefore, is to introduce students to the examination and analysis of historical sources.

FORMAT

To encourage students to think critically about American history, *Thinking Through the Past* brings together primary and secondary sources. It gives students the opportunity to analyze primary sources *and* historians' arguments, and to use one to understand and evaluate the other. By evaluating and drawing conclusions from the sources, students will use the methods and develop some of the skills of critical thinking as they apply to history. Students will also learn about a variety of historical topics that parallel those in U.S. history courses. Unlike most anthologies or collections of primary sources, this book advances not only chronologically, but pedagogically through different skill levels. It provides students the opportunity to work with primary sources in the early chapters before they evaluate secondary sources in later chapters or compare historians' arguments in the final chapters. Students are also able to build on the skills acquired in previous chapters by considering such questions as motivation, causation, and the role of ideas and economic interests in history.

At the same time, this book introduces a variety of approaches to the past. Topics in *Thinking Through the Past* include social, political, cultural, intellectual, economic, diplomatic, and military history. The chapters look at history "from the top down" and "from the bottom up." Thus students have the opportunity to evaluate history drawn from slave quarters as well as from state houses. In the process, they are exposed to the enormous range of sources that historians use to construct arguments. The primary sources in these volumes include portraits, photographs, maps, letters, fiction, music lyrics, laws, oral histories, speeches, movie posters, magazine and newspaper articles, cartoons, and architectural plans.

The chapters present the primary and secondary sources so students can pursue their own investigations of the material. Each chapter is divided into five parts: A brief introduction, which sets forth the problem in the chapter; the Setting, which provides background information pertaining to the topic; the Investigation, which asks students to answer a short set of questions revolving around the problem discussed in the introduction; the Sources, which in most chapters provide a secondary source and a set of primary sources related to the chapter's main problem, and, finally, a brief Conclusion, which offers a reminder of the chapter's main pedagogical goal and looks forward to the next chapter's problem.

CHANGES TO THE SECOND EDITION

In the second edition, there are entirely new chapters in both volumes on provocative topics that have been on the cutting edge of recent historical scholarship. These are topics that are intended to stimulate student interest in American history. In Volume I, the new chapters focus on the subjects of race and religion. The new Chapter 6 explores the issue of race in Jefferson's republic, and the new Chapter 7 presents the Second Great Awakening as a problem of historical causation. In Volume II, there are new chapters on Native Americans and on civil rights. The new Chapter 3 discusses the notion of "saving" the Indians in the late nineteenth century and the new Chapter 10 contemplates history and popular memory with respect to the civil rights movement. Overall, the volumes have been revised with an eye to making the book a more engaging learning tool. To this end, many other chapters contain new sources that provide additional insights for students as they conduct their historical investigations.

INSTRUCTOR'S RESOURCE MANUAL

The format of *Thinking Through the Past* is designed to be effective in various classroom situations. Students in large classes can work through this book with minimal instructor assistance. Yet the format also provides students in seminars, small classes, and discussion sections the opportunity to share with one another the excitement of thinking about the past. The Instructor's Resource Manual is designed to enhance the effectiveness of *Thinking Through the Past* in all these classroom settings. The manual contains discussion of the sources in each chapter and explanations of how they relate to the chapter's main problem and pedagogical goals. It also contains questions to stimulate classroom discussion and suggestions for evaluating students' learning.

ACKNOWLEDGMENTS

Many people contributed to this book. I want to thank my students, without whom it never would have been created.

I owe many thanks to the people who assisted in various ways with this edition. DeAnna Beachley and Michael Green, colleagues at the Community College of Southern Nevada, shared numerous insights, offered useful suggestions, and reviewed portions of the new material. I am grateful for their help. CCSN Interlibrary Loan librarian Marion Martin again provided cheerful and invaluable assistance. Jay Boggis copyedited the manuscript with a careful eye. At Houghton Mifflin, I'd like to thank Heather Hubbard and Colleen Shanley Kyle. Leah Strauss of Houghton Mifflin guided the revision process with useful suggestions, gentle prodding, and welcome humor. Her efforts made my labors more enjoyable and, no doubt, more fruitful. Finally, colleagues around the country offered valuable suggestions regarding revisions and chapter drafts. I am honored by their commitment to *Thinking Through the Past* and thank them for helping to make it a better book. The reviewers were: Lendol Calder, Augustana College; Gary Daynes, Brigham Young University; Marc Dollinger, Pasadena City College; Kim M. Gruenwald, Kent State University; Penelope Harper, Louisiana State University; Richard E. Herrmann, Dyersburg State Community College; Glenn J. Kist, Rochester Institute of Technology; Sean O'Neill, Grand Valley State University; Joseph P. Reidy, Howard University; James D. Rice, SUNY Plattsburgh; and Timothy N. Thurber, SUNY Oswego.

I owe thanks to many others as well for their contribution to the first edition. Richard Cooper and Brad Nystrom at California State University, Sacramento listened patiently to unformed ideas and offered helpful suggestions at the initial stages of this project. Alan Balboni, DeAnna Beachley, Gary Elliott, Michael Green, and Charles Okeke, colleagues at the Community College of Southern Nevada, offered sources, ideas, and encouragement. Marion Martin, Inter-Library Loan librarian at CCSN, provided unfailingly cheerful and efficient assistance. D. C. Heath editors James Miller and Pat Wakeley made many helpful suggestions. Susan Zorn of Houghton Mifflin copyedited the manuscript with extraordinary skill, while Jeffrey Greene and Carol Newman performed their editorial tasks with professionalism and good humor. Numerous colleagues around the country reviewed chapter drafts and offered insightful suggestions. They were very generous with their time, and their ideas were invaluable. The reviewers of the first edition were: Karen Blair, Central Washington University; Joan Chandler, University of Texas—Dallas; Myles Clowers, San Diego City College; Julian Del Gaudio, Long Beach City College; Ronald Faircloth, Abraham Baldwin Agricultural College; Gerald Ghelfi, Rancho Santiago College; David Godschalk, Shippensburg University; Robert Goldman, Virginia Union University; Nancy Isenberg, University of Northern Iowa; John Jameson, Kent State University; Benjamin Newcomb, Texas Technological University; Vince

Nobile, Chaffey Community College; Mario Perez, University of California—Riverside; Edward Pluth, St. Cloud State University; John Rector, Western Oregon State University; David Schmitz, Whitman College; Luther Spoehr, Lincoln School; Emily Teipe, Fullerton College; Stephen Weisner, Springfield Technical Community College; Marianne Wokeck, Indiana University—Purdue University at Indianapolis; Walter Weare, University of Wisconsin—Milwaukee; and Marli Weiner, University of Maine.

As ever, my biggest debt is to Patty for her enduring support and understanding. Once again, therefore, this book is dedicated to her.

J.H.

Thinking Through the Past

INTRODUCTION

"History," said Henry Ford, "is more or less bunk." That view is still shared by many people. Protests about the subject are familiar. Studying history won't help you land a job. And besides, what matters is not the past but the present.

Such protests are not necessarily wrong. Learning about ancient Greece, the French Revolution, or the Vietnam War will hardly guarantee employment, even though many employers evaluate job candidates on critical thinking skills that the study of history requires. Likewise, who can deny the importance of the present compared to the past? In many ways the present and future are more important than the past. Pericles, Robespierre, and Lyndon Johnson are dead; presumably, anyone reading this is not.

Still, the logic behind the history-as-bunk view is flawed because all of us rely upon the past to understand the present, as did even Henry Ford. Besides building the Model T, he also built Greenfield Village outside Detroit because he wanted to recreate a nineteenth-century town. It was the kind of place the automotive genius grew up in and the kind of place he believed represented the ideal American society: small-town, white, native-born, and Protestant. Greenfield Village was Ford's answer to changes in the early twentieth century that were profoundly disturbing to him and to many other Americans of his generation: growing cities, the influx of non-Protestant immigrants, changing sexual morality, new roles and new fashions for women, and greater freedom for young people.

Ford's interest in the past, symbolized by Greenfield Village, reflects a double irony. It was the automobile that helped to make possible many of the changes, like those in sexual morality, that Ford detested. The other irony is that Ford used history—what he himself called "bunk"—to try to better the world. Without realizing it, he became a historian by turning to the past to explain to himself and others what he disliked about the present. Never mind that Ford blamed immigrants, especially Jews, for the changes he decried in crude, hate-filled tirades. The point is that Ford's view of America was rooted in a vision of the past, and his explanation for America's ills was based on historical analysis, however unprofessional and unsophisticated.

All of us use historical analysis all the time, even if, like Ford, we think we don't. In fact, we all share a fundamental assumption about learning from the past: One of the best ways to learn about something, to learn how it came to be, is to study its past. That assumption is so much a part of us that we are rarely conscious of it.

Think about the most recent time you met someone for the first time. As a way to get to know this new acquaintance you began to ask questions about his or her past. When you asked, "Where did you grow up?" or "How long have you lived in Chicago?" you were relying on information about the past to learn about the present. You were, in other words, thinking as a historian. You assumed that a cause-and-effect relationship existed between this person's past and his or her present personality, interests, and beliefs. Like a historian, you began to frame questions and to look for answers that would help to establish causal links.

Because we all use history to make sense of our world, it follows that we should become more skilled in the art of making sense of the past. Ford did it crudely, and ended up promoting the very things he despised. But how exactly do you begin to think more like a historian? For too many students, this challenge summons up images of studying for history exams: cramming names, dates, and facts and hoping to retain some portion of this information long enough to get a passing grade. History seems like a confusing grab bag of facts and events. The historian's job, in this view, is to memorize as much "stuff" as possible. In this "flash-card" approach, history is reduced to an exercise in the pursuit of trivia, and thinking like a historian is nothing but an exercise in mnemonics—a system of improving the memory.

There is no question that the dates, events, and facts of history are important. Without basic factual knowledge historians could no more practice their craft than biologists, chemists, or astrophysicists could practice theirs. But history is not a static recollection of facts. Events in the past happened only once, but the historians who study those events are always changing their minds about them. Like all humans, historians have prejudices, biases, and beliefs. They are also influenced by events in their own times. In other words, they look at the past through lenses that filter and even distort. Events in the past may have happened only once, but what historians think about them, the meaning they give to those events, is constantly changing. Moreover, because their lenses perceive events differently, historians often disagree about the past. The supposedly "static" discipline of history is actually dynamic and charged with tension.

That brings us to the question of what historians really do. Briefly, historians ask questions about past events or developments and try to explain them. Just as much as biology, chemistry, or astrophysics, therefore, history is a problem-solving discipline. Historians, like scientists, sift evidence to answer questions. Like scientists, whose explanations for things often conflict, historians can ask the same questions, look at the same facts, and come up with different explanations because they look at the past in different ways. Or they may have entirely different questions in mind and so come away with very different "pasts." Thus history is a process of constant revision. As historians like to put it, every generation writes its own history.

But why bother to study and interpret the past in our own way if someone else will only revise it again in the future? The answer is sobering: If we don't write our own history, someone else will write it for us. Who today would accept as historical truth the notion that the Indians were cruel savages whose extermination was necessary to fulfill an Anglo-Saxon destiny to conquer the continent for democracy and civilization? Who today would accept the "truth" that slaves were racially inferior and happy with their lot on southern plantations? If we accept these views of Indians and black slaves, we are allowing nineteenth-century historians to determine our view of the past.

Instead, by reconstructing the past as best we can, we can better understand our own times. Like the amnesia victim, without memory we face a bewildering world. As we recapture our collective past, the present becomes more intelligible. Subject to new experiences, a later generation will view the past differently. Realizing that future generations will revise history does not give us a license to play fast and loose with the facts of history. Rather, each generation faces the choice of giving meaning to those facts or experiencing the confusion of historical amnesia.

Finding meaning in the facts of the past, then, is the central challenge of history. It requires us to ask questions and construct explanations—mental activities far different and far more exciting than merely memorizing names, dates, and facts. More important, it enables us to approach history as critical thinkers. The more skilled we become at historical reasoning, the better we will understand our world and ourselves. Helping you to develop skill in historical analysis is the purpose of this volume.

The method of this book reflects its purpose. The first chapter discusses textbooks. History texts have a very practical purpose. By bringing order to the past, they give many students a useful and reassuring "handle" on history. But they are not the Ten Commandments, because, like all works of history, they also contain interpretations. To most readers these interpretations are hard to spot. Chapter 1 examines what a number of college textbooks in American history say and don't say about the Indians at the time of English settlement of the New World. By reading selections from several texts and asking how and why they differ, we can see that texts are not as objective as readers often believe.

If textbooks are not the absolute truth, how can we ever know anything? To answer those questions, we turn next to the raw material of history. Chapter 2, on childhood in Puritan New England, examines the primary sources on which historians rely to reconstruct and interpret the past. What are these sources? What do historians do with them? What can historians determine from them?

With a basic understanding of the nature and usefulness of primary sources, we proceed in Chapter 3 for a closer evaluation. This chapter on the haves and have-nots of colonial Pennsylvania shows how careful historians must be in using primary sources. Does a source speak with one voice or with many? How can historians disagree about the meaning of the same historical facts? By carefully evaluating primary sources in this chapter, you can draw your own conclusions about society in colonial Pennsylvania. You can also better understand how historians often derive different conclusions from the same body of material.

Chapter 3 is good preparation for the evaluation in Chapter 4 of one historian's argument about the Loyalists in the American Revolution. Inasmuch as few people in the American past have suffered more at the hands of historians than Loyalists, the essay and the primary sources in this chapter will also provide another opportunity to see how subjective the craft of history can be.

One of the most important sources of disagreement among historians is the question of motivation. What drove people to do what they did in the past? The good historian, like the detective in a murder mystery, eventually asks that question. And few topics in American history better illustrate the importance of motivation than that in Chapter 5, the Founding Fathers and their purposes in framing the Constitution. As that topic also shows, questions of motive perhaps cause the most arguments among historians.

Motives in history are related to ideas, the subject of Chapter 6. What power do ideas exert in history? What is their relationship, for example, to the economic motives examined in the previous chapter? In Chapter 6 we try to answer these questions by examining the role of ideology in shaping Jeffersonian policies regarding blacks and Native Americans.

The problem of motivation is also closely linked to the study of historical causation. Different historical interpretations usually involve different views about the causes of things. In considering the questions of motivation and ideology, Chapters 5 and 6 move beyond the question of what happened to the question of why it happened. Chapter 7, on the early nineteenth-century religious revivals known as the Second Great Awakening, moves even deeper into the realm of why. It considers how many factors may interact with peoples' economic concerns and ideology to produce historical change.

Once we have considered the questions of motivation and causation in history, Chapter 8 examines what historians call a "grand theory" of history, a sweeping or all-encompassing explanation of historical causation. The topic of this chapter is the causal relationship between America's long frontier experience and the development of democratic political institutions. This chapter also considers the problems historians face in trying to fit historical evidence into sweeping hypotheses.

Chapter 9 turns from the influence of grand forces to the influence of "great" individuals. Few individuals were considered greater, by many Americans in the first half of the nineteenth century, than Andrew Jackson. What influence does a "great" individual like Jackson have on history? Are there extraordinary people who shape an entire era? How much can students of history learn about the past by looking at it from the "top down"? How much do they miss by doing so? Such questions are, of course, related to the topics of previous chapters: historical evidence, motivation, causation, and even grand historical theories.

The next chapter examines history from the opposite perspective—from the "bottom up." What can historians learn by looking at the people at the bottom of a society? What challenges face historians who try? In early American history, the best place for using this approach is the issue of slavery. Chapter 10 examines what slavery was like for slaves and why their lives are important to historians.

Many of the chapters just discussed use a single historical essay and an accompanying set of primary sources. Chapter 11 offers an opportunity to pull together the lessons of previous chapters. It compares what two historians have written about a single topic: the role of women in the abolitionist crusade before the Civil War. Because it involves the attitudes and actions of a small but extraordinary and influential set of individuals, it enables us to consider, in a single topic, such questions as motivation, the role of ideology, and the role of the individual in history.

The goal of Chapter 12 is similar to that of Chapter 11: to synthesize, or pull together, the lessons learned in preceding chapters. Here, however, the emphasis is on the problems of historical evidence, causation, and the use of grand theory. Chapter 12 contains two essays on the outcome of the Civil War as well as a small collection of primary sources. It asks you to compare and analyze conflicting arguments by using not only primary sources but also insights drawn from previous chapters.

All of the chapters in this volume encourage you to think more like a historian and to sharpen your critical thinking skills. Chapter 13 returns to a point emphasized throughout this volume: The pursuit of the past cannot occur apart from a consideration of historical interpretation, and differences in historical interpretation matter not just to historians but to everyone. This final chapter examines various interpretations of the political experience of African Americans during Reconstruction. It contains two accounts of black political involvement in Reconstruction and primary documents that illuminate both interpretations. In addition, it underscores the way our view of the past can be used to justify policies and practices in a later time.

By the end of this volume, you will have sharpened your ability to think about the past. You will think more critically about the use of historical evidence and about such historical problems as motivation, causation, and interpretation. Moreover, by exploring several styles of historical writing and various approaches to the past—from those that emphasize politics or economics to those that highlight social developments or military strategy—you will also learn to understand the importance of the past. In short, you will think more like a historian.

CHAPTER | 1

THE TRUTH ABOUT TEXTBOOKS:

INDIANS AND THE SETTLEMENT OF AMERICA

The textbook selections in this chapter illustrate different assumptions textbook writers have had about American Indians and white-Indian relations during the settlement period.

Sources

1. History of the American People (1927), DAVID S. MUZZEY
2. The American Pageant (1966), THOMAS A. BAILEY
3. The Brief American Pageant (2000), DAVID M. KENNEDY, LIZABETH COHEN, THOMAS A. BAILEY, AND MEL PIEHL

*O*ne of the best aids to learning history is also one of the biggest hindrances to understanding the past. It is the textbook, the traditional authority in American history. Textbooks impose a welcome order on the past by organizing events chronologically and explaining historical relationships. How then do these helpful companions sometimes obscure our understanding of the past?

Readers of textbooks often start with the false assumption that these books simply report facts predetermined by the "dead hand" of the past. That misconception is encouraged by a certain tone: textbooks seem to speak with authority. "To us as children," historian Frances FitzGerald writes,

> . . . texts were the truth of things: they were American history. It was not just that we read them before we understood that not everything that is printed is the truth, or the whole truth. It was that they, much more than other books, had the demeanor and trappings of authority. They were weighty volumes. They spoke in measured cadences: imperturbable, humorless, and as distant as Chinese emperors.[1]

Many college students make the same mistake, even if their textbooks speak in more familiar tones. They too assume that their history textbooks "contain only the truth of things."

Of course, the case is more complicated. Textbook authors select facts and shape history in ways that reflect their own times. Thus, like all works of history, textbooks contain interpretations. Readers who see only the cold, immovable facts of history have difficulty spotting them, yet the interpretations are there, like graveyard ghosts lurking amid the headstones. Comparing the way textbooks present the same topic is one good way to detect these elusive spirits. In this chapter we examine what several textbooks say about the Indians when Europe discovered America and when England settled Virginia.

SETTING

Ravaged by strange diseases, attacked by land-hungry settlers, and dispossessed from their land, Indians were among the biggest losers in the American past. Because history is mostly written by winners, Native Americans have been big losers in history books too. For a long time, historians treated them as little more than "an exotic if melancholy footnote to American history."[2] Worse, their accounts were based on questionable ideas about the Indians' lack of "civilization."

Discussions about population show how historians' assumptions about Indian culture influenced their conclusions. In the early twentieth century, historians believed that 1 million Indians lived north of Mexico in 1492 and that fewer than 10 million lived in the entire Western Hemisphere. In fact, at least 2 million people lived in the United States and Canada, with another 15 million in central Mexico. Some researchers now think the total population of the New World in 1492 was around 60 million. One reason for this difference is that earlier population estimates failed to take into account the devastating effects of Old World germs on Indians. They were also based on an assumption that "uncivilized" Indians were incapable of supporting large numbers of people on their land. Following the lead of anthropologists and ethnographers, historians now understand the sophistication of Native American culture and so have dramatically raised their estimates of the Indian population.

Today's historians also have a much greater understanding of the varied ways that whites and Indians interacted. The Indians' role in American history began with their impact on the environment. English settlers encountered a land already cleared and cultivated, a condition that made English settlement much easier. Cultural exchange began immediately, aided by a rough technological equality between the Europeans and Indians. With the exception of the Europeans' ability to navigate the oceans and make iron into tools and weapons, the technological differences between the English settlers and their indigenous neighbors were not great. While the English learned to cultivate tobacco, corn, squash, and other crops, the Indians quickly learned to use kettles, knives, needles, and guns.

An understanding of Native American culture makes clear that English settlers were influenced by Indians in ways they did not understand. It also puts some familiar events in Virginia's early history in a new light. When the Jamestown settlers fell ill in 1607, the powerful Indian Chief Powhatan provided food to keep the starving colony alive. Captain John Smith could only explain this gift as an act of God, who had "changed the heart of the savages."[3] Later Smith was captured by Indians and saved from death, so he believed, by Powhatan's daughter Pocahontas. Just before Smith's executioners were supposed to strike their fatal blows, the Indian "princess" threw herself at the Englishman's feet and pleaded for his life. Once again, Smith saw only the hand of God. He did not see that his remarkable "rescue" was a ceremony designed to demonstrate Powhatan's power and desire to have friendly relations with the English. Nor did he understand that Powhatan, who wanted to extend his authority over dozens of unruly tribes around the Chesapeake, viewed the English as a useful ally. Within a year the suspicious Smith had begun to burn Indian fields and villages to coerce Powhatan and other chiefs to provide more food to the growing settlement.

Events soon ran their tragic course. After Smith left Virginia in 1609, other settlers continued to use force to extract food from the Indians. In 1613 they also kidnapped Pocahontas and held her ransom. Only when John Rolfe vowed to marry her did Powhatan sign a peace treaty. More settlers poured into Virginia, however, and continued to pressure Indians for land. In 1622 the Indians attacked, wiping out about one-third of Virginia's white population. It was the final blow to the Virginia Company, which soon declared bankruptcy. The attack also led to a new attitude about the Indians. As one settler put it, "Our hands which were before tied with gentleness and fair usage, are now set at liberty by the treacherous violence of the savages. . . . [We] may now . . . invade the Country, and destroy them who sought to destroy us. . . ."[4] Virginians began to exterminate the Indians. Only much later, when they began to examine their own cultural assumptions, would historians question why.

INVESTIGATION

This chapter contains three selections from American history textbooks with varying perspectives about the Indians. The first selection is from a text first published in 1927; the last is from one published in 2000. Two of the selections are from different editions of the same text. *Your primary task is to determine how views of the Indians differ in these accounts. A good analysis will address these main questions:*

1. **What does each text say about Indian culture?** If there is a map, what does it show about cultural differences among the Indians? How are the Indian tribes named? Does the language describing the Indians reflect a belief that one's own culture is superior to others (ethnocentrism)?

2. **Is there evidence of cultural exchange between the Indians and Europeans?** Is relevant information about this exchange left out?

3. **Does the text discuss the Indian population at the time of the European discovery of the new world?** Which text has the higher estimate of this population?

4. **What role do the Indians play in the settlement of Jamestown?** Do the Indians aid the settlers? Why do they attack? Why do the English settlers attack the Indians?

5. **Are individual Indians mentioned? If so, how are they portrayed?** What, if anything, does the selection say about Pocahontas? About Powhatan?

You may not be able to find answers to all of these questions in each text. However, you should be able to find enough evidence to come to a well-supported conclusion about the different ways each text treats the Indians.

Before you begin, some cautions may be helpful. First, there is considerable overlap in these accounts. All of them deal with the Indians on the eve of

European discovery and with white-Indian relations in Virginia. Second, none of these selections contain encyclopedic accounts, but rather information that the authors thought was important to an understanding of these topics.

Third, because historians make interpretations by choosing certain facts, you need to determine what has been left out of each account. Since this task requires some background, before you begin, read what your textbook has to say about the Indians at this time. (Of course, it too contains an interpretation.) Finally, don't dismiss an account simply because it is biased. Your challenge is to make a critical, informed, and fair judgment about the way textbooks have treated the Indians.

SOURCES

1 | History of the American People (1927)
DAVID S. MUZZEY

America is the child of Europe. Until the discoverers and explorers from the maritime nations of western Europe began to come to the shores of these continents, more than four hundred years ago, the vast regions now occupied by the United States, the British Dominion of Canada, and the Latin-American republics of Mexico, Central and South America were a wilderness of tribes of copper-colored barbarians or savages, whose ancestors had crossed by Bering Strait from north-eastern Asia to Alaska, we know not how many centuries before, and had slowly spread southward and eastward to Patagonia and Labrador. These American Indians (or "Amerinds," to use the cable-code name by which scholars distinguish them from the inhabitants of the country of India) showed great diversity of character and attainments, due to differences in climate, soil, food, building material, and the activities necessary to preserve life. The Mayas of Yucatan, the Incas of Peru, the Aztecs of Mexico, the Hopis of New Mexico, the Haidas of Queen Charlotte Island, and the Iroquois of central New York furnish examples of Indian tribes who had learned to construct quite elaborate calendars and temples, to weave beautiful rugs and baskets, to bake pottery, to build houses of clay or of cedar beams, shaped with stone implements and ornamented with huge carved totem poles, to devise rude political institutions, and to raise crops of beans, pumpkins, and Indian

Source: David Saville Muzzey, *History of the American People* (Boston: Ginn and Company, 1927), pp. 1, 2, 39, 40, 43.

corn. Other tribes were sunk in bestial savagery, sheltering themselves from wind and snow behind piles of brushwood, wallowing in the southern mud like hogs, eating roots, grass, snakes, and lizards, and dying by thousands from the ravages of the beasts and the diseases against which they were powerless to protect themselves. Nowhere had they risen above the stage of barbarism. It was for the European settlers to introduce civilization into the New World. They brought hither not only tools for the conquest of the wilderness, such as firearms, iron implements for building and farming, horses, cattle, sheep, and hogs, wheat and barley, vegetables and fruits, but also the forms of government, the religion, the books, and the languages of the Old World. For the ethnologist the American Indians have been a picturesque object of study; for the government, since the days of the earliest settlers, they have been an obstruction to be removed, by methods often unnecessarily cruel, from the path of civilization. They have contributed almost nothing to the making of America. The New World was a virgin continent for the European discoverers and their descendants, to make of it what they would. . . .

. . . On May 6, 1607, three small ships with one hundred and four colonists, of whom a large part were "gentlemen" unused to labor, arrived at the capes guarding the entrance to Chesapeake Bay. Their instructions were to choose a healthful place on a navigable river, by which they might arrive at "some spring which runs the contrary way toward the East India Sea," to avoid giving offense to the Indians, and to conduct themselves "for the good of your country and your own." . . . [T]he colonists' supplies had been almost exhausted during the four and a half months' voyage from England, and they neglected the necessary planting of corn for the search for gold and the passage to the Indies. Indeed, had it not been for the supplies obtained from the Indians, the colony could hardly have lasted through the first winter. As it was, more than half the settlers died of fever from the malarial air and the brackish water of the James. The survivors owed their life, probably, to the energy and resourcefulness of one man, John Smith, a seasoned veteran of many a war in Europe and the hero, in his own tales, of hair-raising adventures among the Turks and the Russians. Smith was a braggart and a martinet, but he made the men work, kept the Indians in awe by a combination of boldness and cleverness, and obtained frequent supplies of corn. . . .

. . . By 1624 there were about a thousand persons in the colony (though more than five times that number had been sent out from England since the first settlement). . . . Yet the results were disappointing. It must be remembered that the colony was not started as an experiment in democracy or a refuge from oppression, but as a business venture. The stockholders were looking for returns on their investment. Hundreds of thousands of dollars had been put into the enterprise and the returns were ridiculously small. . . . An Indian massacre in 1622, which cost the colony three hundred and forty-seven lives, was a good pretext for declaring the government by the company a failure, and two years later [King] James had the charter annulled by the royal judges and took the government into his own hands.

2 | The American Pageant (1966)
THOMAS A. BAILEY

The American republic, which is still relatively young, was from the outset singularly favored. It started from scratch on a vast and virgin continent, which was so sparsely peopled by Indians that they could be eliminated or pushed aside. Such a magnificent opportunity for a great democratic experiment may never come again, for no other huge, fertile, and uninhabited areas are left in the temperate zones of this crowded planet. . . .

As the realization gradually dawned that the American continents were a rich prize in their own right, Spain became the dominant exploring and colonizing power in the 1500s. . . .

The bare statistics of Spain's colonial empire are impressive. By 1574, thirty-three years before the first primitive English shelters in Virginia, there were about two hundred Spanish cities and towns in North and South America. A total of 160,000 Spanish inhabitants, mostly men, had brought some 5,000,000 Indians under their yoke. Majestic cathedrals dotted the land, printing presses were turning out books, and literary prizes were being awarded. Two distinguished universities were chartered in 1551, one at Mexico City and the other at Lima, Peru. Both of them antedated Harvard, the first college established in the English colonies, by eighty-five years.

It is clear that the Spaniards, who had more than a century's head start over the English, were genuine empire builders. As compared with their Anglo-Saxon rivals, their colonial establishment was larger and richer and as an entity lasted a quarter of a century longer. The English settlers, disagreeable though the thought may be, were more successful than the Spaniards in killing off the Indians. . . .

In 1606, two years after peace with Spain, the finger of destiny pointed to Virginia. A joint-stock company, known as the Virginia Company of London, received a charter from King James I of England for a settlement in the New World. The main attraction was hoped-for gold, although there was some desire to convert the heathen Indians to Christianity and to find a passage through America to the Indies.

Source: Thomas A. Bailey, *The American Pageant*, 3rd ed. Copyright © 1966 by D. C. Heath and Company. Reprinted by permission of Houghton Mifflin Company. Photo: North Wind Picture Archives.

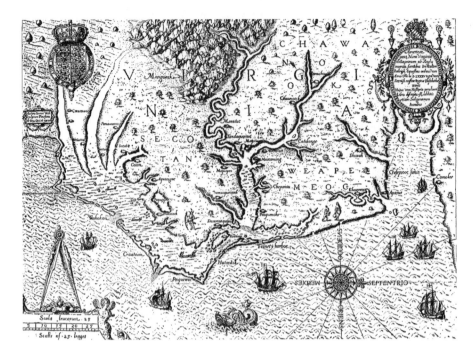

An early map of Virginia.

The early years at Jamestown proved to be a nightmare for all concerned—except the buzzards. Hundreds of wretched souls perished from disease, from actual starvation ("the starving time," 1609–1610), and later from Indian massacres. Ironically, the woods rustled with game and the rivers flopped with fish. Soft-handed English gentlemen and deported criminals wasted valuable time seeking gold when they should have been hoeing corn. They were spurred to their frantic search by edicts from the directors of the company, who threatened to abandon the colonists if they did not strike it rich.

Virginia was saved from going under at the start largely by the leadership and resourcefulness of an incredible young adventurer, Captain John Smith. Taking over in 1608, he whipped the gold-hungry colonists into line with the rule, "He who will not work shall not eat." The dusky Indian maiden Pocahontas may not have saved the captured Smith's life, as he dramatically relates, by suddenly interposing her head between his and the Indian war clubs. But there can be little doubt that Pocahontas, who married John Rolfe in 1613, helped save the colony by enlisting the aid of the Indians and by helping to preserve the peace during these critical years.

3   The Brief American Pageant (2000)

DAVID M. KENNEDY, LIZABETH COHEN, THOMAS A. BAILEY, AND MEL PIEHL

The First Discoverers of America

. . . By the time the Europeans arrived in 1492, perhaps 72 million people inhabited the two American continents. Over the centuries they split into numerous tribes, evolved more than two thousand separate languages, and developed many diverse religions, cultures, and ways of life.

Incas in Peru, Mayans in Central America, and Aztecs in Mexico shaped stunningly sophisticated civilizations. Their advanced agricultural practices, based primarily on the cultivation of maize, which is Indian corn, fed large populations—perhaps as many as 21 million in Mexico alone. Though lacking such technologies as the wheel, these peoples built elaborate cities and carried on far-flung commerce. Talented mathematicians, they made strikingly accurate astronomical observations. The Aztecs also sought the favor of their gods by offering human sacrifices, sometimes cutting the hearts out of the chests of living victims.

The Earliest Americans

Agriculture, especially corn growing, accounted for the size and sophistication of the Native American civilizations in Mexico and South America. About 5000 B.C., hunter-gatherers in highland Mexico developed a wild grass into the staple of corn, which became the foundation of the complex, large-scale, centralized Aztec and Incan nation-states. As cultivation of corn spread across the Americas from the Mexican heartland, it slowly transformed nomadic hunting bands into settled, agricultural villagers.

Corn planting reached the present-day American Southwest by about 1200 B.C. and powerfully molded the Pueblo culture. The Pueblo peoples in the Rio Grande Valley constructed intricate irrigation systems to water their corn-fields, and they built villages of terraced, multistory buildings. Corn cultivation reached other parts of North America considerably later, and the timing of its arrival explains the relative rates of development of different Native American peoples. North and east of the Pueblos, elaborately developed "societies" in the modern sense of the word scarcely existed. The lack of dense concentrations of population or complex nation-states was one of the reasons for the relative ease with which the European colonizers subdued the native North Americans. . . .

Unlike the Europeans, who would soon arrive with the presumption that humans had dominion over the earth and with technologies to alter the very face of the land, Native Americans had neither the desire nor the means to manipulate nature aggressively. They revered the physical world and endowed nature with spiritual properties. Yet they did sometimes ignite massive forest fires, deliberately torching trees to create better hunting habitats, especially for deer. This practice accounted for the open, parklike appearance of the eastern woodlands that so amazed early European explorers.

But in a broad sense the Native Americans did not lay heavy hands on the continent because they were so few in number. In the fateful year 1492, probably no more than 4 million Native Americans padded through the whispering primeval forests and paddled across the sparkling, virgin waters of North America. They were blissfully unaware that the historic isolation of the Americas was about to end forever, as both the land and the native peoples alike felt the full shock of the European "discovery." . . .

England Plants the Jamestown Seedling

In 1606, two years after peace with Spain, the hand of destiny beckoned toward Virginia. A joint-stock company, the Virginia Company of London, received a charter from King James I, who had assumed the English throne in 1603, for a settlement in the New World. The main attractions were the promise of gold and the desire to find a passage through America to the Indies. Like most joint-stock companies of the day, the Virginia Company was intended to endure for only a few years, after which its stockholders hoped to liquidate it for a profit. This arrangement put severe pressure on the luckless colonists, who were threatened with abandonment in the wilderness if they did not quickly strike it rich on the company's behalf. Few of the investors thought in terms of long-term colonization. Apparently no one even faintly suspected that the seeds of a mighty nation were being planted. . . .

The early years of Jamestown proved to be a nightmare for all concerned—except the buzzards. Once ashore, the settlers died by the dozens from disease, malnutrition, and starvation. Ironically, the woods rustled with game and the rivers flopped with fish, but the greenhorn settlers, many of them self-styled "gentlemen" unaccustomed to fending for themselves, wasted valuable time grubbing for nonexistent gold when they should have been gathering provisions.

Virginia was saved from utter collapse at the start largely by the leadership and resourcefulness of an intrepid young adventurer, Captain John Smith. Taking over in 1608, he whipped the gold-hungry colonists into line with the rule "He who shall not work shall not eat." He had been kidnapped in December 1607 and subjected to a mock execution by the Indian chieftain

North American Indian Tribes at the Time of European Colonization. This map illustrates the great diversity of the Indian population—and suggests the inappropriateness of identifying all the Native American peoples with the single label *Indian*. The more than two hundred tribes were deeply divided by geography, language, and lifestyle. The map also identifies geographical areas that are similar in climate and terrain.

Powhatan, whose daughter Pocahontas "saved" Smith by dramatically interposing her head between his and the war clubs of his captors. Pocahontas became an intermediary between the Indians and the settlers, helping to preserve a shaky peace and provide needed food. . . .

Cultural Clash in the Chesapeake

When the English landed in 1607, the chieftain Powhatan dominated the few dozen small tribes in the James River area. Powhatan at first may have considered the English potential allies in his struggle to extend his power over his Indian rivals, and he tried to be conciliatory. But relations between the Indians and the English remained tense, especially as the starving colonists took to raiding Indian food supplies.

The atmosphere grew even more strained after Lord De La Warr arrived in 1610. He carried orders from the Virginia Company that amounted to a declaration of war against the Indians in the Jamestown region. A veteran of the vicious campaigns against the Irish, De La Warr now introduced "Irish tactics" against the Indians. His troops raided their villages, burned houses, confiscated provisions, and torched cornfields. A peace settlement ended this First Anglo–Powhatan War in 1614, sealed by the marriage of Pocahontas to the colonist John Rolfe—the first known interracial union in Virginia.

A fragile peace prevailed for eight years. But the Indians, pressed by the land-hungry whites and ravaged by European diseases, struck back in 1622. A series of Indian attacks left 347 settlers dead, including John Rolfe. Pushed westward by retaliatory settler raids, the Indians made one last effort to dislodge the Virginians in the second Anglo–Powhatan War in 1644. Again they were defeated. The peace treaty of 1646 repudiated any hope of assimilating the native peoples into Virginian society or of peacefully coexisting with them. Instead, it effectively banished the Chesapeake Indians from their ancestral lands and formally separated Indian from white areas of settlement—the origins of the later reservation system. By 1669 an official census revealed that only about two thousand Indians remained in Virginia, perhaps 10 percent of the population the original English settlers had found in 1607. By 1685 the English considered the Powhatan peoples extinct.

It had been the Powhatans' calamitous misfortune to fall victim to three Ds: disease, disorganization, and disposability. Like native people throughout the New World, they were struck down by European epidemics of smallpox and measles. They also lacked the unity to oppose the relatively well-organized and militarily disciplined whites. Finally, the Powhatans served no economic function for the Virginia colonists, having no gold, labor, or valuable commodities to offer in commerce. Indeed the Indian presence frustrated the colonists' desire for a local commodity the Europeans desperately wanted: land.

CONCLUSION

Now that you have examined these selections, several points should be clear. First, there is no such thing as objective history. Even textbooks that seem to be "the whole truth" reflect history's subjectivity. Second, like everyone else, textbook writers are products of their own time. Attitudes about the Indians at different times in the twentieth century surely influenced historians' views about the role of Native Americans in history. Each textbook's publication date is an important clue to why these historians could come to such different conclusions about Indian culture and white–Indian relations. Finally, you may have determined that you need more "firsthand" information to answer the questions in this chapter. That conclusion is a reminder that historians must have more than other historians' accounts to understand the past. They also need primary sources. These valuable sources allow historians to see the past from the perspective of those in it. We turn to them next.

FURTHER READING

William Cronon, *Changes in the Land: Indians, Colonists, and the Ecology of New England* (New York: Hill and Wang, 1983).

Frances FitzGerald, *America Revised: History Schoolbooks in the Twentieth Century* (New York: Vintage, 1979).

James W. Loewen, *Lies My Teacher Told Me: Everything Your American History Textbook Got Wrong* (New York: The New Press, 1995).

Gary B. Nash, *Red, White, and Black: The Peoples of Early America* (Englewood Cliffs: Prentice-Hall, 1982).

Grace Steele Woodward, *Pocahontas* (Norman: University of Oklahoma Press, 1969).

NOTES

1. Frances FitzGerald, *America Revised: History Schoolbooks in the Twentieth Century* (New York: Vintage, 1979), p. 7.
2. James Axtell, *The European and the Indian: Essays in the Ethnohistory of Colonial North America* (New York: Oxford University Press, 1981), p. 274.
3. John Smith, "Generall Historie of Virginia, New-England, and the Summer Isles" (1624), quoted in Jack P. Greene, *Settlements to Society 1584–1763* (New York: McGraw-Hill, 1966), p. 35.
4. Quoted in Gary B. Nash, *Red, White, and Black: The Peoples of Early America,* 2nd ed. (Englewood Cliffs: Prentice-Hall, 1982), p. 61.

CHAPTER | 2

The Raw Materials of History:
Childhood in Puritan New England

The documents in this chapter are primary sources that relate to Puritan child-rearing practices. Three kinds of sources are given—portraits, written material, and architectural drawings.

Sources

1. Elizabeth Eggington (1664)
2. Margaret Gibbs (1670)
3. Henry Gibbs (1670)
4. The Mason Children (1670)
5. Letter of Richard Mather (Age 12) to His Father (ca. 1638)
6. Massachusetts Court Records
7. Lawrence Hammond, Diary Entry for April 23, 1688
8. Samuel Sewall on the Trials of His Fifteen-Year-Old Daughter (1696)
9. The Well-Ordered Family (1719), BENJAMIN WADSWORTH
10. The Duty of Children Toward Their Parents (1727)
11. The Roger Mowry House (ca. 1653)
12. The Eleazer Arnold House (ca. 1684)

*I*n his autobiography, Andrew Carnegie explained what raw materials he needed to produce a pound of steel: two pounds of iron, one and a half pounds of coal, a half-pound of lime, and "a small amount" of manganese ore.[1] Like Carnegie, historians transform raw material into something new. Their "ore" includes such written documents as letters, journals, diaries, legal documents, sermons, speeches, newspapers, and magazines. It can also be furniture, clothing, paintings, posters, coins, motion pictures, and other unwritten artifacts. In fact, historians' primary sources are almost anything from the recorded past. They call these direct links primary sources.

To understand what historians do with primary sources, we turn to the Puritans. Like Andrew Carnegie and all historians, they had high respect for raw material. Theirs, too, had to be refined, cast, and molded. The Puritans' "ore" was their own children, whom they sought to transform through education. As the Massachusetts General Court put it in 1647, reading must be taught in the school because it was "one chief project of that old deluder, Satan, to keep men from the knowledge of the Scriptures."[2] So the Puritans taught their children to read and write. And they *did* write: diaries, journals, tracts, letters, histories, sermons, and notes on sermons. Today libraries, museums, archives, and historical societies are filled with these historical sources.

The Puritans' child-rearing practices were responsible for this wealth of material. For that reason, it is fitting that we begin our examination of primary sources by looking at Puritan childhood. Doing so will also tell us about the Puritan society's important values and ideals. Then, by comparing Puritan and modern childhood, we can learn a great deal about both Puritan society and our own.

SETTING

The Puritans believed that a godly commonwealth was constructed with well-ordered families. Within these "little commonwealths" child rearing was of greatest importance. In addition to ensuring that their children could read and write, parents were expected to teach their children the principles of religion and the fundamental laws. However, because a child's salvation was at stake, child rearing was too important to leave to unsupervised parents. Far more than the schools and government do today, Puritan authorities oversaw the upbringing and education of children.

The Puritan family was, above all, a patriarchy. Drawing on traditional English customs and Old Testament injunctions, the Puritans placed authority within the household in the hands of the husband and father. Thus despite the supervision of family affairs by Puritan authorities, a Puritan father was the divinely ordained ruler of his little commonwealth. In a preindustrial age when most work was done in the home, the father was usually present and his authority was immediate.

Although fathers had final authority in all household matters, mothers of course also played an essential role in the Puritan family. Aside from doing such domestic chores as preparing food and making clothes, wives shared the responsibility for rearing children. The education and spiritual salvation of the children, for example, were primarily the mother's concerns. As the minister Cotton Mather declared, "A mother must give the law of God unto them."[3] Mothers thus exercised a great deal of authority over their children. Although fathers had the power to overrule their wives' decisions regarding their children, they were encouraged not to. Cooperation between husbands and wives was the ideal in the Puritan home. As another writer put it, "Children and Servants are . . . as Passengers are in a boat. Husband and Wife are as a pair of oars, to row them to their desired haven."[4]

The little commonwealth had other important characteristics. One was its size. Compared with families in England or even Virginia, families in New England were large, often with six or more children. In addition, the Puritans followed the common colonial practice of apprenticing their children at a young age. At age fourteen a Puritan child would often be sent for as long as seven years to another family to learn a trade or skill.

Clearly, childhood in Puritan New England was defined by different expectations and values than childhood in a "typical" middle-class American household in the late twentieth century. If historians have the ability to travel instantly to other places and times, when they enter Puritan New England they step into a very different world indeed.

INVESTIGATION

This chapter contains several primary sources relating to the Puritan childhood experience. Some are written sources; others are not. As you read and examine them, answer the following central questions:

1. **How did the experience of growing up in Puritan New England differ from your own experience in the twentieth century?** What values did the Puritans attempt to instill in their children?

2. **What are the main reasons for the differences between Puritan child-rearing practices and those in the late twentieth century?** What forces shaped child rearing then and now?

As you study the sources, you can make a short list of what you think were the most important qualities to be instilled in a Puritan child. List as well the most important influences in shaping a Puritan child. Then list the most important qualities you think your parents tried to instill in you. In comparing these lists, you can begin to frame an answer to the first question: How did the experience of growing up in Puritan New England differ from your own?

Once you have determined those differences, you can begin to consider what these primary sources suggest about the *reasons* for the child-rearing practices in Puritan society. Make a list of the most important influences shaping child-rearing practices in Puritan society and another of the most important influences in your own childhood. This second task will be much easier if you have already read the sections on the Puritans in your textbook. When you are done, some of the important differences between Puritan society and our own should be very clear.

There is no single answer to the central questions of this chapter. Your answers will be determined in part by your biases and experiences. If you compare your answers with those of your classmates, you will quickly discover an axiom of historical inquiry: Even with the same primary sources, historians do not always see the past in the same way.

SOURCES

Portraits

Although artists attempt to capture the likenesses of their subjects, their patrons often want them to do more than that. A portrait may be a view of the subject as he or she wishes to be seen or, in this case, as parents wish their children to be seen. Moreover, as they do today, formal portraits in the seventeenth century captured their subjects' likenesses at special times; historians cannot assume that the subjects looked like this every day. They also have to be careful about using appearances to draw conclusions about personality or emotions. For instance, these Puritan children are not smiling. When modern children have their pictures taken, photographers usually ask them to smile. Yet modern posed photographs of children may not reveal their subjects' feelings either. The question to keep in mind, then, is why the Puritans would prefer to have their children portrayed with facial expressions so different from those in modern photographs. Finally, the dress of these Puritan children may seem odd by modern standards. As you examine it, consider whether it suggests anything about children's roles or about parents' expectations regarding proper behavior.

1 | Elizabeth Eggington (1664)

Source: Courtesy Museum of Fine Arts, Boston.

2 | Margaret Gibbs (1670)

3 Henry Gibbs (1670)

Source: Courtesy Museum of Fine Arts, Boston.

4 | The Mason Children (1670)

Source: Fine Arts Museum of San Francisco. Gift of Mr. and Mrs. John D. Rockefeller 3rd, acc. #1979.7.3.

Written Evidence

The answers to some of the questions in the portrait section may not be obvious from an examination of only the paintings. As you read and analyze the written documents, note what values Puritan parents tried to instill in their children and whether independence or creativity was highly prized. Also look for clues to Puritan attitudes about idleness and play. Try to determine whether Puritan parents and children had an egalitarian relationship and whether they recognized the period of prolonged dependence between childhood and adulthood that we call adolescence. Note any evidence of intense psychological pressure on children. Finally, some observers have argued that children growing up in American society today are often treated like adults by advertisers, Hollywood, parents, schools, and others. Were Puritan children treated more like adults than modern children are?

 ## 5   Letter of Richard Mather (Age 12) to His Father (ca. 1638)

Though I am thus well in my body, yet I question whether my soul doth prosper as my body doth; for I perceive, yet to this very day little growth in grace; and this makes me question, whether grace be in my heart or no. I feel also daily great unwillingness to good duties, and the great ruling sin of my heart; and that God is angry with me, and gives me no answers to my prayers, but many times, he even throws them down as dust in my face; and he does not grant my continual requests for the spiritual blessing of the softning of my hard heart. And in all this I could yet take some comfort, but that it makes me to wonder, what God's secret decree concerning me may be; for I doubt whether ever God is wont to deny grace and mercy to his chosen (though uncalled) when they seek unto him, by prayer, for it; and therefore, seeing he doth thus deny it to me, I think that the reason of it is most like to be, because I belong not unto the election of grace. I desire that you would let me have your prayers, as I doubt not but I have them.

Source: Cotton Mather, *Magnalia Christi Americana* (New York: Russell and Russell, 1967), p. 40, reproduced from 1852 ed., originally published in 1702.

 ## 6   Massachusetts Court Records

[1646]. If any child[ren] above sixteen years old and of sufficient understanding shall curse or smite their natural father or mother, they shall be put to death, unless it can be sufficiently testified that the parents have been very unchristianly negligent in the education of such children, or so provoked them by extreme and cruel correction that they have been forced thereunto to preserve themselves from death or maiming. . . .

Source: From *America Firsthand,* Volume I, edited by Robert D. Marcus and David Burner. Copyright © 1989. Reprinted with permission of St. Martin's Press, Inc.

If a man have a stubborn or rebellious son of sufficient years of understanding, viz. sixteen, which will not obey the voice of his father or the voice of his mother, and that when they have chastened him will not harken unto them, then shall his father and mother, being his natural parents, lay hold on him and bring him to the magistrates assembled in Court, and testify to them by sufficient evidence that this their son is stubborn and rebellious and will not obey their voice and chastisement, but lives in sundry notorious crimes. Such a son shall be put to death.*

[1670]. Ordered that John Edy, Senior, shall go to John Fisk's house and to George Lawrence's and William Priest's houses to inquire about their children, whether they be learned to read the English tongue and in case they be defective to warn in the said John, George, and William to the next meeting of the Selectmen. . . .

William Priest, John Fisk, and George Lawrence, being warned to a meeting of the Selectmen at John Bigulah's house, they making their appearance and being found defective, were admonished for not learning their children to read the English tongue: were convinced, did acknowledge their neglects, and did promise amendment.

[1674]. Agreed that Thomas Fleg, John Whitney, and Joseph Bemus should go about the town to see that children were taught to read the English tongue and that they were taught some orthodox catechism and to see that each man has in his house a copy of the capital laws. For which end the Selectmen agreed there should be copies procured by Captain Mason at the printers and they to be paid for out of the town rate and the men above mentioned to carry them along with them to such of the inhabitants as have none.

Thomas Fleg, John Whitney, and Joseph Bemus gave in an account of what they had found concerning children's education and John Fisk being found wholly negligent of educating his children as to reading or catechizing, the Selectmen agreed that Joseph Bemus should warn him into answer for his neglect at the next meeting of the Selectmen.

[1676]. Ordered that Captain Mason and Simon Stone shall go to John Fisk to see if his children be taught to read English and their catechism.

---

*This penalty was never actually imposed on a child in Puritan Massachusetts.

7 | Lawrence Hammond, Diary Entry for April 23, 1688

This day came into our family Elizabeth Nevenson, daughter of Mr. John Nevinson and Elizabeth his wife, who wilbe 13 yeares of age the 22d day of October next: The verbal Covenant betweene my wife and Mrs. Nevenson is, that she the said Elizabeth shall dwell with my wife as a servant six yeares, to be taught, instructed and provided for as shalbe meet, and that she shall not depart from our family during the said time without my wives consent.

Source: Massachusetts Historical Society Proceedings, XXVII, 146.

8 | Samuel Sewall on the Trials of His Fifteen-Year-Old Daughter (1696)

May 3, 1696. Betty can hardly read her chapter for weeping; tells me she is afraid she is gon back, does not taste that sweetness in reading the Word which once she did; fears that what once upon her is worn off. I said what I could to her, and in the evening pray'd alone with her.

November 12, 1696. I set Betty to read Ezekiel 37. and she weeps so that can hardly read; I talk with her and she tells me of the various Temptations she had; as that she was a Reprobat, Loved not God's people as she should.

Source: Diary of Samuel Sewall, 1674–1729, (Massachusetts Historical Society Collections, 5th series, Vol. V), I, 423, 437.

9 | The Well-Ordered Family (1719)
BENJAMIN WADSWORTH

Parents should govern their children well, restrain, reprove, correct them, and there is occasion. A Christian householder should rule well his own house . . . Children should not be left to themselves, to a loose end, to do as they please; but should be under tutors and governors, *not being fit to govern* themselves . . . Children being bid to obey their parents in all things . . . plainly implies that parents should give suitable precepts to, and maintain a wise government over their children; so carry it, as their children may both fear and love them. You should restrain your children from sin as much as possible . . . You should

Source: From America Firsthand, Volume I, edited by Robert D. Marcus and David Burner. Copyright © 1989. Reprinted with permission of St. Martin's Press, Inc.; originally from Benjamin Wadsworth, The Well-Ordered Family (Boston, 1719).

reprove them for their faults; yea, if need be, correct them too . . . Divide precepts plainly show that, as there is occasion, you should chasten and correct your children; you dishonor God and hurt them if you neglect it. Yet, on the other hand, a father should pity his children . . . You should by no means carry it ill to them; you should not frown, be harsh, morose, faulting and blaming them when they don't deserve it, but do behave themselves well. If you fault and blame your children, show yourself displeased and discontent when they do their best to please you, this is the way to provoke them to wrath and anger, and to discourage them; therefore you should carefully avoid such ill carriage to them. Nor should you ever correct them upon uncertainties, without sufficient evidence of their fault. Neither should you correct them in a rage or passion, but should deliberately endeavor to convince them of their fault, their sin; and that 'tis out of love to God's honor and their good (if they're capable of considering such things) that you correct them. Again, you should never be cruel nor barbarous in your corrections, and if milder ones will reform them, more severe ones should never be used. Under this head of government I might further say, you should refrain your children from bad company as far as possibly you can . . . If you would not have your sons and daughters destroyed, then keep them from ill company as much as may be . . . You should not suffer your children needlessly to frequent taverns, nor to be abroad unseasonably on nights, lest they're drawn into numberless hazards and mischiefs thereby. You can't be too careful in these matters.

10 | The Duty of Children Toward Their Parents (1727)

God hath commanded saying, Honour thy Father and Mother, and whoso curseth Father or Mother, let him die the Death. Mat. 15. 4.

Children obey your Parents in the Lord, for this is right.

2. Honour thy Father and Mother, (which is the first Commandment with Promise).

3. That it may be well with thee, and that thou mayst live long on the Earth.

Children, obey your Parents in all Things, for that is well pleasing unto the Lord. Col. 3, 20.

The Eye that mocketh his Father, and despiseth the Instruction of his Mother, let the Ravens of the Valley pluck it out, and the young Eagles eat it.

Father, I have sinned against Heaven, and before thee. Luke 15, 10.

I am no more worthy to be called thy Son.

Source: Paul Leicester Ford, ed., *The New England Primer* (New York: Dodd, Mead and Co., 1899). Facsimile reprinting of 1727 edition, pp. 20–22.

No man ever hated his own flesh, but nourisheth and cherisheth it. Ephes. 5, 19.

I pray thee let my Father and Mother come and abide with you, till I know what God will do for me. I Sam. 22, 3.

My Son, help thy Father in his Age, and grieve him not as long as he liveth.

And if his Understanding fail, have patience with him, and despise him not when thou art in thy full Strength.

Whoso curseth his Father or his Mother, his Lamp shall be put out in obscure Darkness. Prov. 20, 20.

Architectural Evidence

This section contains sketches and floor plans of two Puritan houses. Like portraits, they must be evaluated carefully. Although floor plans provide only a "bird's eye" view of an interior and by themselves do not answer our primary questions, they can tell us a great deal. First, they reveal the size of the house, a fairly reliable indication of economic circumstances. In addition, they may show the amount of private and common space, thus indicating whether personal privacy was possible. When combined with other sources, they may also indicate whether privacy was even valued. The number and location of fireplaces show how much daytime living space a family had during New England's long winters. Floor plans might even offer clues about the level of household technology, something that would greatly influence the lives of family members. Household sketches give additional information. First, whereas the floor plans here show only the lower floor, the sketches show how much space was provided by the entire house. Second, much like portraits, houses reflect the values of the people who built them. They may be ornate and pretentious or simple and unadorned, qualities that floor plans alone may not reveal.

As you examine the floor plans and sketches of these two houses, think about the impact that these dwellings might have had on the children growing up in them. Also keep in mind how they compare to the "typical" middle-class American home.

11 | The Roger Mowry House (ca. 1653)

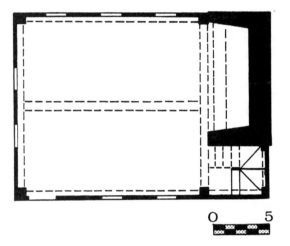

0   5

Source: Drawing by Robert Blair St. George.

NOTE: Addition on the right was added later.
Source: Norman Isham, *Early Rhode Island Houses,* 1895, Courtesy Harvard College Library.

12 | The Eleazer Arnold House (ca. 1684)

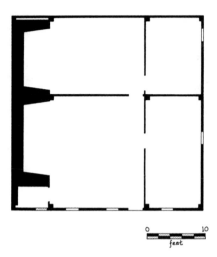

Source: Drawing by Robert Blair St. George.

Source: Norman Isham, *Early Rhode Island Houses,* 1895, Courtesy Harvard College Library.

CONCLUSION

Our first reaction might be to dismiss Puritan child-rearing practices as strange or even cruel. However, it is important to try to understand the way other people saw their world. As one historian has said, "History cannot be written unless the historian can achieve some kind of contact with the mind of those about whom he is writing."[5]

It is not easy to make such "contact" with the Puritans. We do not apprentice children. And it is difficult to imagine a child today writing a letter like the one Richard Mather wrote to his father in 1638. Yet, like us, the Puritans loved their children and, like the Puritans, we recognize the need to "govern" and educate them. Their "raw material" was the same as ours, even if the methods, goals, and results of Puritan child rearing were very different. Young Richard and other Puritan children were formed by their society's beliefs, values, and material conditions, just as children are today. Studying the differences between Puritan and modern child-rearing practices is thus a good way to understand the forces operating in Mather's society and ours.

In the next chapter, we will discover another reason for historians to make "mental contact" with people in the past. As we will see, primary sources rarely speak with one voice; they express opinions as well as facts. To assess these sources critically, historians must understand the strangers who created them on their terms.

FURTHER READING

Edward Hallett Carr, What Is History? (New York: Alfred A. Knopf, 1962).

John Demos, A Little Commonwealth: Family Life in Plymouth Colony (New York: Oxford University Press, 1970).

Philip J. Greven, Four Generations: Population, Land, and Family Life in Colonial Andover, Massachusetts (Ithaca: Cornell University Press, 1970).

Edmund Morgan, The Puritan Family: Religion and Domestic Relations in Seventeenth-Century New England (New York: Harper and Row, 1966).

Alan Simpson, Puritanism in Old and New England (Chicago: University of Chicago Press, 1955).

NOTES

1. Andrew Carnegie, The Autobiography of Andrew Carnegie (Boston: Houghton Mifflin, 1920), pp. 217–218.

2. Quoted in Edmund Morgan, *The Puritan Family: Religion and Domestic Relations in Seventeenth-Century New England* (New York: Harper and Row, 1966), p. 88.

3. Cotton Mather, *A Family Well-Ordered* (Boston: Bartholomew Green and J. Allen, 1699), p. 37.

4. William Secker, *A Wedding Ring* (Boston: T. G. Green, 1705), p. 52.

5. Edward Hallett Carr, *What Is History?* (New York: Alfred A. Knopf, 1962), p. 27.

CHAPTER | 3

EVALUATING PRIMARY SOURCES: WAS PENNSYLVANIA "THE BEST POOR MAN'S COUNTRY"?

This chapter presents various kinds of primary sources on Pennsylvania before the Revolution. The documents relate to the question of whether Pennsylvania was indeed the land of opportunity that one source claims it was.

Sources

1. An Historical and Geographical Account of Pennsylvania (1698), GABRIEL THOMAS
2. Plantations in Pennsylvania (1743), WILLIAM MORALEY
3. Journey to Pennsylvania (1756), GOTTLIEB MITTELBERGER
4. Advertisement for a Runaway (1759)
5. American Husbandry (1775)
6. William Penn on House Construction in Pennsylvania (1684)
7. Cabin, Berks County
8. Fairhill
9. Charles Norris's Mansion, Chestnut Street
10. Early Settlements in Pennsylvania (1696)
11. Newtown, Chester County (1696)
12. Wealth Distribution in Philadelphia, 1693–1774
13. Slaveholding in Philadelphia in 1767
14. Acquisition of Land by Former Indentured Servants, 1686–1720

*T*o the Englishman William Moraley, Pennsylvania was a paradise. Moraley was an indentured servant who went to Pennsylvania in 1729 and found "woods and well-manured farms" everywhere. He claimed to have traveled hundreds of miles at no expense because the inhabitants outdid one another in providing him food and "charity." The colony was "the best poor man's country in the world," Moraley asserted in his autobiography. "If this was sufficiently known by the miserable objects we have in our streets," he concluded, "multitudes would be induced to go thither."[1]

As we know, multitudes from many lands did go there. Did they settle in the "best poor man's country"? Or was Moraley's conclusion unwarranted? Historians want to know how much opportunity the countless immigrants to colonial Pennsylvania found. Just as many Americans today worry about their own opportunities, historians are interested in the extent of equality, wealth, and poverty in colonial America. They are curious if opportunities for economic advancement were increasing or declining in the colonial period and if some people succeeded at others' expense. Because the people living in that society eventually revolted against Great Britain, historians also want to know whether economic and social conditions in the colonies helped to bring on the American Revolution. In this chapter, we use primary sources to investigate wealth holding and opportunity in this "best poor man's country."

SETTING

By the eighteenth century, Pennsylvania was in many ways a prototype of American development. Blessed with a favorable climate, rich soil, and a policy of toleration introduced by Quaker proprietor William Penn, the colony attracted large numbers of English, Irish, German, and Swiss settlers. The Quakers' egalitarianism may not have made them popular in England, but it was appealing to many Europeans looking for a better life. Indeed, many of those drawn to Pennsylvania were indentured servants. In 1685, about half of the adult males arriving in the colony were indentured. Although that percentage declined by the eighteenth century, the number of servants in Pennsylvania remained high throughout the colonial period. In 1750, for example, nearly 20 percent of Philadelphia's work force was indentured.

Like its sister colonies, Pennsylvania was overwhelmingly rural, and its farmers produced crops for faraway markets. That trade sped the growth of Philadelphia, which served the same commercial function as other colonial ports. By the middle of the eighteenth century, the City of Brotherly Love challenged Boston as the most important commercial center in the colonies.

The colony was also typical in other ways. Under English common law, which prevailed in Pennsylvania and throughout the colonies, a married woman had almost no legal rights. She was known as a *femme coverte,* covered by the husband. Under *coverture,* married women had no property or money, including wages, of their own. Since their economic opportunities were limited to those of their husbands, the questions of wealth holding and economic advancement did not apply to them. The situation was even worse for the colony's African-American population. Slavery was legal in Pennsylvania, as it was in all other American colonies. By 1750 there were more than one thousand slaves in Philadelphia, where most of Pennsylvania's bondsmen lived as the colony's ultimate have-nots. The distribution of wealth and the extent of economic opportunity were irrelevant for them.

If wealth holding and economic advancement in colonial Pennsylvania pertained only to some people, conclusions about the opportunities there must be carefully qualified. The available sources make generalizations even more difficult. Because evidence regarding opportunity in the colonies is limited, historians traditionally have relied on "literary" sources—that is, written descriptions of economic or social conditions. Yet such evidence usually reflects only one person's views. Roughly two and a half million people lived in the colonies by the middle of the eighteenth century, and their economic circumstances varied greatly. Making valid generalizations from a limited number of individual observations is therefore difficult. So to obtain larger samples, historians frequently turn to such legal documents as tax rolls and wills, which often reflect the experiences of people who seldom left written records and which are often free of the biases seen in literary sources. To make sense of these legal documents, however, researchers usually limit their studies to a particular colony, county, or town. That narrow focus, in turn, makes it difficult to generalize about other places.

The passage of time creates still more difficulties. Nearly a century separated the founding of Pennsylvania and the Declaration of Independence, and opportunities for advancement changed over that time. The expansion of trade, population growth, overcrowding, and urban growth created dynamic patterns of wealth holding and economic advancement. Because colonial society was not static, historians must know how these patterns changed.

To determine if William Moraley was correct about Pennsylvania is thus not easy. It requires careful evaluation of primary sources. We must separate fact from opinion, reconcile conflicting evidence, determine whether sources are representative, and understand the outlook of our subjects.

INVESTIGATION

Imagine that you rent a small plot of land in rural England in the mid-eighteenth century. You wish to settle in a place without extreme wealth or poverty where you can improve your fortunes. An acquaintance in Pennsylvania has just sent you a packet of documents about the colony. It contains an offer for paid passage to Pennsylvania in exchange for a four-year term of service. You must use the information in the documents to decide whether or not to go. In other words, you must evaluate the documents in order to determine the extent of social stratification and opportunities for economic advancement in Pennsylvania. Thus you will need to determine whether the documents contain facts or unsubstantiated opinions, and whether they are representative or atypical. When you are finished, you should be able to answer these main questions about Pennsylvania society:

1. **What was the pattern of wealth distribution?** How much equality and inequality existed in this society? How large was the gap between the haves and the have-nots?

2. **What were the opportunities for an individual to improve his lot in this society?** Was this a fluid or rigid, class-bound society?

3. **Was there greater or less equality as time went on?** Is there evidence that some people were getting rich at the expense of others?

How you answer these questions will determine whether you move to Pennsylvania. Not every document will answer each of these questions, but together they should give you enough evidence to come to some conclusions about the opportunities in colonial Pennsylvania. Because you need to evaluate a large number of sources, creating a chart like the one below will help keep track of the evidence. As you examine each source, write down the selection number in the appropriate boxes.

Evidence of Stratification	Evidence of Social Equality
Evidence of Rigid Class Structure	**Evidence of Economic Mobility**

When you have finished the chart, your decision should be clearer.

SOURCES

1 | Gabriel Thomas was a Welsh yeoman farmer who spent fifteen years in Pennsylvania before departing for England, where this account of the colony was published. In 1706, Thomas returned to Sussex County near Philadelphia, where he owned a thousand-acre plantation. Note the reasons why he thought that conditions were better in Pennsylvania than in England or Wales.

An Historical and Geographical Account of Pennsylvania (1698)
GABRIEL THOMAS

I must needs say, even the present Encouragements are very great and inviting, for Poor People (both Men and Women) of all kinds, can here get three times the Wages for their Labour they can in England or Wales.

I shall instance in a few, which may serve; nay, and will hold in all the rest. The first was a Black-Smith (my next Neighbour), who himself and one Negro Man he had, got Fifty Shillings in one Day, by working up a Hundred Pound Weight of Iron, which at Six Pence per Pound (and that is the common Price in that Countrey) amounts to that Summ.

And for Carpenters, both House and Ship, Brick-layers, Masons, either of these Trades-Men, will get between Five and Six Shillings every Day constantly. As to Journey-Men Shooe-Makers, they have Two Shillings per Pair both for Men and Womens Shooes: And Journey-Men Taylors have Twelve Shillings per Week and their Diet. Sawyers get between Six and Seven Shillings the Hundred for Cutting of Pine-Boards. And for Weavers, they have Ten or Twelve Pence the Yard for Weaving of that which is little more than half a Yard in breadth. . . .

Corn and Flesh, and what else serves Man for Drink, Food and Rayment, is much cheaper here than in England, or elsewhere; but the chief reason why Wages of Servants of all sorts is much higher here than there, arises from the great Fertility and Produce of the Place; besides, if these large Stipends were refused them, they would quickly set up for themselves, for they can have Provision very cheap, and Land for a very small matter, or next to nothing in comparison of the Purchase of Lands in England; and the Farmers there, can better afford to give that great Wages than the Farmers in England can, for several Reasons very obvious.

As First, their Land costs them (as I said but just now) little or nothing in comparison, of which the Farmers commonly will get twice the encrease of

Source: Albert Cook Myers, ed., *Narratives of Early Pennsylvania, West New Jersey, and Delaware 1630–1707* (New York: Barnes and Noble, Inc., 1912), pp. 326–327, 328–329.

Corn for every Bushel they sow, that the Farmers in England can from richest Land they have.

In the Second place, they have constantly good price for their Corn, by reason of the great and quick vent [passage] into Barbadoes and other Islands; through which means Silver is become more plentiful than here in England, considering the Number of People, and that causes a quick Trade for both Corn and Cattle; and that is the reason that Corn differs now from the Price formerly, else it would be at half the Price it was at then; for a Brother of mine (to my own particular knowledge) sold within the compass of one Week, about One Hundred and Twenty fat Beasts, most of them good handsom large Oxen.

 William Moraley spent nearly five years in the colonies, where he traveled widely. His autobiography describes the relationship between the haves and the have-nots in colonial Pennsylvania. In other passages, Moraley also reveals that he was a drunkard and a thief. Does his character influence his creditability?

Plantations in Pennsylvania (1743)
WILLIAM MORALEY

At the first Peopling [of] these Colonies, there was a Necessity of employing a great Number of Hands, for the clearing the Land, being over-grown with Wood for some Hundred of Miles; to which Intent, the first Settlers not being sufficient of themselves to improve those Lands, were not only obliged to purchase a great Number of *English* Servants to assist them, to whom they granted great Immunities, and at the Expiration of their Servitude, Land was given to encourage them to continue there; but were likewise obliged to purchase Multitudes of Negro Slaves from *Africa,* by which Means they are become the richest Farmers in the World, paying no Rent, nor giving Wages either to purchased Servants or Negro Slaves; so that instead of finding the Planter Rack-rented, as the *English* Farmer, you will taste of their Liberality, they living in Affluence and Plenty.

The Condition of the Negroes is very bad, by reason of the Severity of the Laws, there being no Laws made in Favour of these unhap[p]y Wretches: For the least Trespass, they undergo the severest Punishment; but their Masters make them some amends, by suffering them to marry, which makes them easier, and often prevents their running away. The Consequence of their

Source: Reprinted from Susan E. Klepp and Billy G. Smith, eds., *The Infortunate: The Voyage and Adventures of William Moraley, an Indentured Servant* (University Park: Pennsylvania State University Press, 1992), pp. 93–95. Copyright 1992 by The Pennsylvania State University Press. Reproduced by permission of the publisher.

marrying is this, all their Posterity are Slaves without Redemption; and it is in vain to attempt an Escape, tho' they often endeavour it; for the Laws against them are so severe, that being caught after running away, they are unmercifully whipped; and if they die under the Discipline, their Masters suffer no Punishment, there being no Law against murdering them. So if one Man kills another's Slave, he is only obliged to pay his Value to the Master, besides Damages that may accrue for the Loss of him in his Business.

The Masters generally allow them a Piece of Ground, with Materials for improving it. The Time of working for themselves, is *Sundays*, when they raise on their own Account divers Sorts of Corn and Grain, and sell it in the Markets. They buy with the Money Cloaths for themselves and Wives; as for the Children, they belong to the Wives Master, who bring them up; so the Negro need fear no Expense, his Business being to get them for his Master's use, who is as tender of them as his own Children. On *Sundays* in the evening they converse with their Wives, and drink Rum, or Bumbo, and smoak Tobacco, and the next Morning return to their Master's Labour.

They are seldom made free, for fear of being burthensome to the Provinces, there being a Law, that no Master shall manumise them, unless he gives Security they shall not be thrown upon the Province, by settling Land on them for their Support.

 Gottlieb Mittelberger was a German immigrant who returned to Germany four years after arriving in America in 1756.

Journey to Pennsylvania (1756)
GOTTLIEB MITTELBERGER

When the ships have landed at Philadelphia after their long voyage, no one is permitted to leave them except those who pay for their passage or can give good security; the others, who cannot pay, must remain on board the ships till they are purchased, and are released from the ships by their purchasers. The sick always fare the worst, for the healthy are naturally preferred and purchased first; and so the sick and wretched must often remain on board in front of the city for 2 or 3 weeks, and frequently die, whereas many a one, if he could pay his debt and were permitted to leave the ship immediately, might recover and remain alive. . . .

The sale of human beings in the market on board the ship is carried on thus: Every day Englishmen, Dutchmen and High-German people come from the city of Philadelphia and other places, in part from a great distance, say 20, 30,

Source: Frederick M. Binder and David M. Reimers, *The Way We Lived* (Lexington, Mass.: D. C. Heath and Co., 1988), pp. 59–61.

or 40 hours away, and go on board the newly arrived ship that has brought and offers for sale passengers from Europe, and select among the healthy persons such as they deem suitable for their business, and bargain with them how long they will serve for their passage money, which most of them are still in debt for. When they have come to an agreement, it happens that adult persons bind themselves in writing to serve 3, 4, 5 or 6 years for the amount due by them, according to their age and strength. But very young people, from 10 to 15 years, must serve till they are 21 years old.

Many parents must sell and trade away their children like so many head of cattle; for if their children take the debt upon themselves, the parents can leave the ship free and unrestrained; but as the parents often do not know where and to what people their children are going, it often happens that such parents and children, after leaving the ship, do not see each other again for many years, perhaps no more in all their lives. . . .

It often happens that whole families, husband, wife, and children, are separated by being sold to different purchasers, especially when they have not paid any part of their passage money.

When a husband or wife has died at sea, when the ship has made more than half of her trip, the survivor must pay or serve not only for himself or herself, but also for the deceased.

When both parents have died over half-way at sea, their children, especially when they are young and have nothing to pawn or to pay, must stand for their own and their parents' passage, and serve till they are 21 years old. When one has served his or her term, he or she is entitled to a new suit of clothes at parting; and if it has been so stipulated, a man gets in addition a horse, a woman, a cow. . . .

If some one in this country runs away from his master, who has treated him harshly, he cannot get far. Good provision has been made for such cases, so that a runaway is soon recovered. He who detains or returns a deserter receives a good reward.

If such a runaway has been away from his master one day, he must serve for it as a punishment a week, for a week a month, and for a month half a year. But if the master will not keep the runaway after he has got him back, he may sell him for so many years as he would have to serve him yet. . . .

However hard he may be compelled to work in his fatherland, he will surely find it quite as hard, if not harder, in the new country. Besides, there is not only the long and arduous journey lasting half a year, during which he has to suffer, more than with the hardest work; he has also spent about 200 florins which no one will refund to him. If he has so much money, it will slip out of his hands; if he has it not, he must work his debt off as a slave and poor serf. Therefore let every one stay in his own country and support himself and his family honestly. Besides I say that those who suffer themselves to be persuaded and enticed away by the man-thieves, are very foolish if they believe that roasted pigeons will fly into their mouths in America or Pennsylvania without their working for them.

4 Masters frequently put advertisements in colonial newspapers for runaway indentured servants. As you read this advertisement from the *Pennsylvania Gazette,* you can look for what it reveals about the conditions of indentured servants.

Advertisement for a Runaway (1759)

Germantown, July 18, 1759

Run away on the 13th of this Instant, at Night, from the Subscriber, of said Town, an Apprentice Lad, named Stophel, or Christopher Hergesheimer, about 19 Years of Age, by Trade a Blacksmith, middle sized of his Age, has a sour down-looking Countenance, is of Dutch Extraction, but can talk good English; Had on, and took with him, when he went away, a bluish Cloath Coat, green Nap Jacket, Snuff coloured Breeches, and Linen Jacket and Breeches, all about half wore, two pair of Ozenbrigs Trowsers, two Ditto Shirts, and one pretty fine, a Pair of old Shoes, a Pair of Thread, and a Pair of Cotton Stockings, a good Athlone Felt Hat, and yellowish Silk Handkerchief, wore his own dark brown short Hair, but may cut it off: He had a Hurt on the Inside of his Left-hand, not quite cured, at his going away. Whoever takes him up, and brings or conveys him to his Master, or secures him in the Jail of Philadelphia, shall have Forty Shillings Reward, and reasonable Charges, paid by

Matthew Potter, *junior.*

Source: Pennsylvania Gazette, August 2, 1759.

5 This guide to life in the English colonies was written anonymously and published in London in 1775 as a promotional tract to encourage potential settlers to move to America. Does this purpose make its information suspect?

American Husbandry (1775)

THIS country is peopled by as happy and free a set of men as any in America. Out of trade there is not much wealth to be found, but at the same time there

Source: Reprinted by permission of the author from Jack P. Greene, *Settlements to Society.* Copyright © 1966. Published by the McGraw-Hill Companies.

is very little poverty, and hardly such a thing as a beggar in the province. This is not only a consequence of the plenty of land, and the rate of labour, but also of the principles of the Quakers, who have a considerable share in the government of the country. It is much to the honour of this sect that they support their own poor in all countries, in a manner much more respectable than known in any other religion.

There are some country gentlemen in Pennsylvania, who live on their estates in a genteel and expensive manner, but the number is but small. . . . [M]oney is scarce in this country, and all the necessaries and conveniences of life cheap, except labour. But in general the province is inhabited by small freeholders, who live upon a par with great farmers in England; and many little ones who have the necessaries of life and nothing more.

In the settled parts of the colony, there are few situations to be found that are without such a neighbourhood as would satisfy country gentlemen of small estates, or country parsons in Britain. There are, besides Philadelphia, many small towns in which are found societies that render the country agreeable; and the country itself is scattered with gentlemen at moderate distances, who have a social intercourse with each other, besides occasional parties to Philadelphia.

The most considerable of the freeholders that do not however rank with gentlemen, are a set of very sensible, intelligent, and hospitable people, whose company, in one that is mixed, improves rather than lessens the agreeableness of it; a circumstance owing to many of them being foreigners, which even gives something of a polish to the manners when we find ourselves in the midst of a country principally inhabited by another people. The little freeholders (there are not many farmers, except near Philadelphia) are in ease and circumstances much superior to the little farmers in England.

The method of living in Pennsylvania in country gentlemen's families, is nearly like that of England: the only business is to ride about the plantation now and then, to see that the overseers are attentive to it; all the rest of the time is filled up with entertaining themselves; country sports, in the parts of the province not fully settled, are in great perfection; they have hunting, but their horses are unequal to those of England; shooting and fishing are much more followed, and are in greater perfection than in England, though every man is allowed both to shoot and fish throughout the province, except the latter in cultivated grounds. . . . It must be at once apparent, that a given income would go much further here than in Britain; this is so strongly a truth, that an income of four or five hundred pounds a year, and a plantation, can hardly be spent without extravagance, or indulging some peculiar expence; whereas that income from an estate in Britain will hardly give a man the appearance of a gentleman. . . .

<table>
<tr><td>6</td><td>After returning from Pennsylvania, William Penn wrote a tract directed at people interested in moving to the colony. What does it reveal about living conditions? Using evidence in Source 1, try to calculate how</td></tr>
</table>

much labor would be required to accumulate the amounts shown in Penn's table. (Keep in mind that twenty shillings equals one pound.)

William Penn on House Construction in Pennsylvania (1684)

. . . I propose to speak my own Knowledg, and the Observation of others, as particularly as I can; . . . This done, I take my two men, and go to my Lot . . . and then go to felling of Trees, proper for a first House, which will very well serve for the present occasion, and afterwards, be a good out House, till plenty will allow me to build a Better.

To build them, a House of thirty foot long and eighteen broad, with a partition neer the middle, and an other to divide one end of the House into two small Rooms, there must be eight Trees of about sixteen Inches square, and cut off, to *Posts* of about fifteen foot long, which the House must stand upon; and four pieces, two of thirty foot long, and two of eighteen foot long, for *Plates*, which must lie upon the top of those Posts, the whole length and bredth of the House, for the *Gists* [joists] to rest upon. There must be ten *Gists* of twenty foot long, to bear the Loft, and two false *Plates* of thirty foot long to lie upon the ends of the *Gists* for the *Rafters* to be fixed upon, twelve pare of *Rafters* of about twenty foot, to bear the Roof of the House, with several other smaller pieces; as *Wind-Beams, Braces, Studs,* etc. which are made of the Waste Timber. For Covering the House, Ends, and Sides, and for the Loft, we use *Clabboard,* which is *Rived feather-edged,* of five foot and a half long, that well Drawn, lyes close and smooth: The Lodging Room may be lined with the same, and filld up between, which is very Warm. These houses usually endure ten years without Repair.

	l.	s.	d.*
For the Carpenters work for such an House, I and my Servants assisting him, together with his diet	07	00	00
For a Barn of the same Building and Dimensions,	05	10	00
For Nailes, and other things to finish Both	03	10	00

The lower flour is the *Ground,* the upper *Clabbord:* This may seem a mean way of Building, but 'tis sufficient and safest for ordinary beginners.

*pounds, shillings, pence

Source: From Harold R. Shurtleff, *The Log Cabin Myth: A Study of the Early Dwellings of the English Colonists in North America* (Gloucester, Mass.: Peter Smith, 1967), pp. 124–125; originally from William Penn, *Information and Direction to Such Persons as are inclined to America, more Especially Those related to the Province of Pennsylvania* (London, 1684).

Views of Early Pennsylvania Houses

As you study these pictures of houses in colonial Pennsylvania, note what they reveal about social classes there.

 This stone cabin was of an Old World style frequently copied by British immigrants in Pennsylvania until about 1760.

Cabin, Berks County

Source: From Henry Glassie, *Pattern in the Material Folk Culture of the Eastern United States* (Philadelphia: University of Pennsylvania Press, 1968), p. 52.

Isaac Norris I built Fairhill, a country estate, around 1716.

Fairhill

Source: Historical Society of Pennsylvania.

9 │ Charles Norris was Isaac's son.

Charles Norris's Mansion, Chestnut Street

Source: Historical Society of Pennsylvania.

Maps of Early Pennsylvania (1696)

These two sources are parts of a map of the settled portion of Pennsylvania made in 1696. Source 10 is a section of the settled area of the colony around Philadelphia. Source 11 shows in greater detail one township from the larger map. Like floor plans, maps can be an important primary source for historians and with careful analysis can reveal something about the way people lived. They are especially valuable for determining wealth-holding patterns in colonial society, where most of the wealth was held as land.

In Pennsylvania, proprietor William Penn, the wealthy Quaker land-grant holder, wanted farms to be 450 acres and grouped into townships of about fifty people. In the center of each township was to be a common area of meadows and pasturelands. The scale of miles in these maps will give you a rough idea of the size of the settlers' holdings. (One square mile equals 640 acres.) Locate

Philadelphia and Newtown on the map in Source 10. The large parcels around Philadelphia are actually townships rather than individual holdings. Keep in mind that such developments as growing population and commerce gave some land on the map of the settled area around Philadelphia greater value than other land. As you examine these maps, ask yourself if the settlers followed Penn's wishes regarding land distribution, or if there was inequality in landholding.

10 │ Early Settlements in Pennsylvania (1696)

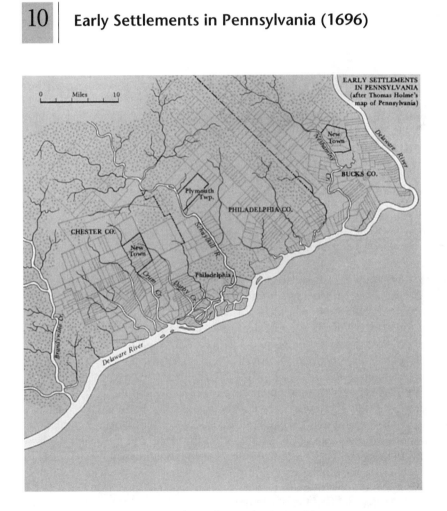

Source: Rare Books Section, State Library of Pennsylvania, Harrisburg.

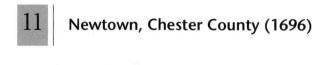

11 | Newtown, Chester County (1696)

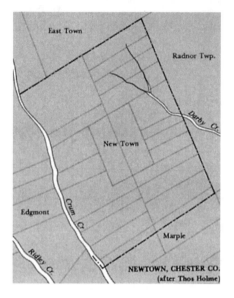

Source: Rare Books Section, State Library of Pennsylvania, Harrisburg.

12   This table is a distillation of large numbers of primary documents. It shows the percentage of the wealth held by different segments of the free adult property holders at various times in Philadelphia. The table divides the sample into two general groups: the lower 90 percent of wealth holders and the upper 10 percent. These groups are then further divided. The lower 90 percent are divided into thirds. (For instance, the 0–30 group is the lowest 30 percent of the total sample of Philadelphia property holders in terms of their individual wealth.) The upper 10 percent is divided in half to show the wealth holding of the richest 5 percent of the population. The figures under each date are the percentage of the wealth owned by each segment of the population. As you examine this table, look for a trend in the distribution of wealth. Then turn back to the map of the settled area around Philadelphia (Source 10). Locate Philadelphia County, Bucks County, and Chester County and consider whether it is likely that the distribution of wealth in Bucks and Chester counties in 1774 was similar to that in Philadelphia County.

Source: Adapted from table in Gary B. Nash, *Race, Class, and Politics: Essays on American Colonial and Revolutionary Society* (Urbana: University of Illinois Press, 1986), p. 176.

Wealth Distribution in Philadelphia, 1693–1774

Segments of Wealth-Holding Population	Percentage of Total Wealth		
	1693	1767	1774
0–30 (poorest)	2.2	1.8	1.1
31–60	15.2	5.5	4.0
61–90	36.6	27.0	22.6
91–100 (richest)	46.0	65.7	72.3
91–95	13.2	16.2	16.8
96–100	32.8	49.5	55.5

 13 The table below shows the number of slaveholders by occupation group and the number of slaves owned by each group. It also reveals the percentage of the roughly 900 slaves owned by each group. (Philadelphia's estimated population was 16,000 in 1767.) Which groups owned the most slaves?

Slaveholding in Philadelphia in 1767

Occupational Group	Number and Percent of Slaveowners		Number and Percent of Taxable Slaves Owned	
Merchants and retailers	161	31.2%	291	32.2%
Professionals (including doctors, lawyers, officeholders)	39	7.5%	95	10.5%
Service trades (including tavernkeepers, barbers, printers)	30	5.6%	48	5.2%
Wood-, metal-, and stone-workers	66	12.6%	104	11.5%
Cloth- and leatherworkers	56	10.7%	97	10.7%

(cont on next page)

Occupational Group	Number and Percent of Slaveowners		Number and Percent of Taxable Slaves Owned	
Food processors (including butchers, bakers, brewers, millers)	31	6.0%	70	7.7%
Maritime trades (including captains, mariners, shipwrights, and sail-, rope-, and blockmakers)	75	14.2%	122	13.5%
Miscellaneous (including widows)	31	6.1%	44	4.9%
Unknown	32	6.1%	34	3.8%
	521		905	

Source: Gary B. Nash, *Race, Class, and Politics: Essays on American Colonial and Revolutionary Society* (Urbana: University of Illinois Press, 1986), p. 106.

14 This table illustrates how much land former indentured servants in Pennsylvania acquired over a period of thirty years after completion of their terms of service. The servants were indentured between 1682 and 1686. What does this table suggest about poor individuals' opportunities to accumulate property?

Acquisition of Land by Former Indentured Servants, 1686–1720

Number of Acres	Number of Former Servants	%
1–50	27	46.6
51–100	14	20.6
101–150	5	7.4
151–200	10	14.7
200–	12	17.7
Total (Total sample = 196)	68	

Source: Sharon V. Salinger, *To serve well and faithfully: Labor and Indentured Servants in Pennsylvania, 1682–1800* (Cambridge: Cambridge University Press, 1987), p. 39.

CONCLUSION

Albert Einstein said that a person who dropped a stone from the window of a moving railroad car would see it descend toward the railroad embankment in a straight line. An observer standing on the embankment, however, would see the same stone fall in a parabolic curve, down and forward in the same direction as the train. Our vantage point determines what we see.

The sources in this chapter also reflect that axiom. Historical evidence rarely supports only one conclusion because people in the past saw things differently. Your decision about the wisdom of moving to Pennsylvania also illustrates Einstein's lesson. You and your classmates may not come to the same decision, but that does not necessarily mean you are wrong. The lesson of Einstein's falling stone thus applies to both primary sources and historians' own writings. We can ask the same question of each: Do they reflect the view from the railroad window or from the embankment? Remembering that question will make it easier, starting in the next chapter, to evaluate the writings of historians and the primary sources on which they are based.

FURTHER READING

James A. Henretta and Gregory H. Nobles, *Evolution and Revolution: American Society, 1600–1820* (Lexington, Mass.: D. C. Health, 1987).

Richard Hofstadter, *America at 1750: A Social Portrait* (New York: Alfred A. Knopf, 1971).

James T. Lemon, *The Best Poor Man's Country: A Geographical Study of Early Southeastern Pennsylvania* (Baltimore: Johns Hopkins University Press, 1972).

Gottlieb Mittelberger, *Journey to Pennsylvania,* ed. Oscar Handlin and John Clive (Cambridge: Harvard University Press, 1960).

Sharon V. Salinger, *"To serve well and faithfully": Labor and Indentured Servants in Pennsylvania, 1682–1800* (New York: Cambridge University Press, 1987).

John Van Der Zee, *Bound Over: Indentured Servitude and American Conscience* (New York: Simon and Schuster, 1985).

NOTE

1. Susan E. Klepp and Billy G. Smith, eds., *The Infortunate: The Voyage and Adventures of William Moraley, an Indentured Servant* (University Park: Pennsylvania State University Press, 1992), p. 89.

CHAPTER | 4

EVALUATING ONE HISTORIAN'S ARGUMENT:
LOYALISTS AND THE MEANING OF THE REVOLUTION

The documents in this chapter are a combination of primary and secondary sources. The chapter presents an essay on the Loyalists and then gives several primary sources that can be used to judge the validity of the essay's position.

Secondary Source

Primary Sources

*T*he fireworks on the Fourth of July celebrate what very few people actually understand. More than two hundred years after the muskets of the American Revolution fell silent, there is still misunderstanding and myth about the struggle for independence.

One of the biggest misconceptions about the Revolution is that almost everyone supported it. Thomas Jefferson may have proclaimed in the Declaration of Independence that Americans were "one people," but they were not. As Jefferson well knew, the Revolution was a civil war as well as a war for independence. Many blacks and most Indians lined up with the British. Perhaps as much as 20 percent of the white population also opposed independence. As one observer at the time put it, "Neighbor was against neighbor."[1]

Today it seems strange, even baffling, that anyone would reject the idea of America as an independent nation. Yet hundreds of thousands of Americans did just that. The arguments for independence are well known, but what were those against it? What led Loyalists to side with the British? What were their interests? What did they believe? What did they fear? Answers to these questions illuminate conflicts at the heart of a revolution that "disloyal" Americans could not support.

SETTING

Whatever we may think about the Loyalists, we know they often paid dearly for their convictions. Roughly 100,000 of them fled to Britain or Canada during and after the Revolution. Their property was confiscated, and they were harassed, beaten, tarred and feathered, and hung. Women were not exempt. Revolutionaries stripped and dragged one Loyalist woman to the "Drawing Room window . . . exposing her to many Thousands of People Naked."[2] The prevailing view of the Loyalists was summed up by the popular revolutionary assertion that a Tory is a thing "whose head is in England, whose body is in America, and whose neck ought to be stretched."[3]

For a long time historians were hardly more charitable. In the period of intense patriotism after the Revolution, many Americans celebrated the war as the triumph of virtue over vice. At the same time, historians pictured Loyalists as scoundrels. Thus Mercy Otis Warren, who wrote one of the earliest histories of the Revolution, saw Loyalist Massachusetts Governor Thomas Hutchinson as "dark, intriguing, insinuating, haughty, and ambitious."[4] Later in the nineteenth century, nationalist historian George Bancroft characterized Loyalists as traitors who stood in the way of America's inevitable progress.

That view came under sharp attack in the early twentieth century, when many Americans feared powerful, mostly Eastern corporations and trusts. At the same time, such progressive historians as Vernon Louis Parrington, Carl Becker, and

Charles Beard emphasized economic and sectional conflict in American history. These historians saw the Revolution as a contest over property and power rather than a moral struggle between righteousness and treachery. As they put it, the Revolution was a battle to gain home rule *and* to determine "who should rule at home." Wealthy Loyalists were pictured as a powerful elite against which the revolutionaries had to fight.

Eventually Progressive historians also came in for attack. The end of the Depression as well as struggles against fascism and communism made it easier for historians to see the importance of ideological conflict in the nation's past. By the 1960s, such historians as Bernard Bailyn and Gordon Wood argued that republican political ideas rather than economic and social struggles were at the heart of the American Revolution. New interpretations of the Revolution led many historians to reject the Progressive view that Loyalists were merely people of property resisting a democratic uprising.

Today, most historians emphasize the tremendous diversity of the colonial population. As a result, they conclude that numerous factors explain Loyalism. For instance, some scholars argue that religious and ethnic conflict was a powerful influence on revolutionary loyalties in many states. Because contemporary historians emphasize the factious nature of colonial society, they are often more sympathetic to the Loyalists' position than were Mercy Otis Warren, George Bancroft, or the Progressives. Yet in one way their accounts have not changed. Modern historians' conclusions about the Loyalists remain a key to their views of the Revolution.

INVESTIGATION

Unlike previous chapters, this one contains a historian's essay—a *secondary source*—and a set of primary documents. Because both types of sources deal with the Loyalists, the primary sources shed light on the arguments in the essay. Your challenge is to use these sources to evaluate the essay's conclusions regarding the nature of Loyalism. Your evaluation should address the following main questions:

1. **According to Source 1, why did Loyalists side with the British?** What were the primary concerns of the Loyalist writers discussed there? What were the Loyalists' fears about tyranny?

2. **According to Source 1, in what ways was Loyalism conservative?** How do black and Indian Loyalists fit into an argument that it was?

3. **Do the primary sources support a different interpretation of Loyalism?** To what extent are the concerns of Loyalists in the essay reflected in the primary

sources? What additional reasons for Loyalism do these primary sources reveal?

To complete this assignment, first read Source 1 and determine its argument about Loyalist fears. Then turn to the primary sources to see what they suggest about opposition to the Revolution. When you are finished, you should be able to explain whether you agree with the author's explanation for Loyalism.

SECONDARY SOURCE

1   In this selection, historian Janice Potter discusses the ideas and fears of a small group of Loyalist spokesmen. They included Anglican clergymen Samuel Seabury, Charles Inglis, and Thomas Chandler; lawyer and Massachusetts attorney general Jonathan Sewall; Massachusetts lieutenant governor Andrew Oliver; Bay Colony chief justice Peter Oliver; and others. All of these men were articulate and had thought much about social disorder, tyranny, and equality. As you read Potter's analysis, look for evidence regarding the Loyalists' views about Patriots and why they opposed independence. Were these men or their concerns typical of Loyalists? Note whether Potter explains why some people adhered to Loyalist principles in the first place.

The Loyalist Argument (1983)
JANICE POTTER

. . . The American Revolution was a civil war in which Americans were deeply divided over fundamental issues. Loyalist and Patriot writers differed in their views of the British-American empire, in their ideas about contemporary American society, and in their basic intellectual assumptions. . . .

[The Loyalist argument] rested on certain basic assumptions about man's nature and government's role. It provided a well-reasoned defense of the imperial status quo at the same time as it outlined ways of improving both the British Empire and British institutions in America. Tying together these various dimensions of Loyalist thought was the pervasive theme that Americans had more to fear from self-interested factions in their midst than from the power of the British government. Loyalists, like Patriots, cautioned their readers about the imminence of oppression, but the tyranny they warned of was, in the words of Jonathan Sewall, a "democratic tyranny." . . .

Source: Reprinted by permission of the publisher from *The Liberty We Seek* by Janice Potter, Cambridge, Mass.: Harvard University Press. Copyright © 1983 by the President and Fellows of Harvard College.

. . . Before independence many writers had warned in very stark terms of the dangers confronting America. "Discord and tyranny, in the guise of liberty, stalk forth among us," a New York Loyalist proclaimed in early 1775. Others from the same colony voiced fears of oppression, slavery, or "tumultuous tyranny" and one spoke ominously of a design "to make us worse than slaves." . . .

The Loyalists' highly colorful imagery resembled that employed by the Patriots. Both groups of writers warned of a plot to deprive Americans of their freedom, yet the chasm between the two views of the Revolution was unbridgeable. To Patriots the threat to colonial freedom was an external one, from government. Britain, enervated by luxury, corruption, and tyranny, was conspiring to enslave the colonies: evil or designing ministers, a corrupt Parliament, and by 1776 the king himself were masterminding the insidious plots against American freedom. Loyalists were equally convinced that self-interested men plotted to subvert American liberty, but the threat they pointed to was an internal one, from below rather than above. Loyalist spokesmen outlined the historical origins and contemporary manifestations of an American-based conspiracy to destroy colonial freedom and happiness, and they beseeched their fellow subjects to wake up and realize the real source of their danger.

Warnings that Americans were in danger because they were obsessed with potential external threats to their liberty while being oblivious to the actual and more serious violations of freedom occurring in their midst abounded in the mid-1770s. As early as 1773, the New York Loyalist Myles Cooper cautioned his fellow colonists: "While we are watchful against *external* attacks on our freedom, let us be on our guard, lest we become *enslaved* by tyrants within." "Take heed," another wrote, "that while the words tyranny and oppression are bandied about, and fixed on Britain, you are not unawares enthralled at home." Peter Oliver was amazed that the colonists would, on the one hand, "trample upon the laws of the mildest Government upon earth," and on the other hand, "submit to a tyranny uncontrolled either by the laws of *God* or man." Other Loyalists stressed that while tyranny could be imposed by a few, it could also emanate from the many, or as Samuel Seabury put it, "The *tyranny* of a mob, is the *freedom* of America." . . .

. . . [F]rom Loyalist tracts the Patriots emerge as an aspiring and self-interested faction. That they sought their own betterment at the expense of the well-being of their country was illustrated, Loyalists contended, in their motives for criticizing public leaders and institutions. Honest criticism would have been public spirited. But the Patriots attacked established institutions and leaders because this suited their purposes. . . .

The charge that they were aspiring reflected the Loyalists' prejudicial assumptions about the characters of the Patriots and in some cases about their socioeconomic status. Loyalists suggested that some leaders . . . were from humble or disreputable backgrounds. They were described as being "ignorant men, bred to the lowest occupations" or as people "either having nothing to lose; or having wasted their own substance, would gladly become the masters of yours." . . . They were not "industrious artizans," "honest farmers," or "frugal tradesmen"; they either had never been successful in their callings or had squandered whatever good fortune they had had.

Especially galling to many Loyalists was that such men aspired to become leaders of the community, replacing what [Daniel] Leonard called "the ancient, trusty and skilful pilots," and were thrusting themselves—"bankrupts in fortune, business and fame"—into public prominence. The Loyalists' elitist view of political leadership showed through in their sense of outrage that men so ill-suited to guide the community were rising at the expense of those who were the natural leaders of society. "I feel indignation and shame mingling in my Bosom," Myles Cooper declared, "when I reflect that a few men (whom only the political storm could cast up from the bottom into notice) have presumed to act in the character of *representatives and substitutes of the Province.*" . . .

Despite the disreputable ambitions, backgrounds, and motives of the Patriot leaders, there was no doubt that by the mid-1770s they were accomplishing their designs to create confusion and to thrust themselves into leadership roles. How could such undeserved success be explained? The answer most commonly given by Loyalist writers was that the Patriots were crafty, hypocritical and manipulative. Loyalist sketches frequently described them as designing, crafty, artful, unprincipled, or cunning. . . . [Peter] Oliver's literary genius was revealed in his magnificent description of Samuel Adams, the epitome of the cunning Patriot, duping the highly esteemed President of the United Colonies, John Hancock, whose gullibility was not a product of innocence but of stupidity: "With his oily tongue he duped a man whose brains were shallow and pockets deep, and ushered him to the public as a patriot too: He filled his head with importance and emptied his pockets, and as a reward hath kicked him up the ladder, where he now presides over the twelve united provinces, and where they both are at present plunging you, my countrymen, into the depths of distress."

The Patriots' manipulative abilities were used with greatest effect on people whom they deftly maneuvered to achieve their self-interested aims. According to Daniel Leonard, they "applied themselves to work upon the imagination, and to inflame the passions; for this work they possessed great talents; I will do justice to their ingenuity; they were intimately acquainted with the feelings of man, and knew all the avenues to the human heart." . . .

The populace was easily deceived, it was argued, because the avenue to the human heart chosen by the Patriots was so effective. Playing upon fears of oppression kindled by British actions in the decade before independence, they fabricated the specter of imminent enslavement and deviously wormed their way into public confidence by posing as the saviors of their country's freedom. The Patriots, it was charged, wore the "mask of patriotism" and used civil liberty as the bait that was "flung out to catch the Populace at large, & engage them in the Rebellion." Peter Oliver and Samuel Seabury agreed that the merchants who had accumulated large inventories stood to benefit by the nonimportation schemes, but they had hypocritically masked their "selfish Designs" by, in Oliver's words, "mouthing it for Liberty." Probably an unknown Loyalist captured the essence of the attitude toward the Patriots' manipulation of the populace when he declared that they conjured up the "bugbear" of slavery to "usher in the demon of sedition."

Thus, Loyalist spokesmen provided a comprehensive, consistent, and compelling explanation of the origins of the Revolution. Ironically, they countered the Patriot version of a British design against colonial liberty with their own conspiracy theory of an American-based plot against freedom. While the villains in the Patriot piece were Loyalists and their allies in the British government, the conspirators in the Loyalist interpretation were self-interested, aspiring Patriot leaders who manipulated the people by playing upon fears of oppression to undermine popular support for the status quo. The British-American dispute fostered anxieties about oppression and gave the Patriots an excellent opportunity to set their design in motion. The aim of the conspirators, according to the Loyalist version of the Revolution, was the same as the goal of the plotters in the Patriot view of events—to oppress Americans. With the colonies reduced to chaos, the Patriots would take advantage of the confusion to erect their own regime—a democratic or popular tyranny—on the ruins of their country. . . .

Loyalists assumed that deference and respect for authority were vital to the long-term health of the body politic. . . . If the masses ever came to question seriously the power of traditional leaders or institutions, then the essential mortar of the body politic would begin to crumble. That is, once people were taught to distrust rather than trust authority, leaders and government would be deprived of a vital ingredient of their power, and the door would be open to anarchy. And chipping away at the legitimacy of symbols of authority was exactly what the Patriots were accused of doing.

This point was made very effectively by an anonymous Loyalist who lashed out at John Hancock for declaring in his oration on the anniversary of the Boston Massacre that the British soldiers who had been acquitted of murder were in fact guilty of the crime. What was so dangerous about Hancock's charge was that it "lessen[ed] the consequence and authority of the superior court . . . and [brought] into contempt, trials by juries." If the soldiers were indeed guilty of murder but were acquitted by the courts, either the court and jury were "invincibly ignorant and stupid, or incorrigibly vicious and wicked." Either conclusion, if generally accepted, would be dangerous since the "characters of both judges and jurors ought to be held in veneration"; otherwise their authority would not be respected or obeyed, they would no longer be able to uphold the law and maintain order, and soon "the strongest arm and longest sword will triumph over justice."

Fears that a decline in deference and respect for authority would lead to anarchy were reinforced by concrete evidence. By the mid-1770s Loyalists had no difficulty finding manifestations of chaos in their midst. Mobs pressured judges to close courts or prevented the courts from sitting, and magistrates lacked either courage or virtue to enforce the law. Grand juries were packed with Patriot partisans who regularly acquitted their cohorts. The legally constituted colonial governments were either ineffective or greatly weakened. "Libertinism," riot, and robbery were everyday occurrences for Loyalists such as Peter Oliver, who decried the fact that "houses were plundered and demolished, persons were beat, abused, tarred and feathered." . . .

Besides fears about an oppression imposed by Patriot committees and congresses, Loyalists were concerned that the whole American continent would suffer from a tyranny rooted in anarchy. Britain, for most Loyalists, was the cohesive bond which united the colonies and upheld the interests of the empire. However, as the Patriots challenged the authority of Britain to legislate for America and undermined public respect for British power, this vital tie joining the colonies would be broken. Instead, the self-interest of each colony would prevail, resulting in disunity, chaos, and eventually civil war. Jonathan Sewall predicted that "intestine jars and jealousies" would result from the difficulty of deciding on a form of government. "You will," he declared, "soon have as many forms of Government contended for, as there are men who have ambition, resolution, and ability sufficient to conduct their cause." Ultimately, he believed, either "a set of petty tyrants" would rule with "a rod of iron," or the colonists would "live in a state of perpetual war with your neighbours, and suffer all the calamities and misfortunes incident to anarchy, confusion, and bloodshed."

But just as anarchy was seen as being a stepping stone for tyranny within each colony, chaos on a continent-wide scale, it was warned, would be a prelude to oppression. The general argument was that once the central power in a political unit was emasculated and no longer able to regulate its members, then powerful, self-interested groups would have free rein to impose their will on others in the unit. . . . Alternatively, Loyalists warned that after America was reduced to utter confusion, there would be a power vacuum into which would step either an internal or more probably an external tyrant. . . . A most frightening picture of an independent America was painted by Peter Oliver. America, he wrote, would be "cantoned out into petty states," plagued by perpetual wars; fertile fields would be "deluged with blood"; wives and children would be "involved in the horrid scene" and the crowning blow would be that "foreign powers will step in and share in the plunder that remains, and those who are left to tell the story will be reduced to a more abject slavery than that which you now dread."

PRIMARY SOURCES

The sources in this section express a variety of viewpoints. As you evaluate them, consider what they reveal about Loyalist fears and to what extent they reflect the concerns of the Loyalist writers depicted in Potter's essay.

 2 Charles Inglis was a prominent Loyalist pamphleteer and a minister in the Church of England, which was headed by the British monarch. As you read this selection, consider what role that may have played in shaping his views.

Reverend Charles Inglis on Revolutionary Tyranny (1777)

Never, I will boldly and without hesitation pronounce it, never was a more just, more honorable, or necessary cause for taking up arms than that which now calls you into the field. It is the cause of truth against falsehood, of loyalty against rebellion, of legal government against usurpation, of Constitutional Freedom against Tyranny—in short it is the cause of human happiness of millions against outrage and oppression. Your generous efforts are required to assert the rights of your amiable, injured sovereign—they are required to restore your civil constitution which was formed by the wisdom of the ages, and was the admiration and envy of mankind—under which we and our ancestors enjoy liberty, happiness and security—but is now subverted to make room for a motley fabric, that is perfectly adapted to popular tyranny. Your bleeding country, through which destitution and ruin are driving in full career, from which peace, order, commerce, and useful industry are banished—your loyal friends and relations groaning in bondage under the iron scourge of persecution and oppression—all these now call upon you for succor and redress.

It is not wild, insatiable ambition which sports with lives and fortunes of mankind that leads you forth, driven from your peaceful habitations for no other cause than honoring your King, as God has commanded; you have taken up the sword to vindicate his just authority, to support your excellent constitution, to defend your families, your liberty, and property, to secure to yourselves and your posterity that inheritance of constitutional freedom to which you were born; and all this against the violence of usurped power, which would deny you even the right of judgment or of choice, which would rend from you the protection of your parent state, and eventually place you . . .

Source: John Wolfe Lydekker, *The Life and Letters of Charles Inglis* (London: The Society for Promoting Christian Knowledge, 1936), p. 257.

under the despotic rule of our inveterate Popish enemies, the inveterate enemies of our religion, our country and liberties.

3 | Samuel Seabury, a physician, farmer, and Anglican rector, was from an old New England family. As you read this selection, note the relationship between Seabury's views about authority and his position on independence.

A View of the Controversy Between Great Britain and Her Colonies (1774)

SAMUEL SEABURY

I wish you had explicitly declared to the public your ideas of the *natural rights of mankind*. Man in a *state of nature* may be considered as perfectly free from all restraints of law and government: And then the *weak* must submit to the *strong*. From such a state, I confess, I have a violent aversion. I think the form of government we lately enjoyed a much more eligible state to live in: And cannot help regretting our having *lost* it, by the *equity, wisdom*, and *authority* of the Congress, who have introduced in the room of it, confusion and violence; where all must submit to the power of a mob.

You have taken some pains to prove what would readily have been granted you—that *liberty* is a very *good* thing, and *slavery* a very *bad* thing. But then I must think that liberty under a *King, Lords* and *Commons* is as good as liberty under a republican Congress: And that slavery under a republican Congress is as bad, at least, as slavery under a *King, Lords* and *Commons:* And upon the whole, that *liberty* under the supreme authority and protection of Great-Britain, is infinitely preferable to *slavery* under an American Congress. . . .

The right of colonists to exercise a legislative power, is no natural right. They derive it not from nature, but from the indulgence or grant of the parent state, whose subjects they were when the colony was settled, and by whose permission and assistance they made the settlement.

Upon supposition that every English colony enjoyed a legislative power independent of the parliament; and that the parliament has no just authority to make laws to bind them, this absurdity will follow—that there is no power in the British empire, which has authority to make laws for the whole empire; i.e. we have an empire, without government; or which amounts to the same thing, we have a government which has no supreme power. All our colonies

Source: Leslie F. S. Upton, *Revolutionary Versus Loyalist: The First American Civil War, 1774–1784* (Waltham, Mass.: Blaisdell Publishing Company, 1968), pp. 24–25, 27–28; originally from New York, *Rivington*, 1774; pages cited in original were 8–11, 14–19, 21, 32–33.

are independent of each other: Suppose them independent of the British Parliament,—what power do you leave to govern the whole? None at all. You split and divide the empire into a number of petty insignificant states. This is the direct, the necessary tendency of refusing submission to acts of Parliament. Every man who can see one inch beyond his nose, must see this consequence. And every man who endeavours to accelerate the independency of the colonies on the British Parliament, endeavours to accelerate the ruin of the British empire.

To talk of being liege subjects to King GEORGE, while we disavow the authority of Parliament is another piece of whiggish nonsense. I love my King as well as any whig in America or England either, and am as ready to yield him all lawful submission: But while I submit to the King, I submit to the authority of the laws of the state, whose guardian the King is. The difference between a good and bad subject, is only this, that the one obeys, the other transgresses the law. The difference between a loyal subject and a rebel, is, that the one yields obedience to, and faithfully supports the supreme authority of the state, and the other endeavours to overthrow it. If we obey the laws of the King, we obey the laws of the Parliament. If we disown the authority of the Parliament, we disown the authority of the King.

 Ann Hulton was a Boston Loyalist. As you read her account of an attack on one Loyalist, think about the fears it reflects.

A Loyalist Woman on the Licentiousness of the Times (1774)

ANN HULTON

The most shocking cruelty was exercised a few nights ago, upon a poor old man, a tidesman, one Malcolm. . . . A quarrel was picked with him. He was afterward taken, and tarred and feathered. There's no law that knows a punishment for the greatest crimes beyond what this is, of cruel torture. And this instance exceeds any other before it. He was stripped stark naked, one of the severest cold nights this winter, his body covered all over with tar, then with feathers, his arm dislocated in tearing off his clothes. He was dragged in a cart, with thousands attending, some beating him with clubs and knocking him out of the cart, then in again. They give him several severe whippings, at different parts of the town. This spectacle of horror and sportive cruelty was exhibited for about five hours.

Source: Reprinted by permission of the publisher from *Letters of a Loyalist Lady* by Ann Hulton, Cambridge, Mass.: Harvard University Press, Copyright © 1927 by the President and Fellows of Harvard College, 1955 by Kenneth B. Murdock.

The unhappy wretch they say behaved with the greatest intrepidity and fortitude. All the while before he was taken, he defended himself a long time against numbers; and afterwards, when under torture they demanded of him to curse his masters, the king, governors, etc. which they could not make him do, but he still cried, Curse all Traitors. They brought him to the gallows and put a rope about his neck saying they would hang him; he said he wished they would, but that they could not for God was above the Devil. The doctors say that it is impossible that this poor creature can live. They say his flesh comes off his back in stakes.

It is the second time he has been tarred and feathered and this is looked upon more to intimidate the judges and others than a spite to the unhappy victim, though they owe him a grudge for some things, particularly, he was with Governor Tryon in the Battle with the Regulators. . . . The Governor has declared that he was of great service to him in that affair, by his undaunted spirit encountering the greatest dangers.

Governor Tryon had sent him a gift of ten guineas just before this inhuman treatment. He has a wife and family and an aged father and mother who, they say, saw the spectacle which no indifferent person can mention without horror.

These few instances among many serve to show the abject state of government and the licentiousness and barbarism of the times. There's no magistrate that dare or will act to suppress the outrages. No person is secure. There are many objects pointed at, at this time, and when once marked out for vengeance, their ruin is certain.

 As you read this poem, note whether its image of Patriots is similar to that advanced by the Loyalist spokesmen depicted in Potter's essay. What is the significance of the refrain "hunting-shirts and rifle-guns"?

A Loyalist Ode (1778)

Ye brave, honest subjects, who dare to be loyal,
And have stood the brunt of every trial,
    Of hunting-shirts, and rifle-guns:
Come listen awhile, and I'll sing you a song;
I'll show you, those Yankees are all in the wrong,
Who, with blustering look and most awkward gait,
'Gainst their lawful sovereign dare for to prate,
    With their hunting-shirts, and rifle-guns.
    . . . .
With loud peals of laughter, your sides, airs, would crack,

Source: Frank Moore, ed., *Songs and Ballads of the American Revolution* (New York, 1855), pp. 196–199.

To see General Convict and Colonel Shoe-black,
    With their hunting-shirts, and rifle-guns.
See cobblers and quacks, rebel priests and the like,
Pettifoggers and barbers, with sword and with pike,
All strutting, the standard of Satan beside,
And honest names using, their black deeds to hide.
    With their hunting-shirts, and rifle-guns.
    . . . .
For one lawful ruler, many tyrants we've got,
Who force young and old to their wars, to be shot,
    With their hunting-shirts, and rifle-guns.
Our good king, God speed him! never used men so,
We then could speak, act, and like freemen could go;
But committees enslave us, our Liberty's gone,
Our trade and church murder'd; our country's undone,
    By hunting-shirts, and rifle-guns.

Come take up your glasses, each true loyal heart,
And may every rebel meet his due desert,
    With his hunting-shirt, and rifle-gun.
May Congress, Conventions, those damn'd inquisitions,
Be fed with hot sulphur, from Lucifer's kitchens,
May commerce and peace again be restored,
And Americans own their true sovereign lord.
    Then oblivion to shirts, and rifle-guns.
        God save the King.

 6 In 1775 Lord Dunmore, the royal governor of Virginia, declared that slaves fighting for Britain would be freed. What does this brief newspaper report reveal about slaves' views of tyranny during the Revolution?

Liberty to Slaves (1775)

Williamsburg, December 2

Since lord [sic] Dunmore's proclamation made its appearance here, it is said he has recruited his army, in the counties of Princess Anne and Norfolk, to the amount of about 2100 men, including his black regiment, which is thought to be a considerable part, with this inscription on their breasts:—"Liberty to slaves."—However, as the rivers will henceforth be strictly watched, and every

Source: Maryland Gazette, December 14, 1775, Maryland Historical Society.

possible precaution taken, it is hoped others will be effectually prevented from joining those his lordship has already collected.

7 | Joseph Brant, also known as Thayendanegea, was an Iroquois chief who was half white. In 1776 Brant was in London and declared his loyalty to the colonial secretary, Lord George Germain. As you read this selection, keep in mind what Thayendanegea sought to gain from his loyalty to Britain.

Chief Thayendanegea Pledges His Loyalty (1776)

Brother.

When we delivered our speech you answered us in few words, that you would take care and have the grievances of the Six Nations on account of their lands, particularly those of the Mohocks and Oughquagas, removed; and all those matters settled to our satisfaction whenever the troubles in America were ended, and that you hoped the Six Nations would continue to behave with that attachment to the King they had always manifested; in which case they might be sure of his Majesty's favour and protection.

Brother. We return you thanks for this promise, which we hope will be performed, and that we shall not be disappointed, as has often been the case, notwithstanding the warm friendship of the Mohocks to his Majesty and his government, who are so immediately concerned, that the same has been often mentioned by the Six Nations and their getting no redress a matter of surprize to all the Indian Nations.

We are not afraid Brother, or have we the least doubt but our brethren the Six Nations will continue firm to their engagements with the King their father. Our Superintendent knows that in order to keep true to their treaties they have at times punished their friends and Allies.

Brother. The troubles that prevail in America and the distance we are from our country, allows us only to say that on our return we shall inform our Chiefs and Warriors what we have seen and heard and join with them in the most prudent measures for assisting to put a stop to those disturbances notwithstanding reports of their generally taking the strongest side. Which was not the case last Summer when we offered to prevent the invasion of Canada and lost several of our people in defending it. The only reason we mentioned the conduct of the Six Nations at that time was, that they might have credit for what they actually did, as we have heard much that affair has been attributed to the Nippissings and other Indians of Canada.

Source: Documents Relative to the Colonial History of the State of New-York, VIII, 678.

Brother. As we expect soon to depart for our own Country having been long here, we request you, and the great men who take charge of the affairs of government, not to listen to every story that may be told about Indians; but to give ear only to such things as come from our Chiefs and wise men in Council; which will be communicated to you by our Superintendent.

 Benjamin Rush was a Philadelphia physician and a Patriot. In this selection, he categorizes Loyalist motives. Compare his explanation of Loyalism to that in Source 1.

Benjamin Rush Categorizes Loyalists (1777)

I had frequent occasion to observe that the Tories and Whigs were actuated by very different motives in their conduct, or by the same motives acting in different degrees of force. The following classes of each of them was published by me in the early stages of the war. . . . There were Tories (1) from an attachment to power and office. (2) From an attachment to the British commerce which the war had interrupted or annihilated. (3) From an attachment to kingly government. (4) From an attachment to the hierarchy of the Church of England, which it was supposed would be abolished in America by her separation from Great Britain. This motive acted chiefly upon the Episcopal clergy, more especially in the Eastern states. (5) From a dread of the power of the country being transferred into the hands of the Presbyterians. This motive acted upon many of the Quakers in Pennsylvania and New Jersey, and upon the Episcopalians in several of those states where they had been in possession of power, or of a religious establishment. . . .

Source: George W. Corner, ed., *The Autobiography of Benjamin Rush, Memoirs of the American Philosophical Society* (1948), XXV, 117–119. Reprinted by permission of the America Philosophical Society.

 In this illustration, an engraving based on a painting by the American artist Benjamin West, Britannia welcomes her loyal subjects from the colonies. Although he was an outspoken supporter of the American Revolution, West was also a friend of George III and in 1772 had become a royal painter of history in England. When the engraving was published in 1815, the following explanation accompanied it:

Religion and Justice are represented extending the mantle of Britannia, whilst she herself is holding out her arm and shield to receive the Loyalists. Under the shield is

Source: Courtesy Harvard College Library.

the crown of Great Britain, surrounded by Loyalists. This group of figures consists of various characters, representing the Law, the Church, and the Government, with other inhabitants of North America; and, as a marked characteristic of that quarter of the globe, an Indian chief extending one hand to Britannia, and pointing the other to a Widow and Orphan, rendered so by the civil war: also a Negro and Children looking up to Britannia in grateful remembrance of their emancipation from Slavery. . . .

The two figures on the right are the painter, Mr. West[,] the President of the Royal Academy, and his Lady, both natives of Pennsylvania.[5]

Compare West's picture of the Loyalists with Benjamin Rush's view in the previous source. What does it reveal about the basis of Loyalism? Is this merely propaganda, or an accurate depiction of Loyalism's appeal?

A British View of the Loyalists (1815)

CONCLUSION

Several points should be clear from your analysis of the sources in this chapter. First, primary sources are useful tools to help assess historical arguments. They may reinforce or contradict historians' conclusions, add insights, and raise new questions. Second, historians must be careful when generalizing about the past. This chapter's sources demonstrate that the American revolutionaries were not the only ones who desired liberty during the conflict. They reveal that Loyalism was rooted in both principle and self-interest. Beyond that, however, it is not easy to make sweeping assertions about Loyalists, whose ranks included ministers, colonial officeholders, slaves, and Indians. They all opposed tyranny, but that term had different meanings for them.

Finally, these sources demonstrate that historians must understand their subjects' motives. Were Loyalists driven by a desire to protect their property and social position, a fear of social disorder, or a desire to end their oppression? Interpretations of the Revolution cannot ignore this question. If Loyalism sprang from a desire to throw off slavery, for instance, the definition of the Revolution as a struggle against tyranny must be qualified. The question of motives is central to historians' interpretations, and, as we will see next, much of history's detective work is a search for clues to explain motives.

FURTHER READING

Wallace Brown, *The Good Americans: Loyalists in the American Revolution* (New York: William Morrow, 1969).
Donald Barr Chidsey, *The Loyalists: The Story of Those Americans Who Fought Against Independence* (New York: Crown Publishers, 1973).
Francis Jennings, "The Indians' Revolution," in Alfred F. Young, ed., *The American Revolution: Explorations in the History of American Radicalism* (DeKalb: Northern Illinois University Press, 1976).
William H. Nelson, *The American Tory* (Oxford: Clarendon Press, 1961).
Mary Beth Norton, "Eighteenth-Century American Women in Peace and War: The Case of the Loyalists," *William and Mary Quarterly,* 33 (July 1976).

NOTES

1. Quoted in Kenneth S. Lynn, *A Divided People* (Westport, Conn.: Greenwood Press, 1961), p. 3.

2. Quoted in Mary Beth Norton, "Eighteenth-Century American Women in Peace and War: The Case of the Loyalists," *William and Mary Quarterly,* 33 (July 1976), 398.

3. Quoted in Richard B. Morris, "Foreword," in Catherine S. Crary, *The Price of Loyalty: Tory Writings from the Revolutionary Era* (New York: McGraw-Hill, 1973).

4. Mercy Otis Warren, *History of the Rise, Progress, and Termination of the American Revolution,* 3 vols. (Boston, 1805), I, 79.

5. Quoted in Helmut von Erffa and Allen Staley, *The Paintings of Benjamin West* (New Haven: Yale University Press, 1986), p. 219.

CHAPTER | 5

MOTIVATION IN HISTORY: CHARLES BEARD AND THE FOUNDING FATHERS

This chapter raises the question of motive in historical interpretation. It presents Charles Beard's revolutionary thesis about the Founding Fathers and gives several primary sources by which to judge that thesis.

Secondary Source

1. An Economic Interpretation of the Constitution of the United States (1913), CHARLES BEARD

Primary Sources

2. Public Security Holdings of the Delegates at the Constitutional Convention (1788)
3. Occupations of the Delegates to the New York State Ratifying Convention (1788)
4. The Founding Fathers Debate the Establishment of Congress (1787)
5. Federalist #10 (1788), JAMES MADISON
6. Federalist #15 (1788), ALEXANDER HAMILTON
7. Address of the Albany Antifederal Committee (1788)

*A*t the end of one of their cases, Sherlock Holmes and his associate Dr. Watson learn of another murder. Of course, Holmes knows that the culprit is his arch-nemesis, Professor Moriarty. This knowledge, however, is less important than Watson's question: "But for what motive?"[1]

That question is essential to both detective work and historical inquiry. Unfortunately, it is not always an easy question to answer because historical sources rarely reveal clear-cut motives. Motivation is one reason that historians argue about the past.

There are few better examples of this disagreement than views about the creation of the Constitution. Why was this document drafted, accepted by the Convention, and ratified? Were the Constitution's backers simply concerned for the nation? Or were they interested in protecting their own material interests? Or was it some combination of idealistic and materialistic motives? As we will see in this chapter, even the Founding Fathers have not been able to escape Dr. Watson's question.

SETTING

Until the early twentieth century, the Founding Fathers were venerated as demigods. As one American history textbook said in 1892, the Constitutional Convention was an "eminent assemblage of America's noblest patriots and most illustrious historic characters, 'all, all, honorable men.' "[2] Then in 1913, during the heyday of muckrakers intent on uncovering political corruption and exposing the practices of corporations, historian Charles Beard published *An Economic Interpretation of the Constitution of the United States.* Whereas earlier writers saw a group of patriots, Beard saw a group of men who were personally interested in the fruits of their labor. As merchants, creditors, and public security holders, he concluded, the framers of the Constitution stood to gain materially from a strong government that would protect private property and pay off depreciated public securities.

Beard also argued that the clash over the Constitution reflected a struggle between economic classes. On the one side were holders of "paper" wealth—creditors; on the other were the holders of "real" or landed wealth—farmers and debtors. The Constitution was thus backed by a minority of Americans. Women, blacks, Indians, and those without sufficient property had no voice. More to the point, Beard contended that no more than one-sixth of qualified voters supported the Constitution. Thus it was hardly a democratic document, but rather was created by a propertied elite who sought protection from popular majorities.

Beard's argument caused an uproar. One historian charged that Beard was intent on "demonstrating the Socialist theory of . . . class struggle."[3] The Seattle public schools banned Beard's book from the classroom. Ohio newspaper publisher and future president Warren G. Harding denounced it as filled with "filthy lies and rotten perversions." Beard's study, Harding said, was "libelous, vicious, and damnable in its influence."[4] Because Progressives were interested in limiting property rights, conservatives saw his work as another Progressive attack on private property. In a speech before an audience that included Supreme Court justices, U.S. senators, governors, and a J.P. Morgan and Company partner, former president William Howard Taft blasted Beard's book as a "muckraking investigation" that was intended to demonstrate the "sinister[,] reactionary nature of the Constitution."[5]

Beard paid a high price for his "politically incorrect" conclusions. In 1917, with the United States at war with Germany, Columbia University's trustees decided to investigate the faculty for disloyalty and subversion. Beard was called before a committee of trustees and instructed to warn his colleagues that "teachings likely to inculcate disrespect for American institutions would not be tolerated."[6] Later that year he resigned, citing the efforts of Columbia's president and the board of trustees to "drive out or humiliate or terrorize every man who held progressive, liberal, or unconventional views on political matters in no way connected with the war."[7] Beard's study had touched a sensitive nerve. By questioning the motives of the Constitution's supporters, it also demonstrated how important our interpretations of the past can be.

INVESTIGATION

In this chapter we analyze the argument that enraged school boards, college trustees, and a former and future president. The sources are a short excerpt from *An Economic Interpretation* by Charles Beard and primary documents related to the debates over the Constitution and to the property holdings and occupations of the Constitution's supporters. As you consider these sources, your job is to determine whether Charles Beard satisfactorily answered the question "For what motive?" Formulating answers to the following questions will help you complete this assignment:

1. **What was the Founding Fathers' motive for creating the Constitution, according to Beard (Source 1)?** What evidence does he use in attempting to demonstrate it?

2. **Does Beard make a convincing case about the origins of the Constitution?** Are his conclusions justified by the evidence? Is he consistent about the Founding Fathers' motives?

3. **Do the primary sources support or contradict Beard's argument?** Can you use them to make an alternative case about the creation of the Constitution?

SECONDARY SOURCE

1 In this selection, *real property* refers to such property as land and buildings. *Personalty* refers to such personal property as cash, bonds, capital invested in business enterprises or slaves, and capital invested to speculate in undeveloped lands. Keep in mind that it is generally in the interest of debtors to have currency devalued. If more money is printed, they can repay their loans with cheap currency. During the revolutionary and Confederation periods, the national and most of the state governments were large borrowers. Beard assumes that their creditors did not want the currency devalued. As you read this selection, keep in mind whether it is possible to be motivated by *economic* concerns without being driven by personal *financial* gain and if Beard carefully distinguishes between these motives. Also, consider whether he was correct in assuming that the identification of people's interests explains their actions. Are people usually driven by just one economic interest? Could the Constitution have been created to protect property and for other reasons as well? Is it possible to offer an economic interpretation of the Constitution without examining the economic standing of its framers?

An Economic Interpretation of the Constitution of the United States (1913)

CHARLES BEARD

A Survey of Economic Interests in 1787

The whole theory of the economic interpretation of history rests upon the concept that social progress in general is the result of contending interests in society—some favorable, others opposed, to change. On this hypothesis, we are required to discover at the very outset of the present study what classes and social groups existed in the United States just previous to the adoption of the Constitution and which of them, from the nature of their property, might have expected to benefit immediately and definitely by the overthrow of the old system and the establishment, of the new. . . .

Groups of Real Property Holders

The real property holders may be classified into three general groups: the small farmers, particularly back from the sea-coast, scattered from New Hampshire

Source: Reprinted with the permission of Simon & Schuster from *An Economic Interpretation of the Constitution of the United States* by Charles Beard. Copyright © 1935 by Macmillan Publishing Company, Copyright © renewed 1963 by William Beard and Mrs. Marion Beard Vagts.

to Georgia, the manorial lords, such as we find along the banks of the Hudson, and the slaveholding planters of the south.

Groups of Personal Property Interests

A second broad group of interests was that of personal property as contrasted with real property. This embraced, particularly, money loaned, state and continental securities, stocks of goods, manufacturing plants, soldiers' scrip, and shipping. The relative proportion of personalty to realty in 1787 has not been determined and it is questionable whether adequate data are available for settling such an important matter.

Personalty in Money.— Although personalty in the form of money at interest or capital seeking investment did not constitute in 1787 anything like the same amount, relative to the value of real estate, which it does to-day, it must not be thought that it was by any means inconsiderable in any state. . . .

Money capital was suffering in two ways under the Articles of Confederation. It was handicapped in seeking profitable outlets by the absence of protection for manufactures, the lack of security in investments in western lands, and discriminations against American shipping by foreign countries. It was also being positively attacked by the makers of paper money . . . and other devices for depreciating the currency or delaying the collection of debts. In addition there was a widespread derangement of the monetary system and the coinage due to the absence of uniformity and stability in the standards. . . .

Personalty in Public Securities.— Even more immediately concerned in the establishment of a stable national government were the holders of state and continental securities. The government under the Articles of Confederation was not paying the interest on its debt and its paper had depreciated until it was selling at from one-sixth to one-twentieth of its par value. Grave uncertainties as to the actions of legislatures kept state paper at a low price, also, even where earnest attempts were being made to meet the obligations.

The advantage of a strong national government that could discharge this debt at its face value is obvious; and it was fully understood at the time. The importance of this element of personalty in forcing on the revolution that overthrew the Articles of Confederation is all the more apparent when it is remembered that securities constituted a very large proportion of the intangible wealth. . . .

Personalty in Manufacturing and Shipping.— The third group of personalty interests embraced the manufacturing population, which was not inconsiderable even at that time. A large amount of capital had been invested in the several branches of industry and a superficial study of the extensive natural resources at hand revealed the immense possibilities of capitalistic enterprise. . . .

In the survey of the economic interests of the members of the federal Convention . . . it is shown that a few leading men were directly connected with industrial concerns, although it is not apparent that the protection of industries was their chief consideration, in spite of the fact that they did undoubtedly contemplate such a system. . . .

That innumerable manufacturing, shipping, trading, and commercial interests did, however, look upon the adoption of the Constitution as the sure guarantee that protection could be procured against foreign competition, is fully evidenced in the memorials laid before Congress in April, May, and June, 1789, asking for the immediate enactment of discriminatory tariff laws.

Capital Invested in Western Lands.— Although companies had been formed to deal in western lands on a large scale before the Revolution, it was not until the close of the War that effective steps were taken toward settlement. . . .

The situation was this: Congress under the Articles of Confederation adopted a policy of accepting certificates in part payment for lands; and it was hoped by some that the entire national debt might be extinguished in this way. However, the weakness of the Confederation, the lack of proper military forces, the uncertainty as to the frontiers kept the values of the large sections held for appreciation at an abnormally low price. Those who had invested their funds in these lands or taken stocks in the companies felt the adverse effects of the prevailing public policy, and foresaw the benefits which might be expected from a new and stable government. Their view was tersely put by Williamson, a member of the Convention from North Carolina, in a letter to Madison on June 2, 1788: "For myself, I conceive that my opinions are not biassed by private Interests, but having claims to a considerable Quantity of Land in the Western Country, I am fully persuaded that the Value of those Lands must be increased by an efficient federal Government."

The weight of the several species of property in politics is not determined by the amount, but rather by the opportunities offered to each variety for gain and by the degree of necessity for defence against hostile legislation. . . . When viewed in this light the reason for the special pressure of personalty in politics in 1787 is apparent. It was receiving attacks on all hands from the depreciators. . . .

It should be remembered also that personalty is usually more active than real property. It is centralized in the towns and can draw together for defence or aggression with greater facility. The expectation of profits from its manipulation was much larger in 1787 than from real property. It had a considerable portion of the professional classes attached to it; its influence over the press was tremendous, not only through ownership, but also through advertising and other patronage. It was, in short, the dynamic element in the movement for the new Constitution.

The Movement for the Constitution

Certain tentative conclusions emerge at this point.

Large and important groups of economic interests were adversely affected by the system of government under the Articles of Confederation, namely, those of public securities, shipping and manufacturing, money at interest; in short, capital as opposed to land.

The representatives of these important interests attempted through the regular legal channels to secure amendments to the Articles of Confederation which would safeguard their rights in the future, particularly those of the public creditors.

Having failed to realize their great purposes through the regular means, the leaders in the movement set to work to secure by a circuitous route the assembling of a Convention to "revise" the Articles of Confederation with the hope of obtaining, outside of the existing legal framework, the adoption of a revolutionary programme.

Ostensibly, however, the formal plan of approval by Congress and the state legislatures was to be preserved.

The Economic Interests of the Members of the Convention

Having shown that four groups of property rights were adversely affected by the government under the Articles of Confederation, and that economic motives were behind the movement for a reconstruction of the system, it is now necessary to inquire whether the members of the Convention which drafted the Constitution represented in their own property affiliations any or all of these groups. In other words, did the men who formulated the fundamental law of the land possess the kinds of property which were immediately and directly increased in value or made more secure by the results of their labors at Philadelphia? Did they have money at interest? Did they own public securities? Did they hold western lands for appreciation? Were they interested in shipping and manufactures?

The purpose of such an inquiry is not, of course, to show that the Constitution was made for the personal benefit of the members of the Convention. Far from it. Neither is it of any moment to discover how many hundred thousand dollars accrued to them as a result of the foundation of the new government. The only point here considered is: Did they represent distinct groups whose economic interests they understood and felt in concrete, definite form through their own personal experience with identical property rights, or were they working merely under the guidance of abstract principles of political science? . . .

A survey of the economic interests of the members of the Convention presents certain conclusions:

A majority of the members were lawyers by profession.

Most of the members came from towns, on or near the coast, that is, from the regions in which personalty was largely concentrated.

Not one member represented in his immediate personal economic interests the small farming or mechanic classes.

The overwhelming majority of members, at least five-sixths, were immediately, directly, and personally interested in the outcome of their labors at Philadelphia, and were to a greater or less extent economic beneficiaries from the adoption of the Constitution.

1. Public security interests were extensively represented in the Convention. Of the fifty-five members who attended no less than forty appear on the Records of the Treasury Department for sums varying from a few dollars up to more than one hundred thousand dollars. . . .

    It is interesting to note that, with the exception of New York, and possibly Delaware, each state had one or more prominent representatives in the Convention who held more than a negligible amount of securities, and who could therefore speak with feeling and authority on the question of providing in the new Constitution for the full discharge of the public debt. . . .

2. Personalty invested in lands for speculation was represented by at least fourteen members. . . .

3. Personalty in the form of money loaned at interest was represented by at least twenty-four members. . . .

4. Personalty in mercantile, manufacturing, and shipping lines was represented by at least eleven members. . . .

5. Personalty in slaves was represented by at least fifteen members. . . .

It cannot be said, therefore, that the members of the Convention were "disinterested." On the contrary, we are forced to accept the profoundly significant conclusion that they knew through their personal experiences in economic affairs the precise results which the new government that they were setting up was designed to attain. . . . [A]s practical men they were able to build the new government upon the only foundations which could be stable: fundamental economic interests.

Conclusions

The movement for the Constitution of the United States was originated and carried through principally by four groups of personalty interests which had been adversely affected under the Articles of Confederation: money, public securities, manufactures, and trade and shipping.

The first firm steps toward the formation of the Constitution were taken by a small and active group of men immediately interested through their personal possessions in the outcome of their labors.

No popular vote was taken directly or indirectly on the proposition to call the Convention which drafted the Constitution.

A large propertyless mass was, under the prevailing suffrage qualifications, excluded at the outset from participation (through representatives) in the work of framing the Constitution.

The members of the Philadelphia Convention which drafted the Constitution were, with a few exceptions, immediately, directly, and personally interested in, and derived economic advantages from the establishment of the new system.

The Constitution was essentially an economic document based upon the concept that the fundamental private rights of property are anterior to government and morally beyond the reach of popular majorities. . . .

The leaders who supported the Constitution in the ratifying conventions represented the same economic groups as the members of the Philadelphia Convention; and in a large number of instances they were also directly and personally interested in the outcome of their efforts.

In the ratification, it became manifest that the line of cleavage for and against the Constitution was between substantial personalty interests on the one hand and the small farming and debtor interests on the other.

The Constitution was not created by "the whole people" as the jurists have said; neither was it created by "the states" as Southern nullifiers long contended; but it was the work of a consolidated group whose interests knew no state boundaries and were truly national in their scope.

PRIMARY SOURCES

The primary sources in this section are debates from the Constitutional Convention, arguments in favor of the Constitution, and tables illustrating the property and occupations of the Constitution's supporters. As you read and analyze these sources, consider what they reveal about the motives of the Founding Fathers and whether they support Beard's argument or offer an alternative explanation for the framing of the Constitution.

2 This table lists the value of the public security holdings (bonds) of the delegates at the Constitutional Convention. As you examine it, keep in mind that bonds such as those issued by the central government to finance the Revolutionary War are simply IOUs, that is, promises by the issuer (borrower) to pay back the amount loaned plus interest to the bearer (lender). Thus, the column under the heading "Face Value" does not refer to the amount the delegate paid for the bonds, but to the total value of his bond holdings if the government were to pay all of the principal and interest due. (For instance, the

Source: Forrest McDonald, *We the People: The Economic Origins of the Constitution* (Chicago: University of Chicago Press, 1958), p. 90.

government owed Robert Morris $11,000.) Also remember that bonds issued to finance the Revolution changed hands after the war at prices considerably lower than their face value—a reflection of investors' fears about the inability of the government under the Articles of Confederation to pay back its debts. The second and third columns of the table reveal the *market* value of the delegates' bonds in 1787 and 1791. Those delegates whose names are marked with an asterisk (*) either refused to sign the Constitution or walked out before the proceedings were over. There were fifty-five delegates at the Constitutional Convention. Determine the total percentage of delegates who held public securities. Then figure the total value of the holdings of the delegates who either walked out or refused to sign the Constitution. Compare those holdings to the holdings of pro-Constitution delegates. Does the table support Beard's argument?

Public Security Holdings of the Delegates at the Constitutional Convention (1788)

Delegate	Face Value	Approximate Market Value		Appreciation or Paper Profit
		1787	December 1791	
Gerry	$ 50,000	$10,000	$ 32,500	$ 22,500*
McClurg	32,000	6,500	20,800	14,300
Langdon	28,000	3,500	18,200	14,700
Clymer	15,500	6,350	10,100	3,750
C. C. Pinckney	15,000	2,500	9,750	7,250
Randolph	13,800	3,450	8,900	5,450*
Robert Morris	11,000	4,500	7,150	2,650
Strong	11,000	2,200	7,150	4,950
Blair	10,800	2,500	7,100	4,600
King	10,000	5,000	6,300	1,300
Fitzsimons	8,300	3,300	5,400	2,100
Franklin	8,100	3,250	5,250	2,000
Sherman	7,800	1,000	5,000	4,000
Mercer	7,200	2,150	4,600	2,450*
Lansing	7,000	3,500	4,550	1,050*
Ellsworth	6,000	750	3,800	3,050
Dayton	5,500	1,000	3,600	2,600
Luther Martin	4,400	1,300	2,850	1,550*
Bedford	2,900	360	1,875	1,515
Williamson	2,600	300	1,700	1,400
Mifflin	2,500	1,000	1,600	600
Baldwin	2,500	300	1,600	1,300

(cont on next page)

Public Security Holdings of the Delegates at the Constitutional Convention (1788) (con't)

Delegate	Face Value	Approximate Market Value		Appreciation or Paper Profit
		1787	December 1791	
Wythe	$ 1,600	$ 350	$ 1,050	$ 700
Gilman	1,000	125	625	500
Few	650	80	425	345
Washington	500	75	325	250
Read	350	50	225	175
Carroll	225	90	150	60
Broom	40	10	25	15
Brearley	15	5	10	5
Total	$266,275	$65,495	$172,610	$107,115

3 As you examine this table, consider what it reveals about the economic position of those who supported and opposed the Constitution in New York. Does it support or contradict Beard's argument?

Occupations of the Delegates to the New York State Ratifying Convention (1788)

	Federal	Elected Anti, voted Fed.	Elected Anti, did not vote	Anti-federal
Merchants	5	1	0	0
Lawyers and large landowners	3	3	0	1
Lawyers	5	0	4	7
Large landowners	2	1	1	2
Millers	0	1	0	1
Obscure men	4	3	2	9
Farmers	0	3	0	6

Source: Jackson T. Main, "Charles A. Beard and the Constitution: A Critical Review of Forrest McDonald's *We the People*," *William and Mary Quarterly,* Ser. 3, 17 (1960), 99.

4 | This selection presents different opinions on popular representation in the House of Representatives. Refer to Source 2 to determine the public security holdings, if any, of the participants in this debate. Then determine if their positions on this issue support Beard's argument.

The Founding Fathers Debate the Establishment of Congress (1787)

Thursday, May 31

Resol: 4. first clause "that the members of the first branch of the National Legislature ought to be elected by the people of the several States" being taken up,

Mr. **Sherman** opposed the election by the people, insisting that it ought to be by the State Legislatures. The people he said, immediately should have as little to do as may be about the Government. They want [lack] information and are constantly liable to be misled.

Mr. **Gerry** The evils we experience flow from the excess of democracy. The people do not want virtue, but are the dupes of pretended patriots. In Massts. it had been fully confirmed by experience that they are daily misled into the most baneful measures and opinions by the false reports circulated by designing men, and which no one on the spot can refute. One principal evil arises from the want of due provision for those employed in the administration of Governmt. It would seem to be a maxim of democracy to starve the public servants. He [Mr. Gerry] mentioned the popular clamour in Massts. for the reduction of salaries and the attack made on that of the Govt. though secured by the spirit of the Constitution itself. He had he said been too republican heretofore: he was still however republican, but had been taught by experience the danger of the levelling spirit.

Mr. **Mason** argued strongly for an election of the larger branch by the people. It was to be the grand depository of the democratic principle of the Govts. It was, so to speak, to be our House of Commons—It ought to know & sympathise with every part of the community; and ought therefore to be taken not only from different parts of the whole republic, but also from different districts of the larger members of it, which had in several instances particularly in Virga., different interests and views arising from difference of produce, of habits &c &c. He admitted that we had been too democratic but was afraid we ... incautiously run into the opposite extreme. We ought to attend to the rights

Source: Gaillard Hunt and James Brown Scott, eds., *The Debates in the Federal Convention of 1787 Which Framed the Constitution of the United States* (New York: Oxford University Press, 1920), pp. 31–33.

of every class of people. He had often wondered at the indifference of the superior classes of society to this dictate of humanity & policy; considering that however affluent their circumstances, or elevated their situations, might be, the course of a few years, not only might but certainly would, distribute their posterity throughout the lowest classes of Society. Every selfish motive therefore, every family attachment, ought to recommend such a system of policy as would provide no less carefully for the rights and happiness of the lowest than of the highest orders of Citizens.

Mr. Wilson contended strenuously for drawing the most numerous branch of the Legislature immediately from the people. He was for raising the federal pyramid to a considerable altitude, and for that reason wished to give it as broad a basis as possible. No government could long subsist without the confidence of the people. In a republican Government, this confidence was peculiarly essential. He also thought it wrong to increase the weight of the State Legislatures by making them the electors of the national Legislature. All interference between the general and local Governmts. should be obviated as much as possible. On examination it would be found that the opposition of States to federal measures had proceeded much more from the officers of the States, than from the people at large.

Mr. Madison considered the popular election of one branch of the National Legislature as essential to every plan of free Government. He observed that in some of the States one branch of the Legislature was composed of men already removed from the people by an intervening body of electors. That if the first branch of the general legislature should be elected by the State Legislatures, the second branch elected by the first—the Executive by the second together with the first; and other appointments again made for subordinate purposes by the Executive, the people would be lost sight of altogether; and the necessary sympathy between them and their rulers and officers, too little felt. He was an advocate for the policy of refining the popular appointments by successive filtrations, but thought it might be pushed too far. He wished the expedient to be resorted to only in the appointment of the second branch of the Legislature, and in the Executive & judiciary branches of the Government. He thought too that the great fabric to be raised woult be more stable and durable, if it should rest on the solid foundation of the people themselves, than if it should stand merely on the pillars of the Legislatures.

Mr. Gerry did not like the election by the people. The maxims taken from the British constitution were often fallacious when applied to our situation which was extremely different. Experience he said had shewn that the State legislatures drawn immediately from the people did not always possess their confidence. He had no objection however to an election by the people if it were so qualified that men of honor & character might not be unwilling to be joined in the appointments. He seemed to think the people might nominate a certain number out of which the State legislatures should be bound to choose.

Mr. Butler thought an election by the people an impracticable mode.

On the question for an election of the first branch of the national Legislature by the people.

Massts. ay. Connect. divd. N. York ay. N. Jersey no. Pena. ay. Delawe. divd. Va. ay. N. C. ay. S. C. no. Georga. ay.

---

5 | *The Federalist* was a collection of documents written by James Madison, John Jay, and Alexander Hamilton to win ratification of the Constitution in New York State. Beard argued that it presented "the finest study in the economic interpretation of politics which exists in any language."[8] In Federalist #10, Madison explains why liberty is better protected in a large republic than in a smaller, more democratic state. As you read, determine whether Madison's concerns about factions were exclusively economic in nature. Also keep in mind where Madison was from. Was he a holder of public securities?

Federalist #10 (1788)

JAMES MADISON

Among the numerous advantages promised by a well-constructed Union, none deserves to be more appreciated than its tendency to break and control the violence of class interest, or faction. The advocate of popular governments never finds himself so much alarmed for their character and fate as when he contemplates their weakness for this dangerous vice.

The instability, injustice, and confusion introduced by faction into public councils have, in truth, been the mortal diseases under which popular governments have everywhere perished.

By a faction I understand a number of citizens, whether amounting to a majority or minority of the whole, who are united and actuated by some common impulse of passion, or of interest, adverse to the rights of other citizens, or to the permanent and aggregate interests of the community. . . .

From the protection of differing and unequal abilities for the acquiring of property, there results the possession of different degrees and kinds of property; and from the influence of these differences there follows a division of society into different interests and parties.

Source: Excerpted from *The Federalist Papers: A Contemporary Selection, Abridged and Edited* by Lester DeKloster. Copyright 1976 Wm. B. Eerdmans Publishing Co. Used by permission.

The causes of faction are thus sown in the very nature of man. A zeal for different opinions concerning religion, concerning government and on many other points; an attachment to different leaders ambitiously contending for pre-eminence and power: these have divided mankind into parties, inflamed them with mutual animosity, and made them much more disposed to vex and to oppress each other than to co-operate for their common good. Even the most frivolous and fanciful distinctions have been sufficient to kindle the most unfriendly passions and to excite the most violent conflicts.

Withal, the most common and durable source of factions has ever been the unequal distribution of property. Those who hold as opposed to those who are without property have ever formed distinct interests in society. Those who are creditors, and those who are debtors, likewise share different concerns. A landed interest, a manufacturing interest, a mercantile interest, a moneyed interest, with many lesser interests, grow up of necessity in civilized nations, and divide them into different classes, actuated by different sentiments and views. The regulation of these various and interfering interests forms the principal task of modern legislation, and involves the spirit of party and faction in the necessary and ordinary operations of government. . . .

A common passion or interest will, in almost every case, be felt by a majority of the whole; and there is nothing to check the inducements to sacrifice the weaker party or individual. Hence it is that such pure democracies have ever been spectacles of turbulence and contention; have ever been found incompatible with personal security or the rights of property; and have in general been as short in their lives as they have been violent in their deaths. . . .

A republic, on the other hand, by which I mean a government in which a scheme of representation takes place, opens a different prospect and promises the cure for which we are seeking. Let us examine the points in which it varies from pure democracy, and we shall comprehend both the nature of the cure and the efficacy it must derive from the Union.

The two great points of difference between a pure democracy and a republic are: first, the delegation of the government in a republic to a smaller number of citizens elected by the rest; secondly, the greater number of citizens and greater sphere of country over which the republic may be thus extended.

The effect of the first difference is, on the one hand, to refine and enlarge the public views by passing them through the medium of a chosen body of citizens, whose wisdom may best discern the true interest of their country and whose patriotism and love of justice will be least likely to sacrifice it to temporary or partial considerations. Under such conditions it may well happen that the public voice, pronounced by the representatives of the people, will be more consonant to the public good than if pronounced by the people themselves. It is possible, of course, that the effect may unhappily be inverted. Men of factious tempers, of local prejudices or of sinister designs, may, by intrigue, by corruption, or by other means, first obtain the votes and then betray the interests of the people. The question resulting is, then, whether small or extensive republics are most favorable to the election of proper guardians of the public weal; and it is clearly decided in favor of the larger.

For, as each representative will be chosen by a greater number of citizens in the large than in the small republic, it will be more difficult for unworthy candidates to practise with success the vicious arts by which elections are too often carried. Moreover, the suffrages of the people being more free, they will be more likely to center on men who possess the most attractive merit and the most diffusive and established characters.

Hence, it clearly appears that the same advantage which a republic has over a pure democracy in controlling the effects of faction is enjoyed by a large over a small republic—is enjoyed, that is, by the Union over the States composing it. . . .

The influence of factious leaders may kindle a flame within their particular States but will be unable to spread a general conflagration through the other States. A religious sect may degenerate into a political faction in a part of the United States, but the variety of sects dispersed over the entire face of the nation must secure the national councils against any danger from that source. A rage for paper money, for an abolition of debts, for an equal division of property, or for any improper or wicked project, will be less apt to pervade the whole body of the Union than a particular member of it, in the same proportion as such a malady is more likely to taint a particular county or district than an entire State.

In the extent and proper structure of the Union, therefore, we behold a republican remedy for the diseases most incident to republican government.

6 | As you read this selection, ask whether Hamilton's concern for the nation's economic conditions betrays self-interest. Was he a security holder?

Federalist #15 (1788)

ALEXANDER HAMILTON

We may indeed with propriety be said to have reached almost the last stage of national humiliation. There is scarcely any thing that can wound the pride, or degrade the character of an independent nation, which we do not experi-

Source Michael Kammen, ed., *The Origins of the American Constitution: A Documentary History* (New York: Viking Penguin, 1986), pp. 158–159.

ence. Are there engagements to the performance of which we are held by every tie respectable among men? These are the subjects of constant and unblushing violation. Do we owe debts to foreigners and to our own citizens contracted in a time of imminent peril, for the preservation of our political existence? These remain without any proper or satisfactory provision for their discharge. Have we valuable territories and important posts in the possession of a foreign power, which by express stipulations ought long since to have been surrendered? These are still retained, to the prejudice of our interests not less than of our rights. . . . Are we entitled by nature and compact to a free participation in the navigation of the Mississippi? Spain excludes us from it. Is public credit an indispensable resource in time of public danger? We seem to have abandoned its cause as desperate and irretrievable. Is commerce of importance to national wealth? Ours is at the lowest point of declension. Is respectability in the eyes of foreign powers a safeguard against foreign encroachments? The imbecility of our Government even forbids them to treat with us: Our ambassadors abroad are the mere pageants of mimic sovereignty. Is a violent and unnatural decrease in the value of land a symptom of national distress? The price of improved land in most parts of the country is much lower than can be accounted for by the quantity of waste land at market, and can only be fully explained by that want of private and public confidence, which are so alarmingly prevalent among all ranks and which have a direct tendency to depreciate property of every kind. Is private credit the friend and patron of industry? That most useful kind which relates to borrowing and lending is reduced within the narrowest limits, and this still more from an opinion of insecurity than from the scarcity of money.

 As you read this Antifederalist argument against the ratification of the Constitution, note the major concerns that it raises. Do the drafters share Beard's conclusions about the Founders' work, or do they focus on other issues? *The focus on other issues: states right, civil liberties fear of consolidated government, taxation*

Address of the Albany Antifederal Committee (1788)

As we have been informed, that the advocates for the new constitution, have lately travelled through the several districts in the county, and propogated an opinion, that it is a good system of government: we beg leave to state, in as few words as possible, some of the many objections against it.—

Source: Herbert J. Storing, ed., *The Complete Anti-Federalist* (Chicago: The University of Chicago Press, 1981), V1: 122–123, 124; originally from *New York Journal* (April 26, 1788).

The convention, who were appointed for the sole and express purpose of revising and amending the confederation, have taken upon themselves the power of making a new one.

They have not formed a *federal* but a *consolidated* government, repugnant to the principles of a republican government: not founded on the preservation but the destruction of the state governments.

The great and extensive powers granted to the new government over the lives, liberties, and property of every citizen.

These powers in many instances not defined or sufficiently explained, and capable of being interpreted to answer the most ambitious and arbitrary purposes.

The small number of members who are to compose the general legislature, which is to pass laws to govern so large and extensive a continent, inhabited by people of different laws, customs, and opinions, and many of them residing upwards of 400 miles from the seat of government.

The members of the senate are not to be chosen by the people, but appointed by the legislature of each state for the term of six years. This will destroy their responsibility, and induce them to act like the masters and not the servants of the people.

The power to alter and regulate the time, place, and manner of holding elections, so as to keep them subjected to their influence.

The power to lay poll taxes, duties, imposts, excises, and other taxes.

The power to appoint continental officers to levy and collect those taxes.

Their laws are to be *the supreme law of the land*, and the judges in every state are to be bound thereby, notwithstanding *the constitution or laws* of any state to the contrary—A sweeping clause, which subjects every thing to the controul of the new government.

Slaves are taken into the computation in apportioning the number of representatives, whereby 50,000 slaves, give an equal representation with 30,000 freemen. . . .

The power to raise, support, and maintain a standing army *in time of peace.* The bane of a republican government; by a standing army most of the once free nations of the globe have been reduced to bondage; and by this Britain attempted to inforce her arbitrary measures. . . .

Men conscienciously scrupulous of bearing arms, made liable to perform military duty. . . .

The not securing the rights of conscience in matters of religion, of granting the liberty of worshipping God agreeable to the mode thereby dictated; whereas the experience of all ages proves that the benevolence and humility inculcated in the gospel, are no restraint on the love of domination.

CONCLUSION

Charles Beard is a good example of the way a generation rewrites history in the light of the dominant ideas and events of its day. Beard turned to the past with a Progressive-era conviction that discovering hidden economic motives was necessary both to understand the past and to change the present. As confident as Progressive historians were about the power of ideas to change society, however, Beard never claimed that his study was the last word on the Constitution. He was careful to call it *an* economic interpretation, not the economic interpretation. Moreover, Beard always called *An Economic Interpretation* "fragmentary." He hoped it would stimulate further research by other scholars.

It did. Since the publication of Beard's study, numerous historians have been inspired to investigate the Founding Fathers. Many would challenge Beard's evidence and his conclusions. For more than eighty years, however, they have yet to put the Founding Fathers back on the pedestal where they stood when *An Economic Interpretation* shocked the nation. Beard's study transcends its own time because after 1913 historians would never again look at the Founding Fathers merely as public-spirited men. Indeed, it remains the starting point for studies of the Constitution. It is also relevant because it dealt with a problem that all historians must confront: the relationship between ideas and economic interests. It is to this problem that we turn next.

FURTHER READING

Catherine Drinker Bowen, *Miracle at Philadelphia: The Story of the Constitutional Convention* (Boston: Little, Brown, 1966).

Richard Hofstadter, *The Progressive Historians: Turner, Beard, Parrington* (New York: Alfred A. Knopf, 1968).

Forrest McDonald, *Novus Ordo Seclorum: The Intellectual Origins of the Constitution* (Lawrence: University Press of Kansas, 1985).

Edmund S. Morgan, *Inventing the People: The Rise of Popular Sovereignty in England and America* (New York: W. W. Norton & Company, 1988).

Garry Wills, *Interpreting America: The Federalist* (Garden City, N.Y.: Doubleday & Company, 1981).

NOTES

1. Sir Arthur Conan Doyle, *The Complete Sherlock Holmes* (Garden City, N.Y.: Doubleday, 1930), p. 866.

2. Richard Miller Devens, *American Progress: or The Great Events of the Greatest Century* (Springfield, Mass.: C. A. Nichols, 1892), p. 80.

3. Quoted in Forrest McDonald, "Introduction," in Charles A. Beard, *An Economic Interpretation of the Constitution of the United States* (New York: The Free Press, 1986), p. xx.

4. Ibid., p. xix.

5. *New York Times,* December 14, 1913, IV, 5:1.

6. Quoted in Richard Hofstadter, *The Progressive Historians: Turner, Beard, Parrington* (New York: Alfred A. Knopf, 1968), p. 285.

7. Richard Hofstadter and Wilson Smith, eds., *American Higher Education: A Documentary History* (Chicago: University of Chicago Press, 1961), II, 891.

8. Charles A. Beard, *An Economic Interpretation of the Constitution of the United States* (New York: Macmillan Company, 1941), p. 153.

CHAPTER | 6

IDEAS IN HISTORY:
RACE IN JEFFERSON'S REPUBLIC

The historian's essay in this chapter discusses Thomas Jefferson's racial views. The primary sources can be used to evaluate the essay's argument.

Secondary Source

1. Within the "Bowels" of the Republic (1979), RONALD T. TAKAKI

Primary Sources

2. Thomas Jefferson on Indians and Blacks (1784)
3. Thomas Jefferson on the Indians' Future (1803)
4. A Jeffersonian Treaty with the Delaware Indians (1804)
5. Indian Land Cessions, 1800–1812 (1982)
6. A Denunciation of White Tyranny (1811)
7. Thomas Jefferson on Black Colonization (1801)
8. A Petition to the Virginia Legislature (1810)
9. A Letter from a Man of Colour (1813)
10. A Black Response to Colonization (1817)
11. John Vanderlyn, *The Death of Jane McCrea* (1804)
12. John Lewis Krimmel, *Quilting Frolic* (1813)

*E*veryone knows that "the pen is mightier than the sword." With that cliché, we often acknowledge the influence of ideas. Historians must do more than that, however, to understand the past. They have to *demonstrate* the power of ideas. Usually, that is not easy. As we saw in the previous chapter, people rarely explain what influenced their behavior. Moreover, many people are unaware of the impact of ideas in their lives. As the British economist John Maynard Keynes observed, those who "believe themselves quite exempt from any intellectual influences" are often "slaves" to some moldy idea.[1]

Fortunately, the American past provides numerous opportunities to assess the influence of ideas. In early American history, there may be few better places to look for such evidence than in Thomas Jefferson's study. More than most Americans of his day—and most presidents since—Jefferson was a man of ideas. With interests that ranged from architecture to zoology, his mind was rarely at rest. Few problems engaged his thoughts more frequently than the obvious differences that he saw between whites, blacks, and Indians. Those differences were more than a curiosity, for in Jefferson's view race could not be considered apart from another problem. The author of the Declaration of Independence justified American independence with the ideas of equality and natural rights, but he feared that America's fragile experiment in self-government could survive only in a properly ordered society that promoted a virtuous citizenry. The crucial issue raised by race, therefore, was whether blacks and Indians could ever become such citizens. In this chapter, we consider the relationship between Jeffersonian ideas about race and a status for blacks and Indians that reflected something less than the Declaration's lofty sentiments.

SETTING

Modern-day visitors to Monticello—the home Thomas Jefferson designed for himself on a Virginia mountaintop—quickly learn something about the circumstances and mind of its builder. The entrance hall, where Jefferson established a museum to receive guests, provides the first clues about his wide-ranging intellectual pursuits. Walls crowded with mastadon bones and the antlers and skulls of North American mammals attest to his interest in natural history. Various Indian artifacts, gifts from Lewis and Clark to the president who sponsored their daring expedition across the continent, stand as reminders of Jefferson's curiosity about Native Americans. The sitting room—a classroom for Jefferson's eleven grandchildren—is further proof of his interest in education, as is the library next door, home to some 7,000 volumes on history, law, and politics. Nearby, the greenhouse attests to his abiding passion for horticulture and the study to his fascination with astronomy, meteorology, and archaeology.

If Monticello reveals Jefferson's love of learning, it also demonstrates his attachment to Enlightenment ideals. There, he prominently displayed the busts of such Enlightenment thinkers as John Locke, Isaac Newton, and Voltaire. Like other eighteenth-century intellectuals, Jefferson believed that the universe was orderly and balanced, and that it operated according to certain "natural laws." It followed that these natural laws could be understood through empirical investigation. It also followed that societies and individuals in harmony with nature's laws would be guided by the ideals of order and self-control. Designed in the carefully balanced neoclassical style, Monticello itself is a study in architectural restraint. There, Jefferson spent many hours conducting experiments to understand the natural world. There, too, he carefully ordered his own life. Thus, like the busts of Enlightenment thinkers, the clock that Jefferson placed on the wall of his bed alcove was no accident. The Sage of Monticello had to know the time as soon as he awoke.

If Jefferson's home abounds with evidence of the Enlightenment's impact on its owner, it also reflects an eighteenth-century republican ideal of virtuous independence. Jefferson shared with other eighteenth-century republican thinkers a belief that property ownership and political liberties were inseparable. He also assumed that a virtuous citizenry was necessary to maintain republican government and that both could be preserved only in a society in which property holding was widespread. Sturdy, hard-working, independent yeomen who were jealous of their liberties, therefore, represented the only sound foundation upon which to erect republican government. For the same reason, Alexander Hamilton's policies posed a dangerous threat to the republic because they promoted factories and urban "sores." Cities filled with "workshops" were dens of vice populated by mobs of often idle, propertyless dependents. Such people were easily swayed by the appeals of demagogues. "While we have land to labor," Jefferson concluded, "let us never wish to see our citizens occupied at a workbench, or twirling a distaff."²

Set against this ideological backdrop, Monticello was not only Jefferson's home, but a place where he could live beholden to no man. On his mountaintop, where he produced his own food and other necessities, Jefferson had achieved on a grand scale the independence that republican society required to maintain a virtuous citizenry. Of course, he did this by making dependents of many others. On his four farms, up to 135 slaves worked in fields and shops and at household chores. Many of them lived in small rooms beneath terraces that flanked the north and south ends of Monticello, while others lived in huts along "Mulberry Row," the plantation road where the stables and workshops were located. Jefferson may have been deeply disturbed by the "abominable crime" of slavery but he never freed any of his own slaves while he lived because he was, ironically, absolutely dependent on them. Slaves provided the means to live according to Enlightenment and republican ideals. From their labor came the leisure to pursue scientific inquiry and to reason about such questions as the best way to assure the continuation of self-government.

When Jefferson took to his study to ponder the preservation of republican society, the black slaves all around him figured prominently in his mind, as did Native Americans who inhabited the land to the west—land that would eventually have to be brought under cultivation if America were to remain an agrarian republic. Although most Indians were as far removed from Jefferson's Virginia piedmont as blacks were close at hand, Jefferson saw both groups through the same lenses of Enlightenment thought and republican ideology. Thus, he subjected both to empirical analysis as he pondered whether either was capable of fitting into an orderly republican society of rational, self-restrained, and independent citizens. Given Jefferson's eighteenth-century outlook, the prospects for either group would seem bleak, for in his mind black slaves were utter dependents and Indians utterly unrestrained.

INVESTIGATION

The colonists justified their revolt against British rule with a republican ideology based on the idea of equality and natural rights. Historians have long been curious about the impact of that ideology on Americans and their society in the early years of the new nation. In particular, they want to know how ideas unleashed by the American Revolution affected Americans' views about race and whether the Revolution brought about changes in race relations in the postrevolutionary generation. As the author of the Declaration of Independence, the third president of the United States, and a large slaveholder, Thomas Jefferson has frequently been at the center of historians' investigations of these questions. First, they want to know Jefferson's views about Native Americans and blacks and to what extent they were influenced by a republican ideology rooted in the principle of human equality. They are curious about how Jefferson dealt intellectually with his own paradoxical situation as an eloquent spokesman for liberty and a plantation owner who never personally disowned slavery. In other words, they seek to understand to what extent Jefferson's own actions were influenced by his ideas, especially given the longstanding allegations (and recent genetic evidence) regarding Jefferson's sexual relationship with his slave Sally Hemings. Second, they are curious to what extent Jefferson's *policies* regarding blacks and Native Americans, as well as those of his Jeffersonian Republican successors, reflected his views. Finally, they want to know the ways in which the lives of blacks and Native Americans changed because of ideas advanced during the Revolution—ideas that few people are more closely associated with than Jefferson himself.

Source 1 is an exploration of Jefferson's views about blacks and Native Americans. The author argues that the policies advocated by Jefferson toward both groups were influenced by a republican vision of American society. Your job, therefore, is to come to a conclusion about the connection between Jeffersonian ideas and early nineteenth-century policies regarding blacks and Native Americans. To do that, you must come to an understanding of the essay's argument about Jefferson's political and social vision and his racial views. You must then evaluate the views expressed in the primary sources regarding the place of blacks and Indians in American society. Answering the following questions will help you complete this assignment:

1. **How did Jefferson's views regarding blacks and Native Americans differ?** What accounts for the difference, according to historian Ronald Takaki in Source 1?

2. **How were Jefferson's views about each group related to his fears about the preservation of republican society?** What policies did Jefferson advocate toward each?

3. **Do the primary sources provide evidence of Jefferson's fears about the threat posed by blacks and Indians to the republic?** What evidence do the sources provide that Jefferson's concerns were widespread or that they actually influenced policies regarding these groups?

4. **What evidence do the primary sources provide that African Americans or Native Americans themselves were influenced by ideas about race or equality in the early republic?** Do the primary sources indicate that racial prejudice became more or less rigid in this period?

Before you begin, review your textbook's analysis of the political and social impact of the American Revolution and the ideology that supported it. Also read your textbook's discussion of the Jeffersonian Republican vision of American society and the domestic policies of Jefferson and his successors, James Madison and James Monroe. Pay particular attention to what it says about the situation confronting blacks and Native Americans in the early republic and about Jeffersonian Republican policies toward these groups.

SECONDARY SOURCE

In this selection, historian Ronald Takaki argues that Jefferson's views of blacks and Native Americans were influenced by a vision of American society that emphasized the need for the homogeneity, moral purity, and self-control of its citizens. This vision, according to the author, led

Jefferson to argue for the exclusion of one group from a "homogenous" American society and the inclusion of the other in it. As you read this selection, note how Takaki tries to establish a link between Jefferson's vision for the republic and the specific policies that he advocated regarding each group. How do the decisions of many of Jefferson's fellow Virginia slaveholders to voluntarily free slaves in the post-Revolutionary period fit into Takaki's argument regarding Jefferson's racial fears? Also consider what significance he sees in the allegations of a sexual liaison between Jefferson and Sally Hemings. To what extent do Jefferson's actions conform to his ideas?

Within the "Bowels" of the Republic (1979)
RONALD T. TAKAKI

While an enemy is within our bowels, the first object is to expel him.
                            —*Thomas Jefferson,*
                                 Notes on the State of Virginia

As he called for the expulsion of the British "enemy" from the "bowels" of the emerging nation, Jefferson used rhetoric strikingly similar . . . to express his concern for moral purity in the new republican society. . . . Many years after the British had been forced out, President Jefferson told James Monroe that he looked forward to distant times when the American continent would be covered with "a people speaking the same language, governed in similar forms, and by similar laws." Beneath this vision of America's future, which would shortly lead him to expand the republican nation through the purchase of the Louisiana, lay a rage for order, tidiness, and uniformity which made him recoil with horror from the possibility of "either blot or mixture on that surface." The purging of the British only created greater pressures to expel other "enemies" from within the "bowels" of American society, as we shall see in an analysis of Jefferson's republican ideology, his insistence on black colonization, and his views on the assimilation of the Indian. . . .

Republicanism, in Jefferson's view, required a homogeneous population. Unless everyone could be converted into . . . what Dr. [Benjamin] Rush called "republican machines," the republic would surely disintegrate into anarchy. Like Dr. Rush, Jefferson believed peace with England did not mean the end of the Revolution. The people themselves still had to be made uniform and a consensus of values and interests established. This homogeneity might

Source: From Ronald T. Takaki, *Iron Cages: Race and Culture in Nineteenth-Century America* (New York: Alfred A. Knopf, 1979), 36–37, 39, 42, 43–45, 46, 47, 48, 49, 50, 55–56, 58–59, 60, 61, 62, 63, 64.

be achieved by discouraging the rapid increase of immigrants into the country. . . .

But what should be done to render the people already here into a more "homogeneous" body? Like Rush, Jefferson placed much of his faith in education. . . . [E]ducation would render the people—"the ultimate guardian of their own liberty"—independent and self-controlled.

Such education was indispensable in a society where the people ruled. Unless they were properly educated and unless they were trained to restrain vigilantly their passions, they would constitute the greatest threat to order. Indeed, like the immigrants whom Jefferson feared, they could even explode into "unbounded licentiousness" and bring down the curtains of the new republic. . . .

Unless men in America obeyed their moral sense and exercised self-control, Jefferson feared, they would "live at random" and destroy republican order. This was an especially frightening prospect in a slaveholding society where white men like Jefferson had to guard themselves not only against "the strongest of all human passions" but also against "the most boisterous passions." The possessor of inordinate power over black men and women, Jefferson recognized the need for slavemasters, free from the king and external authority, to exercise great vigilance against their own despotism. Both passions, he anxiously believed, would continue to undermine republican self-control as long as the new nation lacked complete purity and as long as blacks remained within the "bowels" of republican society. . . .

Not only did slavery, in Jefferson's view, violate the black's right to liberty, it also undermined the self-control white men had to have in a republican society. In *Notes on the State of Virginia*, he described what he believed was the pernicious influence of slavery upon republican men:

> There must doubtless be an unhappy influence on the manners of our people produced by the existence of slavery among us. The whole commerce between master and slave is a perpetual exercise of the most boisterous passions, the most unremitting despotism on the one part, and degrading submissions on the other. . . .

During the 1780s, after the enactment of the Virginia manumission law, some ten thousand slaves were given their freedom; Jefferson, however, did not manumit his own bondsmen. To have done so would have been financially disastrous for this debt-ridden planter. "The torment of mind," he cried out, "I will endure till the moment shall arrive when I shall not owe a shilling on earth is such really as to render life of little value." Dependent on the labor of his slaves to pay off his debts, Jefferson hoped he would be able to free them and "put them ultimately on an easier footing," which he stated he would do the moment "they" had paid the debts due from the estate, two-thirds of which had been "contracted by purchasing them." Unfortunately, he remained in debt until his death.

As a slavemaster, Jefferson personally experienced what he described as the "perpetual exercise of the most boisterous passions." He was capable of punishing his slaves with great cruelty. He had James Hubbard, a runaway slave who had been apprehended and returned in irons to the plantation, whipped and used as an example to the other slaves. "I had him severely flogged in the presence of his old companions," Jefferson reported. . . .

Like his fellow slaveholders, Jefferson was involved in the buying and selling of slaves and viewed them in economic terms. "The value of our lands and slaves, taken conjunctly, doubles in about twenty years," he observed casually. "This arises from the multiplication of our slaves, from the extension of culture, and increased demands for lands." His was not a merely theoretical observation: Jefferson's ownership of land and slaves made him one of the wealthiest men in his state. Yet he continued to expand his slave holdings. In 1805, he informed John Jordan that he was "endeavoring to purchase young and able negro men." His interest in increasing his slave property was again revealed in a letter to his manager regarding "a breeding woman." Referring to the "loss of 5 little ones in 4 years," he complained that the overseers did not permit the slave women to devote as much time as was necessary to the care of their children. "They view their labor as the 1st object and the raising of their children but as secondary," Jefferson continued, "I consider the labor of a breeding woman as no object, and that a child raised every 2 years is of more profit than the crop of the best laboring man." Little wonder that, by 1822, Jefferson owned 267 slaves.

Yet, despite his view of slave women as "breeders" and slave children as "profits," Jefferson insisted he would be willing to make a sacrifice and free all of his slaves, if they could be removed from the United States. "I can say," he asserted, "with conscious truth, that there is not a man on earth who would sacrifice more than I would to relieve us from this heavy reproach, in any practicable way. . . .

Why not, Jefferson asked in *Notes on the State of Virginia*, emancipate the blacks but keep them in the state? "Deep-rooted prejudices entertained by the whites," he fearfully explained, "ten thousand recollections, by the blacks, of the injuries they have sustained; new provocations; the real distinctions which nature has made and many other circumstances, will divide us into parties, and produce convulsions, which will probably never end but in the extermination of the one or the other race." Unless colonization accompanied emancipation, whites would experience the horror of race war. Yet, unless slavery were abolished, whites would continue to face the danger of servile insurrection and the violent rage springing from "ten thousand recollections" of injuries. "As it is," Jefferson declared, "we have the wolf by the ears, and we can neither hold him, nor safely let him go. Justice is in one scale, and self-preservation in the other." The slave revolt in Santo Domingo intensified his anxieties. "It is high time we should foresee," he wrote to James Monroe in 1793, "the bloody scenes which our children certainly, and possibly ourselves (south of Potomac) have to wade through, and try to avert them." . . . The dread of slave rebellion, which Jefferson and other whites felt, was evident in the violent suppression of the Gabriel Prosser conspiracy of 1800. During the hysteria, twenty-five blacks were hanged. Five years later, Jefferson observed that the insurrectionary spirit among the slaves had been easily quelled, but he saw it becoming general and more formidable after every defeat, until whites would be forced, "after dreadful scenes and sufferings to release them in their own way. . . ." He predicted that slavery would be abolished—"whether brought on by the generous energy of our own minds" or "by the bloody process of St. Domingo" in which slaves would seize their freedom with daggers in their hands. . . .

Even if emancipation could be achieved peacefully, colonization would still be required as one of the conditions for the liberation of slaves. Though Jefferson regarded blacks as members of humankind, endowed with moral sense, he believed that blacks and whites could never coexist in America because of "the real distinctions" which "nature" had made between the two races. "The first difference which strikes us is that of color," Jefferson explained. Regardless of the origins of the Negro's skin color, this difference was "fixed in nature." "And is this difference of no importance? Is it not the foundation of a greater or less share of beauty in the two races? Are not the fine mixtures of red and white, the expressions of every passion by greater or less suffusions of color in the one, preferable to that eternal monotony, which reigns in the countenances, that immovable veil of black which covers the emotions of the other race?" To Jefferson, white was beautiful. . . .

White "superiority," for Jefferson, was also a matter of intelligence. He acknowledged that the "opinion" that blacks were "inferior" in faculties of reason and imagination had to be "hazarded with great diffidence." Evaluation of intelligence was problematical: It was a faculty which eluded the research of all the senses, the conditions of its existence were various and variously combined, and its effects were impossible to calculate. "Great tenderness," he added, was required "where our conclusion would degrade a whole race of man from the rank in the scale of beings which their Creator may perhaps have given them." Thus, Jefferson advanced it as a "suspicion" only that blacks "whether originally a distinct race, or made distinct by time and circumstances," were "inferior" to whites in the endowments of both body and mind. Jefferson stated he was willing to have his "suspicion" challenged, even refuted. . . .

In his investigation of the black's "inferior" intelligence, however, Jefferson was more interested in "proofs" which supported rather than refuted his "suspicion." . . . Unlike Rush, Jefferson did not view black "inferiority" as a consequence of slavery or as a social rather than a biological condition. Instead he seized evidence which set blacks apart as "a distinct race," and which emphasized the importance of biology over conditions or circumstances in the determination of intelligence. . . .

Jefferson's descriptions of the Negro involved more than the assertion of black intellectual inferiority: They depicted blacks as dominated by their bodies rather than their minds, by their sensations rather than their reflections. They appeared to be a libidinal race. "They [black men] are more ardent after their female; but love seems with them to be more an eager desire, than a tender delicate mixture of sentiment and sensation." Blacks, in Jefferson's mind, represented the body and the ascendancy of the instinctual life—those volcanic forces of passions he believed whites had to control in republican society.

Here, for Jefferson, in the midst of the society which had destroyed the authority of the king, expelled the enemy from its "bowels," and established a republic of self-governing men, was the presence of a race still under the rule of the passions, created with moral sense but without sufficient intelligence to serve the conscience. . . .

Still, regardless of whether blacks were to be included or excluded, Jefferson was articulating a general fear. If the republican experiment were to succeed and if the new nation were to realize the vision of a "homogeneous" republic, it had to preserve what Franklin described as the "lovely White." It must not allow its people to be "stained" and become a nation of mulattoes. "Their amalgamation with the other colour," Jefferson warned, "produces a degradation to which no lover of his country, no lover of excellence in the human character can innocently consent." If this mixture were to occur, it would surely mean that whites had lost control of themselves and their lustful passions, and had in their "unbounded licentiousness" shattered the very experiment in self-government which they had undertaken during the American Revolution.

This was precisely why the Thomas Jefferson/Sally Hemings relationship, whether imagined or actual, was so significant. If the philosopher of republicanism could not restrain what he called "the strongest of all the human passions" and if the author of jeremiads against miscegenation were guilty of "staining" the blood of white America, how could white men in the republic ever hope to be self-governing? . . .

The question of the relationship between race and republican society could not ignore the presence of the native American. Jefferson knew this, and his racial concerns did not revolve exclusively around blacks. . . . As a white expansionist and an agrarian philosopher in search of "vacant lands," Jefferson was fully conscious of the Indian's existence.

During the struggle to expel the British, Jefferson had two views of the Indian's future in the new nation: He could be civilized and assimilated, or he could be removed and possibly exterminated. Thus, Jefferson declared to the chief of the Kaskaskias that he hoped "we shall long continue to smoke in friendship together," and that "we, like you, are Americans, born in the same land, and having the same interests." Yet, at the same time, Jefferson did not hesitate to advocate removal of hostile Indians beyond the Mississippi and even total war upon them. "Nothing will reduce those wretches so soon as pushing the war into the heart of their country," he wrote angrily in 1776. "But I would not stop there. I would never cease pursuing them while one of them remained on this side [of] the Mississippi." And he went further. Quoting from the instructions the Congress had given the commissioners to the Six Nations, he continued: "We would never cease pursuing them with war while one remained on the face of the earth." His two views—civilization and extermination—were not contradictory: They were both consistent with his vision of a "homogeneous" American society.

To civilize the Indian meant, for Jefferson, to take him from his hunting way of life and convert him into a farmer. As President of the United States, he told the Potawatomies:

> We shall . . . see your people become disposed to cultivate the earth, to raise herds of the useful animals, and to spin and weave, for their food and clothing. These resources are certain: they will never disappoint you: while those of hunting may fail, and expose your women and children to the miseries of hunger and cold. We will with pleasure furnish you with implements for the most necessary arts, and with persons who may instruct you how to make and use them. . . .

Jefferson believed that Indians, like blacks and all humankind, were endowed with an innate "moral sense of right and wrong," which, like the "sense of tasting and feeling" in every man, constituted "a part of his nature." But while Jefferson assigned conscience to both the Indian and the black, he made a crucial distinction between them in the area of intelligence. "I am safe in affirming," he wrote to the Marquis de Chastellux in 1785, "that the proofs of genius given by the Indians of N. America, place them on a level with whites in the same uncultivated state. . . . I believe the Indian then to be in body and mind equal to the white man. I have supposed the black man, in his present state, might not be so." Thus, what made the Indian "equal" or potentially so was his intelligence. . . . If the Indians' circumstances could be changed, white Americans would "probably" find that the native Americans were "formed in mind as well as body, on the same module with the 'Homo sapiens Europaeus.'" Thus, in Jefferson's mind, Indians had a potential blacks did not have: They had the intelligence capable of development which could enable them to carry out the commands of their moral sense.

This meant that Indians did not have to be a "problem" in America's future: They could be assimilated and their oneness with white America would reaffirm the republican civilization and the "progress" Jefferson hoped to realize. Time and again President Jefferson called upon the Indians to intermarry and live among whites as "one people." To the Delawares, Mohicans, and Munries, he declared:

> When once you have property, you will want laws and magistrates to protect your property and persons, and to punish those among you who commit crimes. You will find that our laws are good for this purpose; you will wish to live under them, you will unite yourselves with us, join in our Great Councils and form one people with us, and we shall all be Americans; you will mix with us by marriage, your blood will run in our veins, and will spread with us over this great island.

In 1803 President Jefferson urged Colonel Benjamin Hawkins to encourage the Indians to give up hunting and turn to agriculture and household manufacture as a new way of life. Indians must learn how a little land, well cultivated, was superior in value to a great deal, unimproved. . . .

What the Indian would be required to amputate was not only his identity and culture but also his land. The civilizing of the Indian was a crucial part of Jefferson's strategy to acquire Indian land for white settlement and the expansion of white agrarian society. . . . In a "Confidential Message" to Congress in 1803, he outlined how this could be done.

> First: to encourage them to abandon hunting, to apply to the raising stock, to agriculture and domestic manufactures, and thereby prove to themselves that less land and labor will maintain them in this, better than in their former mode of living. The extensive forests necessary in the hunting life will then become useless, and they will see advantage in exchanging them for the means of improving their farms. . . . Secondly: to multiply trading-houses among them, and place within their reach those things which will contribute more to their domestic comfort than the possession of extensive but uncultivated wilds. Experience and reflection will develop to them the wisdom of exchanging what they can spare and we want, for what we can spare and they want.

So, for whites to obtain western lands the Indians must be led to agriculture, manufactures, and thus to civilization. . . .

The purchase of the Louisiana Territory in 1803 offered Jefferson the opportunity to pursue at once the two possibilities he saw for the Indian—removal and incorporation. The vast new territory, he calculated, could be "the means of tempting all our Indians on the East side of the Mississippi to remove to the West. . . ." In his draft of an amendment to the Constitution, Jefferson included a specific provision for such a removal: "The legislature of the Union shall have authority to exchange the right of occupancy in portion where the U.S. have full rights for lands possessed by Indians within the U.S. on the East side of the Mississippi: to exchange lands on the East side of the river for those . . . on the West side. . . ." Though the amendment remained in draft form, the Louisiana Territorial Act of 1804 did contain a clause which empowered the President to effect Indian emigration. Not all Indians would be "transplanted," however. If Indians chose civilization, Jefferson explained to the Cherokees, they would be allowed to remain where they were; if they chose to continue the hunter's life, they would be permitted to leave and settle on lands beyond the Mississippi. Calling the Cherokees "my children," he promised them that the United States would be the friends of both parties, and would be willing, as far as could be reasonably asked, to satisfy the wishes of both.

Still, all Indians, whether they were farmers or hunters, were subject to removal, and even extermination, if they did not behave. Should any tribe be foolhardy enough to take up the hatchet against the United States, the President wrote Governor Harrison, the federal government should seize the whole country of that tribe and drive them across the Mississippi as the only condition of peace. As Anglo-American tensions mounted in 1808, President Jefferson told the Ottawas, Chippewas, Potawatomies, and Senecas that white Americans considered them "a part of ourselves" and looked to their welfare as "our own." If they sided with the British, however, they would have to abandon forever the land of their fathers. "No nation rejecting our friendship, and commencing wanton and unprovoked war against us, shall ever after remain within our reach. . . ."

Ultimately, for Jefferson, it made no difference whether Indians were removed to the Rocky Mountains, "extirpated from the earth," or allowed to remain in the United States. Indians as Indians could not be tolerated in the republican civilization the American Revolution had created. The new nation must have a "homogeneous" population—a people with the same language and laws, good cabins and enclosed fields, owners of private property. Diversity itself was dangerous in the republican society, especially diversity which included groups and cultures close to nature and the instinctual life. . . .

Regardless of whether they were viewed in terms of their labor or their land, both blacks and Indians, for Jefferson, were under the domination of the body or the instinctual life. While both of them, like whites, were endowed with moral sense, they were both deficient in reason: Black intelligence was inferior and Indian intelligence was undeveloped. Thus both lacked the self-control and rational command Jefferson believed were essential qualities republicans and civilized men must have. In a republican society, men could not live "at random," and all behavior had to be "a matter of calculation" or else the strongest passions would overwhelm the moral sense and rationality. The hope Jefferson held for white America was the creation of a perfect society through the rule of reason and the expulsion of "enemies" from the "bowels" of the new republic.

PRIMARY SOURCES

The primary sources in this section reflect Jefferson's attitudes toward African Americans and Native Americans as well as their own views about their circumstances. As you read these sources, look for connections between Jeffersonian ideas about race and policies toward these two groups. Also consider what ideas influenced the responses of blacks and Indians to their situations.

| 2 | In these passages from *Notes on the State of Virginia,* Jefferson reveals his view about the differences between blacks and Indians. What bearing would his conclusions about each group have on their "fitness" |

for life in a republican society?

Thomas Jefferson on Indians and Blacks (1784)

Before we condemn the Indians of this continent as wanting genius, we must consider that letters have not yet been introduced among them. Were we to compare them in their present state with the Europeans, north of the Alps, when the Roman arms and arts first crossed those mountains, the comparison would be unequal, because, at that time, those parts of Europe were swarming with numbers; because numbers produce emulation, and multiply the chances of improvement, and one improvement begets another. Yet I may safely ask, how many good poets, how many able mathematicians, how many great inventors in arts or sciences, had Europe, north of the Alps, then produced? And it was sixteen centuries after this before a Newton could be formed. I do not mean to deny that there are varieties in the race of man, distinguished by their powers both of body and mind. I believe there are, as I see to be the case in the races of other animals. . . .

The first difference [between blacks and Indians] which strikes us is that of color. Whether the black of the negro resides in the reticular membrane between the skin and scarf-skin, or in the scarf-skin itself; whether it proceeds from the color of the blood, the color of the bile, or from that of some other secretion, the difference is fixed in nature, and is as real as if its seat and cause were better known to us. And is this difference of no importance? Is it not the foundation of a greater or less share of beauty in the two races? Are not the fine mixtures of red and white, the expressions of every passion by greater or less suffusions of color in the one, preferable to that eternal monotony, which

Source: From Adrienne Koch and William Peden, eds., *The Life and Selected Writings of Thomas Jefferson* (New York: Random House, 1944), pp. 212–213, 256, 257, 258–259.

reigns in the countenances, that immovable veil of black which covers the emotions of the other race? Add to these, flowing hair, a more elegant symmetry of form, their own judgment in favor of the whites, declared by their preference of them, as uniformly as is the preference of the Oran-utan for the black woman over those of his own species. The circumstance of superior beauty, is thought worthy attention in the propagation of our horses, dogs, and other domestic animals; why not in that of man? . . .

A black after hard labor through the day, will be induced by the slightest amusements to sit up till midnight, or later, though knowing he must be out with first dawn of the morning. They are at least as brave, and more adventuresome. But this may perhaps proceed from a want of forethought, which prevents their seeing a danger till it be present. When present, they do not go through it with more coolness or steadiness than the whites. They are more ardent after their female; but love seems with them to be more an eager desire, than a tender delicate mixture of sentiment and sensation. Their griefs are transient. Those numberless afflictions, which render it doubtful whether heaven has given life to us in mercy or in wrath, are less felt, and sooner forgotten with them. In general, their existence appears to participate more of sensation than reflection. To this must be ascribed their disposition to sleep when abstracted from their diversions, and unemployed in labor. An animal whose body is at rest, and who does not reflect must be disposed to sleep of course. Comparing them by their faculties of memory, reason, and imagination, it appears to me that in memory they are equal to the whites; in reason much inferior, as I think one could scarcely be found capable of tracing and comprehending the investigations of Euclid; and that in imagination they are dull, tasteless, and anomalous. . . . Most of them, indeed, have been confined to tillage, to their own homes, and their own society; yet many have been so situated, that they might have availed themselves of the conversation of their masters; many have been brought up to the handicraft arts, and from that circumstance have always been associated with the whites. Some have been liberally educated, and all have lived in countries where the arts and sciences are cultivated to a considerable degree, and all have had before their eyes samples of the best works from abroad. The Indians, with no advantages of this kind, will often carve figures on their pages not destitute of design and merit. They will crayon out an animal, a plant, or a country, so as to prove the existence of a germ in their minds which only wants cultivation. They astonish you with strokes of the most sublime oratory; such as prove their reason and sentiment strong, their imagination glowing and elevated. But never yet could I find that a black had uttered a thought above the level of plain narration; never saw even an elementary trait of painting or sculpture. In music they are more generally gifted than the whites with accurate ears for tune and time, and they have been found capable of imagining a small catch.* Whether they

*A short rhythmical composition.

will be equal to the composition of a more extensive run of melody, or of complicated harmony, is yet to be proved. Misery is often the parent of the most affecting touches in poetry. Among the blacks is misery enough, God knows, but no poetry. Love is the peculiar oestrum of the poet. Their love is ardent, but it kindles the senses only, not the imagination.

 Jefferson wrote this letter to William Henry Harrison, governor of the Indiana territory. As you read it, note how Jefferson proposes to change the Indians' way of life and the advantage he sees in doing so. Does he appear to want what is best for Indians? Does he see Indians as his brothers, or in some other relationship?

Thomas Jefferson on the Indians' Future (1803)

... [T]his letter being unofficial and private, I may with safety give you a more extensive view of our policy respecting the Indians, that you may the better comprehend the parts dealt out to you in detail through the official channel, and observing the system of which they make a part, conduct yourself in unison with it in cases where you are obliged to act without instruction. Our system is to live in perpetual peace with the Indians, to cultivate an affectionate attachment from them, by everything just and liberal which we can do for them within the bounds of reason, and by giving them effectual protection against wrongs from our own people. The decrease of game rendering their subsistence by hunting insufficient, we wish to draw them to agriculture, to spinning and weaving. The latter branches they take up with great readiness, because they fall to the women, who gain by quitting the labors of the field for those which are exercised within doors. When they withdraw themselves to the culture of a small piece of land, they will perceive how useless to them are their extensive forests, and will be willing to pare them off from time to time in exchange for necessaries for their farms and families. To promote this disposition to exchange lands, which they have to spare and we want, for necessaries, which we have to spare and they want, we shall push our trading uses, and be glad to see the good and influential individuals among them run in debt, because we observe that when these debts get beyond what the individuals can pay, they become willing to lop them off by a cession of lands. At our trading houses, too, we mean to sell so low as merely to repay us cost and charges, so as neither to lessen or enlarge our capital. This is what private traders cannot do, for they must gain; they will consequently retire from the competition, and we shall thus get clear of this pest without giving offence or

Source: Merrill D. Peterson, *Thomas Jefferson: Writings* (New York: Literary Classics of the United States, Inc., 1984), pp. 1117–1119.

umbrage to the Indians. In this way our settlements will gradually circum-
scribe and approach the Indians, and they will in time either incorporate with
us as citizens of the United States, or remove beyond the Mississippi. The
former is certainly the termination of their history most happy for themselves;
but, in the whole course of this, it is essential to cultivate their love. As to their
fear, we presume that our strength and their weakness is now so visible that
they must see we have only to shut our hand to crush them, and that all our
liberalities to them proceed from motives of pure humanity only. Should any
tribe be fool-hardy enough to take up the hatchet at any time, the seizing the
whole country of that tribe, and driving them across the Mississippi, as the
only condition of peace, would be an example to others, and a furtherance of
our final consolidation.

 In 1804, William Henry Harrison signed a treaty with the Delaware
tribe, one of eleven Indian treaties negotiated by Harrison between
1803 and 1809. Were its terms consistent with the Jeffersonian ends
described in the previous source?

A Jeffersonian Treaty with the Delaware Indians (1804)

The Delaware tribe of Indians finding that the annuity which they receive from
the United States, is not sufficient to supply them with the articles which are
necessary for their comfort and convenience, and afford the means of intro-
ducing amongst them the arts of civilized life, and being convinced that the
extensiveness of the country they possess, by giving an opportunity to their
hunting parties to ramble to a great distance from their towns, is the principal
means of retarding this desirable event; and the United States being desirous
to connect their settlements on the Wabash with the state of Kentucky: therefore the said United States, by William Henry Harrison, governor of the
Indiana territory, superintendent of Indian affairs, and their commissioner
plenipotentiary for treating with the Indian tribes northwest of the Ohio river;
and the said tribe of Indians, by their sachems, chiefs, and head warriors, have
agreed to the following articles, which when ratified by the President of the
United States, by and with the advice and consent of the Senate, shall be
binding on the said parties.

ARTICLE 1. The said Delaware tribe, for the considerations hereinafter
mentioned, relinquishes to the United States forever, all their right and title to
the tract of country which lies between the Ohio and Wabash rivers, and below

Source: Commissioner of Indian Affairs, *Treaties between the United States of America, and the
Several Indian Tribes, From 1778 to 1837* (1837; reprint, Millwood, N.Y.: Kraus Reprint Co., 1975),
pp. 104–105 (page citations are to the reprint edition).

the tract ceded by the treaty of Fort Wayne, and the road leading from Vincennes to the falls of Ohio.

ARTICLE 2. The said tribe shall receive from the United States for ten years, an additional annuity of three hundred dollars, which is to be exclusively appropriated to the purpose of ameliorating their condition and promoting their civilization. Suitable persons shall be employed at the expense of the United States to teach them to make fences, cultivate the earth, and such of the domestic arts as are adapted to their situation; and a further sum of three hundred dollars shall be appropriated annually for five years to this object. The United States will cause to be delivered to them in the course of the next spring, horses fit for draft, cattle, hogs and implements of husbandry to the amount of four hundred dollars. The preceding stipulations together with goods to the amount of eight hundred dollars which is now delivered to the said tribe, (a part of which is to be appropriated to the satisfying certain individuals of the said tribe, whose horses have been taken by white people) is to be considered as full compensation for the relinquishment made in the first article. . . .

5 As you examine this map of Indian land cessions in the early nineteenth century, locate the general area of the Delaware cession outlined in the previous source. What does this map reveal about the effectiveness of Jeffersonian means for dealing with the Indians?

Indian Land Cessions, 1800–1812 (1982)

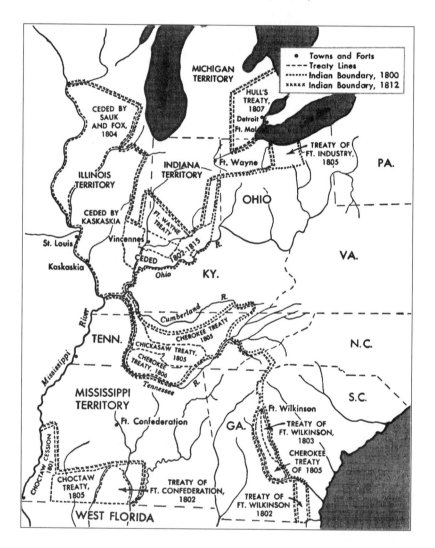

Source: Ray Allen Billington and Martin Ridge, *Westward Expansion: A History of the American Frontier,* 5th ed. (New York: Macmillan Publishing Co., Inc., 1982), p. 273.

6 As settlers advanced into the trans-Appalachian West in the first years of the nineteenth century, the Shawnee chief Tecumseh attempted to unify Indian tribes into a confederation to resist further white encroachment. Note the rhetoric with which he tries to rally the Choctaws and Chickasaws. How would you compare it to the Patriots' during the American Revolution? What does this speech reveal about the outcome of Jeffersonian treaty-making?

A Denunciation of White Tyranny (1811)

. . . [H]ave we not courage enough remaining to defend our country and maintain our ancient independence? Will we calmly suffer the white intruders and tyrants to enslave us? Shall it be said of our race that we knew not how to extricate ourselves from the three most dreadful calamities—folly, inactivity and cowardice? . . . Soon your mighty forest trees, under the shade of whose wide spreading branches you have played in infancy, sported in boyhood, and now rest your wearied limbs after the fatigue of the chase, will be cut down to fence in the land which the white intruders dare to call their own. Soon their broad roads will pass over the grave of your fathers, and the place of their rest will be blotted out forever. The annihilation of our race is at hand unless we unite in one common cause against the common foe. . . .

Sleep not longer, O Choctaws and Chickasaws, in false security and delusive hopes. Our broad domains are fast escaping from our grasp. Every year our white intruders become more greedy, exacting, oppressive and overbearing. Every year contentions spring up between them and our people and when blood is shed we have to make atonement whether right or wrong, at the cost of the lives of our greatest chiefs, and the yielding up of large tracts of our lands. Before the palefaces came among us, we enjoyed the happiness of unbounded freedom, and were acquainted with neither riches, wants nor oppression. How is it now? Wants and oppression are our lot; for are we not controlled in everything, and dare we move without asking, by your leave? Are we not being stripped day by day of the little that remains of our ancient liberty? Do they not even kick and strike us as they do their black-faces? How long will it be before they will tie us to a post and whip us, and make us work for them in their corn fields as they do them? Shall we wait for that moment or shall we die fighting before submitting to such ignominy? . . .

. . . Choctaws and Chickasaws, you have too long borne with grievous usurpation inflicted by the arrogant Americans. Be no longer their dupes. If there be one here tonight who believes that his rights will not sooner or later

Source: From W. C. Vanderwerth, *Indian Oratory: Famous Speeches by Noted Indian Chieftains* (Norman: University of Oklahoma Press, 1971), pp. 62–65.

be taken from him by the avaricious American pale faces, his ignorance ought to excite pity, for he knows little of the character of our common foe.

7 Jefferson wrote this letter to James Monroe, the governor of Virginia, during his first year as president and shortly after a slave rebellion near Richmond, Virginia, organized by a slave named Gabriel Prosser. Although this slave conspiracy was quickly smashed, it renewed whites' fears about the blacks in their midst and led the Virginia legislature to take up the question of colonization. What practical problems does Jefferson see in removing "troublesome" blacks?

Thomas Jefferson on Black Colonization (1801)

Washington, Nov. 24, 1801

Dear Sir—I had not been unmindful of your letter of June 15, covering a resolution of the House of Representatives of Virginia, and referred to in yours of the 17th inst. The importance of the subject, and the belief that it gave us time for consideration till the next meeting of the Legislature, have induced me to defer the answer to this date. . . .

The idea seems to be to provide for these [blacks] by a purchase of lands; and it is asked whether such a purchase can be made of the U S in their western territory? A very great extent of country, north of the Ohio, has been laid off into townships, and is now at market, according to the provisions of the acts of Congress, with which you are acquainted. There is nothing which would restrain the State of Virginia either in the purchase or the application of these lands; but a purchase, by the acre, might perhaps be a more expensive provision than the H of Representatives contemplated. Questions would also arise whether the establishment of such a colony within our limits, and to become a part of our union, would be desirable to the State of Virginia itself, or to the other States—especially those who would be in its vicinity?

Could we procure lands beyond the limits of the U S to form a receptacle for these people? On our northern boundary, the country not occupied by British subjects, is the property of Indian nations, whose title would [have] to be extinguished, with the consent of Great Britain; & the new settlers would be British subjects. It is hardly to be believed that either Great Britain or the Indian proprietors have so disinterested a regard for us, as to be willing to relieve us,

Source: Merrill D. Peterson, *Thomas Jefferson: Writings* (New York: Literary Classics of the United States, Inc., 1984), pp. 1096, 1097–1098.

by receiving such a colony themselves; and as much to be doubted whether that race of men could long exist in so rigorous a climate. On our western & southern frontiers, Spain holds an immense country, the occupancy of which, however, is in the Indian natives, except a few insulated spots possessed by Spanish subjects. It is very questionable, indeed, whether the Indians would sell? whether Spain would be willing to receive these people? and nearly certain that she would not alienate the sovereignty. The same question to ourselves would recur here also, as did in the first case: should we be willing to have such a colony in contact with us? However our present interests may restrain us within our own limits, it is impossible not to look forward to distant times, when our rapid multiplication will expand itself beyond those limits, & cover the whole northern, if not the southern continent, with a people speaking the same language, governed in similar forms, & by similar laws; nor can we contemplate with satisfaction either blot or mixture on that surface. Spain, France, and Portugal hold possessions on the southern continent, as to which I am not well enough informed to say how far they might meet our views. But either there or in the northern continent, should the constituted authorities of Virginia fix their attention, of preference, I will have the dispositions of those powers sounded in the first instance.

The West Indies offer a more probable & practicable retreat for them. Inhabited already by a people of their own race & color; climates congenial with their natural constitution; insulated from the other descriptions of men; nature seems to have formed these islands to become the receptacle of the blacks transplanted into this hemisphere. Whether we could obtain from the European sovereigns of those islands leave to send thither the persons under consideration, I cannot say; but I think it more probable than the former propositions, because of their being already inhabited more or less by the same race. The most promising portion of them is the island of St. Domingo, where the blacks are established into a sovereignty *de facto,* & have organized themselves under regular laws & government. I should conjecture that their present ruler might be willing, on many considerations, to receive even that description which would be exiled for acts deemed criminal by us, but meritorious, perhaps, by him. The possibility that these exiles might stimulate & conduct vindicative or predatory descents on our coasts, & facilitate concert with their brethren remaining here, looks to a state of things between that island & us not probable on a contemplation of our relative strength, and of the disproportion daily growing; and it is overweighed by the humanity of the measures proposed, & the advantages of disembarrassing ourselves of such dangerous characters. Africa would offer a last & undoubted resort, if all others more desirable should fail us. Whenever the Legislature of Virginia shall have brought it's mind to a point, so that I may know exactly what to propose to foreign authorities, I will execute their wishes with fidelity & zeal.

Starting in 1806, the state of Virginia required that all blacks who were freed in the future leave the state, unless they received permission from the state legislature to stay. Blacks who purchased relatives with the intention of freeing them, therefore, had to petition the legislature for them to remain. How might the description of one free black in the petition below have countered the desire of many white Virginians to remove the African Americans in their midst?

A Petition to the Virginia Legislature (1810)

To the Honble. Speaker and other members of the Genl. Assembly of Virginia.

The Petition of Henry Birch most respectfully represents, that he is a free man of Colour. That he has long resided in the County of Hanover, and uniformly supported the character of an Honest, sober and industrious man. That he has two sons who are slaves, whom he purchased of Mr. Wm. Dandridge Claiborne Esq. of King William County, with the view of procuring their freedom. Your Petitioner therefore humbly prays that a law may be passed authorizing his sons John Birch and Bond Birch to reside within the Commonwealth, and will ever pray, etc.

Source: Herbert Aptheker, ed., *A Documentary History of the Negro People in the United States* (Secaucus, N.J.: The Citadel Press, 1973), p. 54; originally from J. J. Johnston, Jr. in *Journal of Negro History,* 13 (1928), pp. 90–91.

9 When the Pennsylvania legislature considered a bill designed to halt the movement of free blacks to the state in 1813, James Forten, a free black Philadelphia sailmaker, wrote a pamphlet against the measure. Due to the efforts of Forten and others, the legislature failed to pass the measure. What principles does he use to support his case? Are they consistent with Thomas Jefferson's republican ideology?

A Letter from a Man of Colour (1813)

We hold this truth to be self-evident, that God created all men equal, and is one of the most prominent features in the Declaration of Independence, and in that glorious fabrick of collected wisdom, our noble Constitution. This idea embraces the Indian and the European, the Savage and the Saint, the Peruvian and the Laplander, the white Man and the African, and whatever measures are adopted subversive of this inestimable privilege, are in direct violation of

Source: From Gary B. Nash, *Race and Revolution* (Madison: Madison House, 1990), pp. 190–192.

the letter and spirit of our Constitution, and become subject to the animadversion of all, particularly those who are deeply interested in the measure.

These thoughts were suggested by the promulgation of a late bill, before the Senate of Pennsylvania, to prevent the emigration of people of colour into this state. It was not passed into a law at this session and must in consequence lay over until the next, before when we sincerely hope, the white men, whom we should look upon as our protectors, will have become convinced of the inhumanity and impolicy of such a measure, and forbear to deprive us of those inestimable treasures, Liberty and Independence. . . . We grant there are a number of worthless men belonging to our colour, but there are laws of sufficient rigour for their punishment, if properly and duly enforced. We wish not to screen the guilty from punishment, but with the guilty do not permit the innocent to suffer. If there are worthless men, there are also men of merit among the African race, who are useful members of Society. The truth of this let their benevolent institutions and the numbers clothed and fed by them witness. Punish the guilty man of colour to the utmost limit of the laws, but sell him not to slavery! If he is in danger of becoming a publick charge prevent him! If he is too indolent to labour for his own subsistence, compel him to do so; but sell him not to slavery. By selling him you do not make him better, but commit a wrong, without benefitting the object of it or society at large. Many of our ancestors were brought here more than one hundred years ago; many of our fathers, many of ourselves, have fought and bled for the Independence of our country. Do not then expose us to sale. Let not the spirit of the father behold the son robbed of that Liberty which he died to establish, but let the motto of our Legislators be: "The Law knows no distinction." . . .

10 In late 1816, the American Colonization Society was formed with the object of transporting free blacks to Africa. Early the next year, a meeting of free blacks in Philadelphia wrote a protest against the aim of the society. On what grounds do they argue against it? How do their ideas compare to Jefferson's?

A Black Response to Colonization (1817)

Whereas our ancestors (not of choice) were the first successful cultivators of the wilds of America, we their descendants feel ourselves entitled to participate in the blessings of her luxuriant soil, which their blood and sweat manured; and that any measure or system of measures, having a tendency to

Source: From Herbert Aptheker, ed., *A Documentary History of the Negro People in the United States: From Colonial Times through the Civil War* (Secaucus, N.J.: The Citadel Press, 1973), pp. 71–72.

banish us from her bosom, would not only be cruel, but in direct violation of those principles, which have been the boast of this republic.

Resolved, That we view with deep abhorrence the unmerited stigma attempted to be cast upon the reputation of the free people of color, by the promoters of this measure, "that they are a dangerous and useless part of the community," when in the state of disfranchisement in which they live, in the hour of danger they ceased to remember their wrongs, and rallied around the standard of their country.

Resolved, That we never will separate ourselves voluntarily from the slave population in this country; they are our brethren by the ties of consanguinity, of suffering, and of wrong; and we feel that there is more virtue in suffering privations with them, than fancied advantages for a season.

Resolved, That without arts, without science, without a proper knowledge of government, to cast into the savage wilds of Africa the free people of color, seems to us the circuitous route through which they must return to perpetual bondage.

Resolved, That having the strongest confidence in the justice of God, and philanthropy of the free states, we cheerfully submit our destinies to the guidance of Him who suffers not a sparrow to fall, without his special providence.

Resolved, That a committee of eleven persons be appointed to open a correspondence with the honorable Joseph Hopkinson, member of Congress from this city, and likewise to inform him of the sentiments of this meeting, when they in their judgment may deem it proper.

Artists' Images of Indians and African Americans

Indians and blacks were frequently depicted in early nineteenth-century art. As you examine these paintings, note the way they are portrayed. Do these images support or contradict themes in Takaki's essay (Source 1)?

11 This painting depicts the death of a young woman at the hands of her Indian guides during the American Revolution. The murder of helpless white females by Indians was a common image in early nineteenth-century art.

John Vanderlyn, *The Death of Jane McCrea* (1804)

Source: From Ellwood Parry, *The Image of the Indian and the Black Man in American Art, 1590–1900* (New York: George Braziller, 1974), p. 59; originally from Wadsworth Atheneum, Hartford, Connecticut.

12   This painting provides not only a detailed look into a middle-class household, but also clues about white attitudes. The servant girl and the fiddler are marks of status. Note their placement and portrayal compared to the whites. According to one art historian, the artist John Lewis Krimmel was one of the first "to utilize physiognomical distortions as a basic element in depiction of African-Americans."[3] As you examine this painting, think about the way it may have reflected—and reinforced—white views of blacks.

John Lewis Krimmel, *Quilting Frolic* (1813)

Source: Stephen F. Eisenman, ed., *Nineteenth Century Art: A Critical History* (London: Thames and Hudson Ltd, 1994), p. 164; The Henry Francis du Pont Winterthur Museum.

CONCLUSION

In 1824, James Fenimore Cooper published *The Pioneers*. Like his other Leatherstocking tales, this popular novel reflected a Romantic view of Native Americans. The Leatherstocking, Cooper's backwoods hero, had learned much from the Indians and, like the self-possessed Mohegan named Indian John, exhibited a primitive nobility. By the 1820s, of course, white–Indian warfare had moved far to the west of Cooper's New York, and many of his readers could sympathize with the fate of the decimated and displaced tribes of the Eastern woodlands. Like most of his readers, however, Cooper had a very different view of African Americans. Thus, another character in *The Pioneers*, a free black named Abraham Freeborn or "Brom," also reflected a stereotypical view embedded in the white imagination by the early nineteenth century. In contrast to the self-confident Leatherstocking and the stoic Indian John, Brom is a buffoon. In one scene, Cooper tells his readers, Brom danced "until his legs wearied with motion . . . exhibit[ing] all that violence of joy that characterized the mirth of a thoughtless negro."[4]

As with Cooper's characters in *The Pioneers*, the fate of blacks and Indians in the nineteenth century was surely influenced by ideas inherited from previous generations. Illustrating the connections between Jeffersonian ideas and the lives of African Americans and Native Americans, however, can be as difficult as tracing the influence of economic interests in the lives of the Founding Fathers. Historians' sources rarely reveal how people's beliefs, values, and prejudices influenced their actions. To complicate things more, ideas and other motivating forces may not be mutually exclusive. Thus, Jeffersonian policies regarding the Indians may have as much reflected white land hunger as assumptions about the need for a virtuous citizenry. Obviously, ideas and economic concerns can be related. For Charles Beard, the former reflects the latter. For Ronald Takaki and many other historians, ideas and beliefs have a life of their own even though they can't be divorced from economic circumstances. In fact, disagreement about the power of ideas and economic interests is one reason why historians come to different conclusions about the causes of things—even, as we will see in the next chapter, of religious movements.

FURTHER READING

Annette Gordon-Reed, *Thomas Jefferson and Sally Hemings: An American Controversy* (Charlottesville: University Press of Virginia, 1997).
John C. Miller, *The Wolf by the Ears: Thomas Jefferson and Slavery* (New York: The Free Press, 1977).

Gary B. Nash, *Race and Revolution* (Madison: Madison House, 1990).

Francis Paul Prucha, *American Indian Policy in the Formative Years: The Indian Trade and Intercourse Acts, 1780–1834* (Cambridge, Mass.: Harvard University Press, 1970).

Bernard W. Sheehan, *Seeds of Extinction: Jeffersonian Philanthropy and the American Indian* (Chapel Hill: The University of North Carolina Press, 1973).

NOTES

1. Quoted in Robert L. Heilbroner, *The Worldly Philosophers* (New York: Simon and Schuster, 1967), p. 12.
2. Thomas Jefferson, *Notes on the State of Virginia,* in Adrienne Koch and William Peden, *The Life and Selected Writings of Thomas Jefferson* (New York: Random House, 1944), p. 280.
3. Quoted in Frances K. Pohl, "Black and White in America," in Stephen F. Eisenman, *Nineteenth Century Art: A Critical History* (London: Thames and Hudson Ltd, 1994), p. 164.
4. James Fenimore Cooper, *The Pioneers* (New York: Dodd, Mead & Company, 1958), p. 198.

CHAPTER | 7

The Problem of Historical Causation:
The Second Great Awakening

The sources in this chapter relate to the question of why so many Americans were drawn to revivalism in the early nineteenth century.

Secondary Source

1. Society and Revivals in Rochester (1987), PAUL E. JOHNSON

Primary Sources

2. Maps of Western New York
3. Alexis de Tocqueville on the Condition of Americans (1835)
4. An Attack on the Revivals (1811)
5. A Defense of Camp Meetings (1814)
6. "On Predestination" (1809)
7. "Negro Methodists Holding a Meeting in Philadelphia" (ca. 1812)
8. *Book of Mormon* (1830)
9. Parley Pratt on Wage-Earning (1874)
10. Philadelphia Journeymen Protest Their Conditions (1828)
11. Occupations of Methodist Converts in Philadelphia, 1830s
12. Frances Trollope's Account of a Camp Meeting (1829)
13. Harriet Martineau on the Condition of American Women (1837)
14. Rebeccah Lee on the Appeal of Christianity (1831)

15. Charles Finney on the Rochester Revival (1876)
16. Charles Finney on the Freedom of Sinners (1836)

N obody knows for sure how many people showed up at the Cane Ridge revival in 1801. Some observers put the crowd at 10,000, while others said it was two and a half times that size. Likewise, no one is certain exactly what happened at this massive Kentucky camp meeting. Enemies of the revival, pointing to the six men lying with a woman under a preacher's stand on Saturday night, claimed that "more souls were begot than saved" at Cane Ridge.[1] If the accounts of most contemporaries are any guide, though, more people experienced ecstasy beside the preacher's stand than below it. Even hard-bitten Kentuckians were astounded. One of them saw a "vast sea of human beings . . . agitated as if by a storm." While seven ministers preached simultaneously, he reported, "some of the people were singing, others praying, some crying for mercy in the most piteous accents, while others were shouting most vociferously." The resulting noise was "like the roar of Niagara."[2] Meanwhile, grown men crawled on all fours barking like dogs. Other men and not a few women rolled on the ground shouting and shrieking. Still other worshippers were overcome with the "jerks," their entire bodies twitching and shaking uncontrollably "as if," according to another witness, "they must . . . fly asunder."[3]

The joint work of Presbyterian, Baptist, and Methodist preachers, Cane Ridge was the biggest camp meeting during the religious revivals known as the Second Great Awakening. Beginning about 1800 and extending into the 1830s, this period of intense religious ferment would leave thousands converted—and not just around frontier campfires. By the 1820s and 1830s, revivalism had spread from the backwoods of Kentucky to New York and beyond. In fact, long after the fires were extinguished at Cane Ridge, the Second Great Awakening's preachers were reaping their most abundant harvests in the bustling commercial and manufacturing centers of the Northeast.

Those same communities have provided a fertile field for historians searching for the origins of this remarkable religious phenomenon amid the economic and social changes of the early nineteenth century. Despite the obvious enthusiasm exhibited at Cane Ridge and elsewhere, modern historians do not trace the Second Great Awakening to supernatural causes—or explain it as merely the work of skilled preachers. Rather, they seek explanations in the lives of the converted. Exploring the roots of the Second Great Awakening thus challenges historians to identify important patterns of historical experience and establish causal links between seemingly unrelated developments. Often, neither task is easy. Yet if the most important job of historians is to explain the causes of events, then their most useful explanations do not merely state the obvious. In this chapter, then, we take up the problem of historical causation by exploring the links between the worldly and otherworldly concerns of Americans drawn to the revival tent in the early nineteenth century.

SETTING

The search for explanations for the Second Great Awakening began even while its fires raged. Echoing defenses heard during the First Great Awakening in the 1740s and 1750s, some clergymen suggested that religious enthusiasm was a response to waning religious zeal, declining church membership, and increasing moral waywardness. Like their counterparts during the colonial revival, ministers often laid much of the blame for this deplorable state of affairs on a decline in respect for religious authorities and the spread of deism and other forms of rational religion, which emphasized the orderly nature of the universe and God's reasonableness. Two circumstances in particular drew their attention: disestablishment of churches after the American Revolution and the triumph of the Jeffersonian Republicans in 1800. The separation of church and state, they argued, removed ministers from their exalted position in American society, while the election of 1800 swept into power rationalists, deists, and supporters of an anticlerical French Revolution. The Awakening's defenders saw an even more disturbing problem when they looked westward. As thousands of pioneers trekked across the Appalachian mountains, alarmed easterners feared that their western cousins had slipped into a sink of violence, vice, and immorality. Often without churches and surrounded, in the words of one Connecticut Methodist, by "the offscouring of the earth," westerners were in urgent need of redemption at the hands of Protestant missionary societies.[4] The Second Great Awakening, according to this view, reimposed sobriety and order on society.

Although historians are less interested in justifying the Second Great Awakening than in explaining it, they often echo some of these conclusions. Many educated Americans, they argue, *had* found Enlightenment rationalism emotionally unsatisfying. Likewise, growing numbers of unlettered and unchurched pioneers in the trans-Appalachian West *were* ripe for conversion at the hands of evangelical preachers whose simple, emotional preaching aimed at the heart rather than the head. Yet many Americans far removed from the frontier also succumbed to religious enthusiasm, and this has led to more comprehensive explanations for the revivals. Some historians conclude that religious enthusiasm was a response to the increasingly democratic nature of American society. They point out that revivals were based on emotional preaching and a theology emphasizing individual free will and the promise of salvation for all rather than logical, finely spun arguments. At a time when all adult white males could vote and increasing numbers were free to make decisions affecting their own well-being, it seemed only natural that they should be able to control their own salvation. In short, enthusiastic religion fit the experience of most Americans far better than Calvinism's doctrine of predestination; that is, salvation by God's election.

Meanwhile, many historians trace the appeal of revival religion to broad and disruptive economic or social changes. Some students, for instance, contend that revivalism was a response to changes associated with a rising market economy in the early nineteenth century. According to this explanation, many Americans pulled up stakes from settled communities in search of economic opportunities in booming towns and cities and then flocked to revivals to reestablish a lost sense of order in their lives. Other historians have extended this analysis to the family. Pointing to the Great Awakening's disproportionate number of female converts, they conclude that revivals helped women develop a separate sphere, free from the male dominance in traditional, patriarchal households. Finally, some historians maintain that the revivals were fueled by class tensions created by the changing relations between employers and workers in workshops and new factories. In this view, the revivals were a way for an emerging capitalist elite to keep the working class in line by promoting within it the values of sobriety and industry and a belief in individual responsibility.

Clearly, historians disagree about the relationship between religious develop-ments and economic or social changes. As a consequence, even today they remain divided on whether revivalism was, as its early defenders suggested, a powerful means for social control. Pointing to the evangelical roots of the temperance and other moral reform movements of the 1820s and 1830s, many historians argue that evangelism reflected a desire to establish order in an unruly society. Whether it arose out of a desire to civilize dissolute westerners or make industrious workers for a growing capitalist economy, they contend, the Second Great Awakening represented a conservative antidote to social disorder. Other historians deny that revivalism was merely a means for social control—or that religious developments are mere responses to economic or social concerns. They argue instead that religious ideas can also be prime movers in history and that those who seek an explanation for the revivals must therefore understand what one scholar called the "ideological universe in which the historical actors lived."[5] Modern historians, in short, continue to disagree about religion's role in society. At the same time, few episodes in American history present a better opportunity to assess the causal relationship between economic, social, and religious developments than the Second Great Awakening. And for that reason, more than for the strange behavior it sometimes elicited, it merits our attention today.

INVESTIGATION

The sources in this chapter illuminate various aspects of the revivals of the Second Great Awakening. The essay by historian Paul Johnson deals with its impact on Rochester, a heavily evangelized community along the Erie Canal in upstate New York. Charles G. Finney, the most famous and successful preacher of the Second Great Awakening, brought revivalism to Rochester in 1830. Near the climax of a generation of religious enthusiasm, Finney's Rochester crusade was, according to Johnson, representative of the revivals' increasingly urban, middle-class character. Notice that this essay does not discuss Cane Ridge or other early revivals, or the rise of the Second Great Awakening in general. Rather, it explores the appeal of religious enthusiasm in a representative, expanding commercial community. Your job, then, is to evaluate the relationship between economic change and revivalism. To do that, you must determine the historian's argument about the function of the revivals in this social setting and assess it with the help of several primary sources. When you are finished, you should be able to offer an explanation for early nineteenth-century revivalism that takes into account important economic and social changes. Your analysis should address the following questions:

1. **What is the causal connection between an expanding capitalist market economy and the appeal of revival religion, according to Paul Johnson's essay (Source 1)?** How did a new "free-labor economy" change social relationships in Rochester? How did revivalism provide a solution to "disordered" social relations there?

2. **Do there appear to have been social bases for the revivalist spirit?** What evidence do the primary sources and the essay provide to support Paul Johnson's explanation regarding the origins of the revivals?

3. **What do the primary documents indicate were the major sources of religious revivalism during the first third of the nineteenth century?** Do they offer alternative explanations for the appeal of revival religion?

4. **What clues does the evidence provide about why different groups were drawn to revivalism?** What special appeals did the Awakening have for women? For African Americans? For white workingmen?

Before you begin, read your textbook's account of changes in early nineteenth-century Protestantism and its discussion of the economic changes associated with a spreading market economy after the War of 1812. Be careful to notice any connections it makes between these religious and economic developments.

SECONDARY SOURCE

1

In this selection, historian Paul E. Johnson discusses economic changes overtaking Rochester between 1815 and the 1830s. These changes, he contends, are essential for understanding the popularity of revivalist preacher Charles Finney. As you read this essay, note the way Johnson attempts to demonstrate that Rochester's economic transformation and revivalism's appeal intersected in particular individuals' lives. What evidence does he use to establish this connection? What do you think Charles Beard would say about Johnson's argument regarding the relationship between Rochester's business owners, their workers, and revival religion?

Society and Revivals in Rochester (1987)
PAUL E. JOHNSON

The rich literature on American revivals contains surprisingly few causal statements. Scholars assume that revivals were responses to widespread spiritual unrest, but few have attempted to describe its specific content. Evangelical America was, after all, the America of Andrew Jackson and Alexis de Tocqueville. The people who flocked to Charles Finney's meetings had experienced an abrupt and decisive commercial revolution in agriculture, rapid territorial expansion, the beginnings of industrialization and sustained urban growth, the democratization of politics—a generation of change that transformed Jefferson's republic of self-governing communities into Jackson's boisterous capitalist democracy. . . .

We have more generalizations and less solid information on society in the years 1815 to 1850 than on any other period in the American past. We know, for instance, that the extension of the market after 1815 revolutionized the ways in which people lived. But what precisely were the effects on ordinary persons, and which of those effects translated into religious tension? We know that Americans are a mobile people and that movement from place to place seems to have accelerated after 1800. But what, really, did migration do to the texture of everyday life, and were the most mobile really more prone to revivalism than others? We know that Jacksonian America was full of men on the make. How many made it? And was it the new rich who swarmed into the

Source: Excerpt from "Society and Revivals in Rochester," from A Shopkeeper's Millennium: Society and Revivals in Rochester, New York, 1815–1837 by Paul E. Johnson. Copyright © 1979 by Paul E. Johnson. Reprinted by permission of Hill and Wang, a division of Farrar, Straus and Giroux, LLC.

churches? We have been told over and over that the early nineteenth century was an age of institutional breakdown. Which institutions broke down? Which persisted? Every student of revivals assumes that they were a response to disorder in the lives of ordinary men and women. But we do not know precisely who joined churches during revivals. Until we do, speculation on the sources of their religious unrest seems a little out of place. Terms such as "culture strain" and "social atomization" are not enough. Most Americans were somehow strained in the 1820s and 1830s. But which ones found comfort in revivals, and why?

Answers to that question will remain vague and unsatisfying until we know more about the people who converted during revivals. Beyond that, we need some conception of the social processes that are tied most sensitively to religious belief, and whose derangement would be likely to elicit a religious response. . . .

. . . As the site of that investigation I have chosen Rochester, New York. . . . The sequence of rapid urbanization, religious revival, and political and social reorganization struck that community with uncommon force. Rochester was the first of the inland cities created after 1815 by the commercialization of agriculture. In 1812 the site of Rochester was unbroken wilderness. By 1830 the forest had given way to a city of 10,000, the marketing and manufacturing center for a broad and prosperous agricultural hinterland. Rochester was the capital of western New York's revival-seared "Burned-over District," and a clearinghouse for religious enthusiasms throughout the 1820s and 1830s. The city holds a special place in the history of revivals, for Charles Finney's triumph there in 1830–31 was the most spectacular event within the national revival of that year. In short, Rochester was the most thoroughly evangelized of American cities. . . .

When asked to explain nineteenth-century revivals, most historians point to social dislocations that attended migration and the expansion of the market after 1790. Young persons dissolved old social ties and worked out their careers far from home, and each was forced to create an identity and a system of ethics pretty much out of whole cloth. The result was a nationwide epidemic of unregulated greed, family collapse, adolescent trauma, status anxiety, cultural confusion, simple loneliness, and—as a result—revival religion. To use an older and more cheerful phrase, revivals were society's antidote to individualism. A systematic test of that proposition is long overdue. . . .

Rochester was America's first inland boom town, certainly a good place to look for normless men on the make. Few Rochester entrepreneurs, however, fit that description. And if we limit attention to men who joined churches during Charles Finney's revival, we shall find even fewer for whom migration and participation in the entrepreneurial world had been an isolating or norm-shattering experience. More than others, Finney's converts were firmly engaged in the country trade and in the elaborate and stability-inducing relationships through which it was conducted. . . .

. . . Both before and during the revival, churches were filled disproportionately with businessmen and master craftsmen and their families—persons who enjoyed far greater residential stability than did other elements of the Rochester population. . . . More revealing, the men who joined churches during the Finney revival were more stable than were others even in the same stability-prone occupations—and this despite their relative youth. Anyone wishing to ascribe the Rochester revival to rootlessness must explain the fact that Finney's converts were the most firmly rooted men in town. . . .

Few American communities—certainly none in which Rochester businessmen had lived—had ever held such a young, unstable, and poor population. Day laborers and journeyman craftsmen made up 71 percent of the adult male work force. In Philadelphia, as late as 1820, the comparable figure was 39 percent. Rochester may have looked like a country town. But underneath, it was a blue-collar city. When Charles Finney arrived late in 1830, he found merchants and master workmen at the top of a city that they owned but could not control. . . .

The loss of social control began, paradoxically, with the imposition of new and tighter controls over the process of labor. For while market operations revolutionized the scale and intensity of work, they freed wage earners from the immediate discipline exerted by older, household-centered relations of production. . . .

. . . [W]hile circumstances varied, journeymen all over the city experienced harsher, more impersonal, and more transparent forms of exploitation than had men in the same trades a few years earlier. At the same time they were freed from controls imposed by the smaller workshops, for the businessmen who bought and controlled their labor were seldom present when the work was performed. They worked together and talked and joked among themselves, and they forged sensibilities that were specific to the class of wage-earning craftsmen. Basic to that mental set was the proposition that master and wage earner were different and opposed kinds of men. In 1829 an editor had occasion to use the word boss, and followed it with an asterisk. "A foreman or master workman," he explained. "Of modern coinage, we believe." Five years later the striking carpenters used the word again. This time, there was no asterisk.

The reorganization of work brought change into the most intimate corners of daily life. For until the coming of merchant capitalism, most Rochester wage earners lived with their employers and shared in their private lives. Evidence is fragmentary and incomplete, and quantifiable data are unavailable, but this much is clear: in 1820 merchants and master workmen lived above, behind, or very near their places of business, and employees boarded in their homes. On most jobs, employment was conditional on co-residence. Even workmen whose fathers and brothers headed households in Rochester lived with employers. Work, leisure, and domestic life were acted out in the same place and by the same people, and relations between masters and men transferred without a break from the workshop to the fireside. . . .

Rochester merchants and masters had grown up in communities in which labor relations and family life were structurally and emotionally inseparable. Most had served resident clerkships and apprenticeships, some of them in Rochester itself. But in the 1820s the nature of work and of the work force made it difficult to provide employees with food, lodgings, behavioral models, and domestic discipline. Even proprietors who kept employees in their homes (and these tended more and more to be the youngest apprentices and clerks) often retained customary forms while neglecting the responsibilities that had given them meaning. An editor addressed these questions to the town's churchgoing businessmen:

> Have apprentices and clerks immortal souls? Are their masters, or employers, being professed Christians, to be considered as having charge of those souls? Is prayer, and especially family prayer, one of the means of grace? Are those masters or employers, being professors of religion, doing their duty, who keep their apprentices or clerks in the shop, or store, during the time of family worship, when those apprentices and clerks reside in, and are members of the family? These apprentices and clerks, being excluded from *family* prayer, is there not reason to fear they are also forgotten in *secret* devotion? May not these questions furnish one reason why there are so many ungodly clerks and apprentices in our country? . . .

By 1830 the household economy had all but passed out of existence, and so had the social order that it sustained. Work, family life, the makeup of neighborhoods—the whole pattern of society—separated class from class: master and wage earner inhabited distinct social worlds. Workmen experienced new kinds of harassment on the job. But after work they entered a fraternal, neighborhood-based society in which they were free to do what they wanted. At the same time masters devised standards of work discipline, domestic privacy, and social peace that were directly antithetical to the spontaneous and noisy sociability of the workingmen. The two worlds stood within a few yards of each other, and they fought constantly. That battle took place on many fronts. But from the beginning it centered on alcohol.

The temperance question was nonexistent in 1825. Three years later it was a middle-class obsession. Sullen and disrespectful employees, runaway husbands, paupers, Sabbath breakers, brawlers, theatergoers: middle-class minds joined them in the image of a drink-crazed proletariat. In 1829 the county grand jury repeated what had become, in a remarkably short time, bourgeois knowledge: strong drink was "the cause of almost all of the crime and almost all of the misery that flesh is heir to." . . .

The drinking problem of the late 1820s stemmed directly from the new relationship between master and wage earner. Alcohol had been a builder of morale in household workshops, a subtle and pleasant bond between men. But in the 1820s proprietors turned their workshops into little factories, moved their families away from their places of business, and devised standards of discipline, self-control, and domesticity that banned liquor. By default, drinking became part of an autonomous working-class social life, and its meaning changed. When proprietors sent temperance messages into the new neighborhoods, they received replies such as this:

> Who are the most temperate men of modern times? Those who quaff the juice of the grape with their friends, with the greatest good nature, after the manner of the ancient patriarchs, without any malice in their hearts, or the cold-water, pale-faced, money-making men, who make the necessities of their neighbors their opportunity for grinding the face of the poor?

An ancient bond between classes had become, within a very short time, an angry badge of working-class status.

The liquor question dominated social and political conflict in Rochester from the late 1820s onward. At every step, it pitted a culturally independent working class against entrepreneurs who had dissolved the social relationships through which they had controlled others, but who continued to consider themselves the rightful protectors and governors of their city. . . .

In 1828, worried gentlemen formed the Rochester Society for the Promotion of Temperance, and affiliated with a national movement led by Lyman Beecher of Boston. These men proposed to end drunkenness through persuasion, example, and the weight of their names. Every old family and every church submerged their differences and contributed leaders to the society. . . .

The temperance reformers were wealthy men, and they possessed enormous power. But they preferred to translate power into authority, and to reform lesser men by persuasion rather than by force. Lyman Beecher, whose *Six Sermons on Intemperance* guided the movement from its beginning, defined the goal as "THE BANISHMENT OF ARDENT SPIRITS FROM THE LIST OF LAWFUL ARTICLES OF COMMERCE BY A CORRECT AND EFFICIENT PUBLIC SENTIMENT . . ." by social pressure and an aroused public opinion. . . . Temperance men did not want to outlaw liquor or to run drunkards and grogsellers out of town. They wanted only to make men ashamed to drink. Reform would come quietly and voluntarily, and it would come from the top down. . . .

By 1830 the temperance crusade was, on its own terms, a success: society's leading men were encouraging abstinence. But even as they preached, they withdrew from the social relationships in which their ability to command obedience was embedded. Wage earners continued to drink. But now they drank only in their own neighborhoods and only with each other, and in direct defiance of their employers. It taught the masters a disheartening lesson: if authority collapsed whenever they turned their backs, then there was in fact no authority. It was a lesson that masters were learning in a wide variety of situations. . . .

Charles Grandison Finney came to Rochester in September 1830. For six months he preached in Presbyterian churches nearly every night and three times on Sunday, and his audience included members of every sect. During the day he prayed with individuals and led an almost continuous series of prayer meetings. Soon there were simultaneous meetings in churches and homes throughout the village. . . . By early spring the churches faced the world with a militance and unity that had been unthinkable only months before, and with a boundless and urgent sense of their ability to change society. In the words of its closest student, ". . . no more impressive revival has occurred in American history." . . .

Both in the 1820s and in the revival of 1830–31, new church members came disproportionately from among businessmen, professionals, and master workmen. During the Finney revival conversions multiplied dramatically within every group. But the center of enthusiasm shifted from the stores and offices to the workshops. Indeed it is the sharp increase in conversions among master craftsmen that accounts for slight declines in every other group. Whatever the problems that prepared the ground for Finney's triumph, they were experienced most strongly by master workmen.

With few exceptions, then, Charles Finney's revival was strongest among entrepreneurs who bore direct responsibility for disordered relations between classes. And they were indeed responsible. The problem of social class arose in towns and cities all over the northern United States after 1820. It would be easy to dismiss it as a stage of urban-industrial growth, a product of forces that were impersonal and inevitable. In some ways it was. But at the beginning the new relationship between master and wage earner was created by masters who preferred money and privacy to the company of their workmen and the performance of old patriarchal duties. Available evidence suggests that it was precisely those masters who filled Finney's meetings. . . .

Perhaps more than any other act, the removal of workmen from the homes of employers created an autonomous working class. . . . Finney's converts kept fewer workmen in their families than did other proprietors, suggesting either that they had removed many of those men or that they had never allowed them into their homes. Table 6 traces households that included "extra" adult men in 1827 over the next three years. The table is compiled from the 1830 census. That document names heads of households and identifies others by age and

TABLE 6. CHANGES IN THE COMPOSITION OF HOUSEHOLDS HEADED BY PROPRIETORS, 1827–30, BY RELIGIOUS STATUS OF HOUSEHOLDERS

	Number of Males over 16 Years		
Householder	1827	1830	Percent Change
Church member in 1829	67	48	−24
Revival convert	74	31	−58
Non-church member	113	80	−29

sex. By counting males over the age of sixteen . . . we may trace the broadest outlines of household change in the years immediately preceding the revival. Most proprietors thinned their families between 1827 and 1830. But while old church members and those who stayed outside the churches removed one in four adult men, converts cut their number by more than half. Thus the analyses of occupations and of household structure point clearly to one conclusion: Finney's converts were entrepreneurs who had made more than their share of the choices that created a free-labor economy and a class-bounded society in Rochester.

The transformation began in the workshops, but it was not contained there. For in removing workmen the converts altered their own positions within families. The relative absence of even boarders and distant kin in their homes suggests a concern with domestic privacy. And within those families housewives assumed new kinds of moral authority. The organization of prayer meetings, the pattern of family visits, and bits of evidence from church records suggest that hundreds of conversions culminated when husbands prayed with their wives. Women formed majorities of the membership of every church at every point in time. But in every church, men increased their proportion of the communicants during revivals, indicating that revivals were family experiences and that women were converting their men. In 1830–31 fully 65 percent of male converts were related to prior members of their churches (computed from surnames within congregations). Traditionalists considered Finney's practice of having women and men pray together the most dangerous of the new measures, for it implied new kinds of equality between the sexes. Indeed some harried husbands recognized the revival as subversive of their authority over their wives. A man calling himself Anticlericus complained of Finney's visit to his home:

> He *stuffed* my wife with tracts, and alarmed her fears, and nothing short of meetings, night and day, could atone for the many fold sins my poor, simple spouse had committed, and at the same time, she made the miraculous discovery, that she had

been "unevenly yoked." From this unhappy period, peace, quiet, and happiness have fled from my dwelling, never, I fear, to return.

The evangelicals assigned crucial religious duties to wives and mothers. In performing those duties, women rose out of old subordinate roles and extended their moral authority within families. Finney's male converts were driven to religion because they had abdicated their roles as eighteenth-century heads of households. In the course of the revival, their wives helped to transform them into nineteenth-century husbands.

The Rochester revival served the needs . . . of entrepreneurs who employed wage labor. And while there are few systematic studies of revivals in other cities, there is reason to believe that the Rochester case was not unique. In towns and cities all over the northern United States, revivals after 1825 were tied closely to the growth of a manufacturing economy. . . . The relation between revivals and manufactures gains strength when we turn from cities to individuals, for in urban places of all types, revivals and their related social movements were disproportionately strong among master workmen, manufacturers, and journeyman craftsmen. There were relatively few merchants and clerks among the converts, and even fewer day laborers and transport workers. Clearly, urban revivals in the 1820s and 1830s had something to do with the growth of manufactures.

In the few towns that have been studied over time, revivals followed the same chronology and served the same functions as they had at Rochester. Everywhere, enthusiasm struck first among masters and manufacturers, then spread through them into the ranks of labor. The workingman's revival of the 1830s was effected through missionary churches, temperance and moral reform societies, and Sunday schools that were dominated by rich evangelicals. The religion that it preached was order-inducing, repressive, and quintessentially bourgeois. In no city is there evidence of independent working-class revivals before the economic collapse of 1837. We must conclude that many workmen . . . were adopting the religion of the middle class, thus internalizing beliefs and modes of comportment that suited the needs of their employers.

The analysis of Rochester, along with evidence from other cities, allows us to hypothesize the social functions of urban revivals with some precision. Evangelicalism was a middle-class solution to problems of class, legitimacy, and order generated in the early stages of manufacturing. Revivals provided entrepreneurs with a means of imposing new standards of work discipline and personal comportment upon themselves and the men who worked for them, and thus they functioned as powerful social controls. . . .

These men demonstrated that paternalistic controls could indeed be replaced by piety and voluntary self-restraint: free labor could generate a well-regulated, orderly, just, and happy society. The only thing needed was more revivals of religion. Workmen who continued to drink and carouse and stay away from church were no longer considered errant children; they were free moral agents who had chosen to oppose the Coming Kingdom. They could be hired when they were needed, fired without a qualm when they were not.

Thus a nascent industrial capitalism became attached to visions of a perfect moral order based on individual freedom and self-government, and old relations of dependence, servility, and mutuality were defined as sinful and left behind. The revival was not a capitalist plot. But it certainly was a crucial step in the legitimation of free labor.

PRIMARY SOURCES

The following primary sources reveal the Second Great Awakening's impact on various groups. These sources may support the argument in Paul Johnson's essay regarding the relationship between economic change and revivalism, or suggest alternative explanations.

| 2 | The maps on the next page are based on the distillation of a large number of primary sources and illustrate several important develop- ments in the western portion of upstate New York. As you examine |

these maps, keep in mind that the Erie Canal (labeled "Grand Canal" on the first map) opened in 1825. Do these maps reveal connections between social, economic, and religious trends in the region?

Maps of Western New York

Source: Barbara K. and Warren S. Walker, eds., *The Erie Canal: Gateway to Empire* (Boston: D. C. Heath and Company, 1963), pp. xii–xiii; a facsimile of a fold-out map facing the first page of the Appendix to David Hosack's *Memoir of De Witt Clinton* (New York: J. Seymour, 1829). (Facsimile drawn by Donald T. Pitcher—cartographer.); Whitney R. Cross, *The Burned-over District: The Social and Intellectual History of Enthusiastic Religion in Western New York, 1800–1850* (New York: Harper & Row, Publishers, 1965), pp. 58, 157.

Gain of more than 20 persons per square
mile between 1820 and 1835

• Places in western New York that asked
  Finney's aid in conducting revivals in 1831 or
  that reported notable sympathetic revivals

3 | Alexis de Tocqueville, a French aristocrat who traveled extensively in the United States in the early 1830s, published his observations about American manners, society, and politics in *Democracy in America*. In what ways did a "general equality of condition" influence Americans' attitudes, according to Tocqueville? How might conditions or attitudes that he perceived encourage revivalism? Are these conditions and attitudes the same as those identified in Paul Johnson's essay?

Alexis de Tocqueville on the Condition of Americans (1835)

Among the novel objects that attracted my attention during my stay in the United States, nothing struck me more forcibly than the general equality of condition among the people. I readily discovered the prodigious influence that this primary fact exercises on the whole course of society; it gives a peculiar direction to public opinion and a peculiar tenor to the laws; it imparts new maxims to the governing authorities and peculiar habits to the governed.

I soon perceived that the influence of this fact extends far beyond the political character and the laws of the country, and that it has no less effect on civil society than on the government; it creates opinions, gives birth to new sentiments, founds novel customs, and modifies whatever it does not produce. The more I advanced in the study of American society, the more I perceived that this equality of condition is the fundamental fact from which all others seem to be derived and the central point at which all my observations constantly terminated. . . .

The men who live at a period of social equality are not therefore easily led to place that intellectual authority to which they bow either beyond or above humanity. They commonly seek for the sources of truth in themselves or in those who are like themselves. . . .

When the ranks of society are unequal, and men unlike one another in condition, there are some individuals wielding the power of superior intelligence, learning, and enlightenment, while the multitude are sunk in ignorance and prejudice. Men living at these aristocratic periods are therefore naturally induced to shape their opinions by the standard of a superior person, or a superior class of persons, while they are averse to recognizing the infallibility of the mass of the people.

The contrary takes place in ages of equality. The nearer the people are drawn to the common level of an equal and similar condition, the less prone does

Source: Alexis de Tocqueville, *Democracy in America* (New York: Alfred A. Knopf, Inc., 1945), I: p. 3; II: pp. 10, 11, 27–28, 105.

each man become to place implicit faith in a certain man or a certain class of men. But his readiness to believe the multitude increases, and opinion is more than ever mistress of the world. . . .

We shall see that of all the passions which originate in or are fostered by equality, there is one which it renders peculiarly intense, and which it also infuses into the heart of every man; I mean the love of well-being. The taste for well-being is the prominent and indelible feature of democratic times.

It may be believed that a religion which should undertake to destroy so deep-seated a passion would in the end be destroyed by it; and if it attempted to wean men entirely from the contemplation of the good things of this world in order to devote their faculties exclusively to the thought of another, it may be foreseen that the minds of men would at length escape its grasp, to plunge into the exclusive enjoyment of present and material pleasures.

The chief concern of religion is to purify, to regulate, and to restrain the excessive and exclusive taste for well-being that men feel in periods of equality; but it would be an error to attempt to overcome it completely or to eradicate it. Men cannot be cured of the love of riches, but they may be persuaded to enrich themselves by none but honest means.

This brings me to a final consideration, which comprises, as it were, all the others. The more the conditions of men are equalized and assimilated to each other, the more important is it for religion, while it carefully abstains from the daily turmoil of secular affairs, not needlessly to run counter to the ideas that generally prevail or to the permanent interests that exist in the mass of the people. For as public opinion grows to be more and more the first and most irresistible of existing powers, the religious principle has no external support strong enough to enable it long to resist its attacks. . . .

As social conditions become more equal, the number of persons increases who, although they are neither rich nor powerful enough to exercise any great influence over their fellows, have nevertheless acquired or retained sufficient education and fortune to satisfy their own wants. They owe nothing to any man, they expect nothing from any man; they acquire the habit of always considering themselves as standing alone, and they are apt to imagine that their whole destiny is in their own hands. . . .

Although the desire of acquiring the good things of this world is the prevailing passion of the American people, certain momentary outbreaks occur when their souls seem suddenly to burst the bonds of matter by which they are restrained and to soar impetuously towards heaven. In all the states of the Union, but especially in the half-peopled country of the Far West, itinerant preachers may be met with who hawk about the word of God from place to place. Whole families, old men, women, and children, cross rough passes and untrodden wilds, coming from a great distance, to join a camp-meeting, where, in listening to these discourses, they totally forget for several days and nights the cares of business and even the most urgent wants of the body.

Here and there in the midst of American society you meet with men full of a fanatical and almost wild spiritualism, which hardly exists in Europe. From time to time strange sects arise which endeavor to strike out extraordinary paths to eternal happiness. Religious insanity is very common in the United States. . . .

 Revivalism often had limited appeal among Congregationalists and others who traced their theological roots back to the Puritans. This attack on revival preachers was published by an organization of Congregationalist ministers in New England in 1811. What did they perceive as the basis of the revivalists' power? How does their analysis of the revivalists' appeal compare to that identified by Paul Johnson?

An Attack on the Revivals (1811)

Liberty is a great cant word with them. They promise their hearers to set them at liberty. And to effect this, they advise them to give up all their old prejudices and traditions which they have received from their fathers and their ministers; who, they say, are hirelings, keeping poor souls in bondage, and under oppression. Hence to use their own language, they say, "Break all those yokes and trammels from off you, and come out of prison; and dare to think, and speak, and act for yourselves."

Source: Walter Harris, *Characteristics of False Teachers* (Concord, N.H., 1811), p. 19.

 Revivalist preacher Lorenzo Dow offered this defense of camp meetings in response to the attacks of orthodox preachers. On what grounds does he defend them?

A Defense of Camp Meetings (1814)

You may support your distinction and feed your pride, but in a religious point of view all men are on a level, and the good man feels it so. The very fact, your

Source: Lorenzo Dow, *History of Cosmopolite; or the Four Volumes of Lorenzo Dow's Journal* (Wheeling, Va., 1848), p. 593.

aversion to worship your Creator with the poor and despised, proves to me that you have neither part nor lot in the matter; that you know not God nor his worship, and that to follow your advice would be the sure road to perdition. The Lord hath declared his intention and purpose to exalt the humble whilst he will pull down high looks.

6 | Verse was a popular form of expression for defenders of revival religion during the Second Great Awakening. What does this doggerel suggest about the sources of revivalism's appeal?

"On Predestination" (1809)

If all things succeed
Because they're decreed
And immutable impulses rule us;
    Then praying and preaching,
    And all such like teaching,
Is nought but a plan to befool us.

If destiny and fate,
    Guide us this way and that,
As the coachman with bits guides his horses;
    There's no man can stray,
    But all go the right way,
As the stars in their different courses.

. . . .

If this be the way,
    As some preachers say,
That all things were order'd by fate;
    I'll not spend my pence,
    To pay for nonsense,
If nothing will alter my state.

. . . .

Then with all he must pass
    For a dull, senseless ass,
Who depends upon predestination.

Source: Elias Smith, *Herald of Gospel Liberty,* September 15, 1809.

7 As this early nineteenth-century painting reveals, revivalism was not confined to whites during the Second Great Awakening. Why might the messages of revivalist preachers have been especially appealing to African Americans? Do scenes like the one pictured here support Paul Johnson's argument in Source 1?

"Negro Methodists Holding a Meeting in Philadelphia" (ca. 1812)

Source: Watercolor by Pavel (Paul) Petovich Svinin, "Negro Methodists Holding a Meeting in Philadelphia," (between 1811 and 1813); in Nathan O. Hatch, *The Democratization of American Christianity* (New Haven: Yale University Press, 1989); Metropolitan Museum of Art.

8 The "burned-over" district was the scene of intense revival activity. It was also the birthplace of the Church of Jesus Christ of Latter-day Saints (Mormons), founded in 1830 by Joseph Smith less than thirty miles from Rochester. Smith claimed to be a prophet and to have translated ancient scripture that told the story of Israelites and other inhabitants in pre-Columbian America. Although Mormon preaching lacked the emotionalism of the revivalists, it initially attracted many people from this area of intense revival activity. In these passages from the *Book of Mormon,* the prophet Nephi explains the path to salvation and indicts churches that will appear in modern times. Are the themes expressed here similar to those emphasized in other sources? Why might they have been appealing to many people in the 1830s, especially in the "burned-over" district?

Book of Mormon (1830)

25 Adam fell that men might be; and men are, that they might have joy.

26 And the Messiah cometh in the fulness of time, that he may redeem the children of men from the fall. And because that they are redeemed from the fall they have become free forever, knowing good from evil; to act for themselves and not to be acted upon, save it be by the punishment of the law at the great and last day, according to the commandments which God hath given.

27 Wherefore, men are free according to the flesh; and all things are given them which are expedient unto man. And they are free to choose liberty and eternal life, through the great Mediator of all men, or to choose captivity and death, according to the captivity and power of the devil; for he seeketh that all men might be miserable like unto himself.

28 And now, my sons, I would that ye should look to the great Mediator, and hearken unto his great commandments; and be faithful unto his words, and choose eternal life, according to the will of his Holy Spirit;

29 And not choose eternal death, according to the will of the flesh and the evil which is therein, which giveth the spirit of the devil power to captivate, to bring you down to hell, that he may reign over you in his own kingdom. . . .

12 Because of pride, and because of false teachers, and false doctrine, their churches have become corrupted, and their churches are lifted up; because of pride they are puffed up.

13 They rob the poor because of their fine sanctuaries; they rob the poor because of their fine clothing; and they persecute the meek and the poor in heart, because in their pride they are puffed up.

14 They wear stiff necks and high heads; yea, and because of pride, and wickedness, and abominations, and whoredoms, they have all gone astray save it be a few, who are the humble followers of Christ; nevertheless, they are led, that in many instances they do err because they are taught by the precepts of men.

Source: Book of Mormon, 2 Nephi 2:25–29; 28:12–15 (Salt Lake City: The Church of Jesus Christ of Latter-day Saints, 1986).

15 O the wise, and the learned, and the rich, that are puffed up in the pride of their hearts, and all those who preach false doctrines, and all those who commit whoredoms, and pervert the right way of the Lord, wo, wo, wo be unto them, saith the Lord God Almighty, for they shall be thrust down to hell!

9 Parley Pratt was one of the Mormon prophet Joseph Smith's original Twelve Apostles. Parley and his brother Orson were born into a poor farm family and boarded out to other farmers. Later, he wrote about his experiences as a young wage earner. How does Pratt's experience on the farm compare to the pattern of experience that Paul Johnson found among Rochester's workmen?

Parley Pratt on Wage-Earning (1874)

The next spring found me in the employment of a wealthy farmer, by the name of Eliphet Bristol. . . . I was then but a lad—being only seventeen years of age—and stood in need of fatherly and motherly care and comfort. But they treated a laborer as a machine; not as a human being, possessed of feelings and sympathies in common with his species. *Work!* WORK! WORK! you are hired to work. . . . I was glad when the time expired; I felt like one released from prison.

Source: The Autobiography of Parley Parker Pratt, One of the Twelve Apostles of the Church of Jesus Christ of Latter-Day Saints, ed. Parley Parker Pratt (son) (New York, Russell Brothers, 1874), pp. 20–21.

Workers and Revivalism in Philadelphia

By the 1820s, such eastern cities as Philadelphia were hotbeds of revival activity. As you examine these sources, keep in mind that journeymen (unlike master craftsmen) were hired workers. Do these sources reveal a possible connection between workers' economic concerns and revivalism's appeal?

10 | Philadelphia Journeymen Protest Their Conditions (1828)

We, the Journeymen Mechanics of the City and County of Philadelphia, conscious that our condition in society is lower than justice demands it should be, and feeling our inability, individually, to ward off from ourselves and families those numerous evils which result from an unequal and very excessive accumulation of wealth and power into the hands of a few, are desirous of forming an Association, which shall avert as much as possible those evils with which poverty and incessant toil have already inflicted, and which threaten ultimately to overwhelm and destroy us. And in order that our views may be properly understood, and the justness of our intention duly appreciated, we offer to the public the following summary of our reasons, principles and objects.

If unceasing toils were actually requisite to supply us with a bare, and in many instances wretched, subsistence; if the products of our industry or an equitable proportion of them, were appropriated to our actual wants and comfort, then would we yield without a murmur to the stern and irrevocable decree of necessity. But this is infinitely wide of the fact. We appeal to the most intelligent of every community, and ask—Do not you, and all society, depend solely for subsistence on the products of human industry? Do not those who labour, while acquiring to themselves thereby only a scanty and penurious support, likewise maintain in affluence and luxury the rich who never labour?

Do not all the streams of wealth which flow in every direction and are emptied into and absorbed by the coffers of the unproductive, exclusively take their rise in the bones, marrow, and muscles of the industrious classes? In return for which, exclusive of a bare subsistence, (which likewise is the product of their own industry,) they receive—not any thing! . . .

The real object, therefore, of this association, is to avert, if possible, the desolating evils which must inevitably arise from a depreciation of the intrinsic value of human labour; to raise the mechanical and productive classes to that condition of true independence and inequality [sic] which their practical skill and ingenuity, their immense utility to the nation and their growing intelligence are beginning imperiously to demand: to promote, equally, the happiness, prosperity and welfare of the whole community—to aid in conferring a due and full proportion of that invaluable promoter of happiness, leisure, upon all its useful members; and to assist, in conjunction with such other institutions of this nature as shall hereafter be formed throughout the union, in establishing a just balance of power, both mental, moral, political and

Source: John R. Commons et al., eds., *A Documentary History of American Industrial Society* (Cleveland, 1910), 5: pp. 84–85, 89–90.

scientific, between all the various classes and individuals which constitute society at large.

11 | Occupations of Methodist Converts in Philadelphia, 1830s

Occupation	No.	%
Gentlemen	0	0
Professional	3	2.9
Merchant and Retailer	16	15.5
Manufacturer	1	0.9
Lower white-collar	4	3.9
Master Craftsman	10	9.7
Journeyman	64	62.1
Unskilled labor and street trade	5	4.9
Total	103	

Source: Bruce Laurie, *Working People of Philadelphia, 1800–1850* (Philadelphia: Temple University Press, 1980), p. 47; originally from First Presbyterian Church in Southwark, Minutes, 1830–1840, Presbyterian Historical Society, Philadephia; First Presbyterian Church of Southwark, Trustees Minutes, 1818–1832, Presbyterian Historical Society, Philadephia; and Centennial Publishing Committee, *History of Ebenezer Methodist Church, Southwark* (Philadelphia: J. B. Lippincott, 1892); and city directories, 1830–1835.

Women and the Revivals

Women played a large role in the Second Great Awakening, an aspect of the revivals noted by many observers. Like Tocqueville, Frances Trollope and Harriet Martineau were Europeans who traveled widely in America in the early nineteenth century. Rebeccah Lee, on the other hand, was the wife of a Connecticut minister. What do these sources reveal about the possible sources of revivalism's appeal to women?

12 | Frances Trollope's Account of a Camp Meeting (1829)

But how am I to describe the sounds that proceeded from this strange mass of human beings? I know no words which can convey an idea of it. Hysterical sobbings, convulsive groans, shrieks and screams the most appalling, burst forth on all sides. I felt sick with horror. As if their hoarse and overstrained voices failed to make noise enough, they soon began to clap their hands violently. . . .

Many of these wretched creatures were beautiful young females. The preachers moved about among them, at once exciting and soothing their agonies. I heard the muttered "Sister! dear sister!" I saw the insidious lips approach the cheeks of the unhappy girls; I heard the murmured confessions of the poor victims, and I watched their tormentors, breathing into their ears consolations that tinged the pale cheek with red. Had I been a man, I am sure I should have been guilty of some rash act of interference; nor do I believe that such a scene could have been acted in the presence of Englishmen without instant punishment being inflicted; not to mention the salutary discipline of the treadmill, which, beyond all question, would, in England, have been applied to check so turbulent and so vicious a scene.

Source: Frances Trollope, *Domestic Manners of the Americans* (New York: Vintage Books, 1949; originally published 1832), pp. 172, 173.

13 | Harriet Martineau on the Condition of American Women (1837)

. . . [H]er husband's hair stands on end at the idea of her working, and he toils to indulge her with money: she has liberty to get her brain turned by religious excitements, that her attention may be diverted from morals, politics, and philosophy; and, especially, her morals are guarded by the strictest observance of propriety in her presence. In short, indulgence is given her as a substitute for justice. . . .

. . .[M]arriage is the only object left open to woman. Philosophy she may pursue only fancifully, and under pain of ridicule: science only as a pastime, and under a similar penalty. Art is declared to be left open: but the necessary learning, and, yet more, the indispensable experience of reality, are denied to her. Literature is also said to be permitted: but under what penalties and

Source: Harriet Martineau, *Society in America* (Gloucester, Mass.: Peter Smith, 1968), pp. 292, 293, 305.

restrictions? Nothing is thus left for women but marriage.—Yes; Religion, is the reply. . . .

As for the occupations with which American ladies fill up their leisure; what has been already said will show that there is no great weight or diversity of occupation. Many are largely engaged in charities, doing good or harm according to the enlightenment of mind which is carried to the work. In New England, a vast deal of time is spent in attending preachings, and other religious meetings: and in paying visits, for religious purposes, to the poor and sorrowful. The same results follow from this practice that may be witnessed wherever it is much pursued. In as far as sympathy is kept up, and acquaintanceship between different classes in society is occasioned, the practice is good. In as far as it unsettles the minds of the visitors, encourages a false craving for religious excitement . . . the practice is bad.

14 | Rebeccah Lee on the Appeal of Christianity (1831)

To the Christian religion we owe the rank we hold in society, and we should feel our obligations. It is that, which prevents our being treated like beasts of burden—which secures us the honourable privilege of human companionship in social life, and raises us in the domestic relations to the elevated stations of wives and mothers. Only seriously reflect upon the state of our sex, in those regions of the globe unvisited and unblessed with the light of Christianity; we see them degraded to a level with the brutes, and shut out from the society of lordly *man;* as if they were made by their Creator, not as the companions, but as the slaves and drudges of domineering masters. . . . Let each one then ask herself, how much do I owe?

Source: Nancy F. Cott, *The Bonds of Womanhood: "Woman's Sphere" in New England, 1780–1835* (New Haven: Yale University Press, 1977), pp. 131–132; originally from Mrs. Rebeccah Lee, *An Address, Delivered in Marlborough, Connecticut, September 7, 1831* (Hartford, 1831).

Charles Finney and the Revivals

Charles Finney, a lawyer by training, preached with great effect in Rochester in 1830 and 1831. No unlettered, backwoods preacher, he also wrote widely on the doctrines and techniques of the revivals. As you read the following two sources, consider what they reveal about the types of people Finney converted and the reasons for his popularity with middle-class audiences. Do they support any of Paul Johnson's conclusions?

15 | Charles Finney on the Rochester Revival (1876)

There were very soon some very marked conversions. The wife of a prominent lawyer in that city, was one of the first converts that was much known in the city. She was a lady of high standing, well-known, a lady of culture and extensive influence. Her conversion was a very marked one. The first that I saw her a lady friend of hers came with her to my room, and introduced her. The lady who introduced her was a Christian woman, who had found that she was very much exercised in her mind, and persuaded her to come and see me. Mrs. —————— had been a gay, worldly woman, and very fond of society. She afterwards told me that when I first came there she greatly regretted it, and feared there would be a revival; and if so it would greatly interfere with the pleasures and amusements that she had promised herself that winter. On conversing with her I found that the Spirit of the Lord was indeed dealing with her in an unsparing manner. She was bowed down with great conviction of sin. After considerable conversation with her, I pressed her hard then and there to give herself to Christ—to renounce sin, and the world, and self, and everything for Christ. I saw that she was a very proud woman, and this struck me as rather the most marked feature of her character. At the conclusion of our conversation we knelt down to pray; and my mind being full of the subject of the pride of her heart as it was manifested, I very soon introduced the text, "Except ye be converted and become as little children, ye shall in no wise enter into the kingdom of heaven." This I seemed to be led to by the Spirit of prayer almost irresistibly. I turned this subject over in prayer; and I almost immediately heard Mrs. Matthews, as she was kneeling by my side, repeating that text: "Except ye be converted and become as little children"—"as *little children*"—"Except ye be converted *and become as little children*." I observed that her mind was taken with that, and the Spirit of God was pressing it upon her heart. I therefore continued to pray and hold that subject before her mind, and holding her up before God as needing that very thing to be converted—to become as a little child. I besought the Lord to convert her, to make her as a little child, to put away her pride and her loftiness of spirit and bring her down into the attitude of a little child. I felt that the Lord was answering prayer. I felt *sure* that He was; and had no doubt, I believe, in my mind, that the Lord was doing the very work that I asked him to do. Her heart broken down, her sensibility gushed forth, and before we rose from our knees she was indeed a little child. When I stopped praying and opened my eyes and looked at her,

Source: Garth M. Rosell and Richard A. G. Dupuis, *The Memoirs of Charles G. Finney* (Grand Rapids, Mich.: Zondervan Publishing House, 1989), pp. 304–308, 318–319.

her face was turned up toward heaven, and the tears streaming over her face; and she was in the attitude of praying that she might be made a little child. She rose up, became peaceful, settled into a joyous faith, and retired. From that moment she was outspoken in her religious convictions, and zealous for the conversion of her friends. Her conversion of course produced much excitement among that class of people to which she belonged. . . .

. . . My meetings soon became thronged with that class. The lawyers, physicians, merchants, and indeed all the most intelligent class of society, became more and more interested, and more and more easily influenced to give their hearts to God. Very soon the work took effect extensively among the lawyers in that city. There has always been a large number of the leading lawyers of the state resident at Rochester. The work soon got hold of numbers of those. They became very anxious, and came freely to our meetings of inquiry; and numbers of them came forward to the anxious seat, as it has since been called, and publicly gave their hearts to God. . . .

There were a good many cases in Rochester in which people were exercised with this spirit of agonizing travail of soul. I have said that the moral aspect of things was greatly changed by this revival. It was a young city, full of thrift and enterprize, and full of sin. The inhabitants were intelligent and enterprizing in the highest degree; but as the revival swept through the town and converted the great mass of the most influential people both male and female, the change in the order, sobriety, and morality of the city was wonderful.

At a subsequent period, which I shall mention in its place, I was conversing with a lawyer who was converted at this revival of which I have been speaking, and who soon after had been made district attorney of the city, the same that some call prosecuting attorney. His business was to superintend the prosecution of criminals. From his position he was made thoroughly acquainted with the history of crime in that city. In speaking of the revival in which he was converted, he said to me many years afterwards: "I have been examining the records of the criminal courts, and I find this striking fact, that whereas our city has increased since that revival three-fold, there is not one third as many prosecutions for crime as there had been up to that time.

"Thus crime," he says, "has *decreased* two thirds, and the population has *increased* two thirds. This is," he said, "the wonderful influence that that revival had had upon the community." Indeed by the power of that revival public sentiment has been molded. The public affairs of the city have been, in a great measure in the hands of Christian men. The great weight of character has been on the side of Christ, and their public business had been conducted accordingly.

16 | Charles Finney on the Freedom of Sinners (1836)

. . . Suppose God should command a man to fly; would the command impose upon him any obligation, until he was furnished with wings? Certainly not. But suppose, on his failing to obey, God should require him to repent of his disobedience, and threaten to send him to hell if he did not heartily blame himself, and justify the requirement of God. He must cease to be a reasonable being before he can do this. He knows that God never gave him power to fly, and therefore he had no right to require it of him. His natural sense of justice, and of the foundation of obligation, is outraged, and he indignantly and conscientiously throws back the requirement into his Maker's face. Repentance, in this case, is a natural impossibility; while he is a reasonable being, he knows that he is not to blame for not flying without wings; and however much he may regret his not being able to obey the requirement, and however great may be his fear of the wrath of God, still to blame himself and justify God is a natural impossibility. As, therefore, God requires men to make to themselves a new heart, on pain of eternal death, it is the strongest possible evidence that they are able to do it. To say that he has commanded them to do it, without telling them they are able, is consummate trifling. Their ability is implied as strongly as it can be, in the command itself. . . .

You see from this subject that a sinner, under the influence of the Spirit of God, is just as free as a jury under the arguments of an advocate.

Here also you may see the importance of right views on this point. Suppose a lawyer, in addressing a jury, should not expect to change their minds by any thing he could say, but should wait for an invisible, and physical agency, to be exerted by the Holy Ghost upon them. And suppose, on the other hand, that the jury thought that in making up their verdict, they must be passive, and wait for a direct physical agency to be exerted upon them. In vain might the lawyer plead, and in vain might the jury hear, for until he pressed his arguments as if he was determined to bow their hearts, and until they make up their minds, and decide the question, and thus act like rational beings, both his pleading, and their hearing is in vain. So if a minister goes into a desk to preach to sinners, believing that they have no power to obey the truth, and under the impression that a direct physical influence must be exerted upon them before they *can* believe, and if his audience be of the same opinion, in vain does he preach, and in vain do they hear, "for they are yet in their sins;" they sit and quietly wait for some invisible hand to be stretched down from

Source: David Grimstead, ed., *American Visions and Revisions, 1607–1865* (Acton, Mass.: Copley Publishing Group, 1999), pp. 366, 367; originally from Charles Grandison Finney, *Sinners Bound to Change Their Own Hearts* (1836).

heaven, and perform some surgical operation, infuse some new principle, or implant some constitutional taste; *after* which they suppose they shall be *able* to obey God. Ministers should labor with sinners, as a lawyer does with a jury, and upon the same principles of mental philosophy; and the sinner should weigh his arguments, and make up his mind as upon oath and for his life, and give a verdict upon the spot, according to law and evidence. . . .

CONCLUSION

By now you have probably decided whether you agree with the conclusions in Paul Johnson's essay. You may have also discovered that the question of historical causation is inseparable from other questions. One such question was the subject of Chapter 5: motivation. To study the appeal of revivalism, as Johnson's essay reveals, necessarily forces us to confront the motives of those who embraced it. Another of those questions is the role of ideology in history. Paul Johnson suggests that Finney's revivals promoted "visions of a perfect moral order based on individual freedom" rather than older paternalistic controls. In effect, he argues that the revivals helped give birth to an ideology conducive to the rise of capitalism. Studying the Second Great Awakening also demonstrates that questions of causation and the role of individuals in history are closely related. Were preachers like Charles Finney prime movers in history, or did they merely serve some large, underlying forces? As we shall see, historians have different answers. Finally, perhaps you found one underlying cause to explain the appeal of revivalism in the early nineteenth century. The search for historical causes sometimes leads historians, as it did Alexis de Tocqueville, to an all-encompassing explanation. In other words, they advance a "grand" theory. In the next chapter, we turn to one such interpretation of history.

FURTHER READING

Nancy F. Cott, *The Bonds of Womanhood: "Woman's Sphere" in New England, 1780–1835* (New Haven: Yale University Press, 1977).

Whitney R. Cross, *The Burned-over District: The Social and Intellectual History of Enthusiastic Religion in Western New York, 1800–1850* (New York: Harper & Row, Publishers, 1965).

Nathan O. Hatch, *The Democratization of American Christianity* (New Haven: Yale University Press, 1989).

Curtis D. Johnson, *Islands of Holiness: Rural Religion in Upstate New York, 1790–1860* (Ithaca: Cornell University Press, 1989).

Bernard A. Weisberger, *They Gathered at the River: The Story of the Great Revivalists and Their Impact upon Religion in America* (Chicago: Quadrangle Books, 1966).

NOTES

1. Quoted in Bernard Weisberger, *They Gathered at the River: The Story of the Great Revivalists and Their Impact upon Religion in America* (Chicago: Quadrangle Books, 1966), p. 36.
2. Quoted in Charles A. Johnson, *The Frontier Camp Meeting: Religion's Harvest Time* (Dallas: Southern Methodist University Press, 1955), p. 64.
3. Quoted in Weisberger, *They Gathered at the River,* p. 34.
4. Ibid., p. 11.
5. Curtis D. Johnson, *Islands of Holiness: Rural Religion in Upstate New York, 1790–1860* (Ithaca: Cornell University Press, 1989), p. 7.

CHAPTER | 8

GRAND THEORY AND HISTORY:
DEMOCRACY AND THE FRONTIER

The documents in this chapter deal with the frontier experience and Frederick Jackson Turner's theory about its importance in American history.

Secondary Source

1. The Significance of the Frontier in American History (1893), FREDERICK JACKSON TURNER

Primary Sources

2. Sketch of Trappers (1837), ALFRED JACOB MILLER
3. N. J. Wyeth's Instructions for Robert Evans at the Fort Hall Trading Post (1834)
4. Daguerreotype of *The Stump Orator* (1847), GEORGE CALEB BINGHAM
5. Autobiography (1833), BLACK HAWK
6. Waneta, a Yanktonai (ca. 1823)
7. On Settling in Missouri (1839), HANS BARLIEN
8. View of the Valley of the Mississippi (1832), ROBERT BAIRD
9. Life in the Gold Fields (1849), ANTONIO FRANCO CORONEL
10. An English-Chinese Phrase Book (1875)
11. A Camp Meeting (n.d.)
12. We Went to Kansas (1862), MIRIAM DAVIS COLT
13. Early View of Salt Lake City (1872)
14. Brigham Young on Land Distribution (1848)

*I*n 1822, a young Ohio clerk named Jedediah Smith joined a fur-trading party heading up the Missouri River for the Yellowstone country. The fearless, Bible-toting Methodist spent three years in the Rockies, braving attacks from grizzly bears and Indians. Still, it was a fruitful outing. While traveling through Wyoming's Wind River Range, he located South Pass, a future gateway through the Rockies for thousands of westward-bound migrants. And when he returned to St. Louis in 1825, he carried 9,000 pounds of beaver pelts. The West had cast its spell on him. Less than a month later, Smith led a party of seventy men back up the Missouri. By the time the trapper returned five years later, he had trekked beyond the Rockies into the wastes of the Great Basin and across the Mojave desert to California—the first American to enter the Mexican province by land.

Smith and other trappers represented the leading edge of American penetration into the West. Yet when he sold his fur business in 1830 to get into the growing Santa Fe trade, the trappers' days were just about over. In fact, when Smith returned to St. Louis that year, he saw many settlers hard on his heels. Drifting back down the Missouri, he passed a host of new towns where none had been before. And more newcomers were on the way. In 1830, more people lived west of the Appalachian Mountains than had lived in the original states in 1790. Indeed, so quickly did settlers displace fur trappers that when Smith died in an Indian attack near the Cimarron River in 1831, he and other mountain men had already become legends—outsized characters from a bygone era.

If Americans' romance with the frontier began in the era of the mountain men, today it has lost little of its ability to evoke powerful images. In the West, whether it was Missouri, Montana, or California, myth and fact merged to create romantic, larger-than-life figures like Jedediah Smith. There, we have often been told, pioneers turned their backs on civilization to face numerous dangers and hard work. Triumphing over nature and the native inhabitants, they brought civilization to the land. As they marched ever westward, so did democracy and progress. In short, the frontier's hold on our imaginations reflects an assumption about its ability to remake people and institutions. Given this story's compelling power, it is not surprising that some historians have seen the frontier as a decisive influence in American history. They argue that the long frontier experience is a unifying thread running through the nation's past. In this chapter we pick up that thread by evaluating one historian's grand theory about the frontier. Like all grand theories, it attributes numerous and far-reaching consequences to a single force.

SETTING

It did not take long for Americans to create its first frontier heroes out of fur traders like Jedehiah Smith. It took historians far longer to acknowledge the influence of the frontier on American society. First the frontier had to become history. In 1890 the U.S. Census Bureau announced the closing of the frontier. Three years later, a young University of Wisconsin historian named Frederick Jackson Turner read a paper called "The Significance of the Frontier in American History" at the World Columbian Exposition in Chicago. Although Turner's "frontier thesis" was ignored at the time, after the turn of the century historians gradually began to acknowledge it.

Even then, many of them were not impressed. In the nineteenth century, most historians ignored the West. They often defined history as "past politics" and emphasized the European roots of American political institutions. Turner, who grew up in rural Wisconsin a generation removed from the frontier, resented the Eastern and European slant to American history. His essay challenged that anti-Western bias and the orthodox definition of history as political narrative. Instead Turner offered nothing less than a sweeping reassessment of the formation of American society. His "frontier thesis" was a grand explanation of American uniqueness from a Western perspective.

Despite its chilly reception, Turner's thesis gradually became historical orthodoxy. His argument may have challenged a conventional definition of history, but it also confirmed popular thinking. As Theodore Roosevelt noted, Turner "put into definite shape a good deal of thought that has been floating around rather loosely."[1] One idea blowing in the late nineteenth-century breezes was a belief in America's "manifest destiny" to spread American culture and institutions abroad. Turner's thesis was published just after the frontier officially closed and when nostalgia over its passing was growing. Just when many Americans saw new "frontiers" overseas, Turner's thesis confirmed a nationalist assumption that American expansion and democracy were inseparable. It also reflected the pervasive influence of Charles Darwin's theory of evolution on American thought. Like many post-Darwinian thinkers, Turner assumed that societies evolved from a primitive to a "civilized" stage. This Darwinian model of social evolution reinforced both expansionist desires and assumptions about Anglo-Saxon superiority. Indeed, many Americans argued that it was their duty as "Anglo-Saxons" to bring civilization to the "backward" peoples of the world.

Given a receptive audience, Turner's thesis became part of popular thought. It was embraced and popularized by many prominent Americans, from T. R. and Woodrow Wilson to Herbert Hoover. Future president Hoover, for instance, would declare in a widely read article in 1922 that "American individualism has received much of its character from our contacts with the forces of nature on a new continent."[2] In addition to crystallizing popular thinking, Turner's argument was comprehensive, comprehensible, and romantic. Reading Turner, Americans for more than a century have discovered a key to their history in a cherished part of the nation's past. In one bold stroke, Turner had broadened Americans' history and captured their imaginations.

INVESTIGATION

Because the frontier thesis gave legend and romance a central role in the nation's past, readers even today are inclined to judge it with their hearts rather than their heads. Your main challenge, therefore, is to evaluate Turner's thesis critically. Using Turner's own evidence (Source 1) and that in the primary sources, determine whether his thesis is a useful tool to explain Americans' institutions and character. Your evaluation should address the following questions:

1. **What important effects did the frontier have on American society and character, according to Turner?** What is his evidence that the frontier promoted individualism and a "composite nationality"?

2. **What was the relationship between the frontier and American political institutions?** How does Turner attempt to demonstrate a relationship between democracy and the frontier?

3. **What is Turner's evidence for social breakdown and evolution on the frontier?** What role do the government, corporations, cities, or religious organizations play in Turner's frontier?

4. **How do the experiences of specific groups of people, as reflected in the primary sources, support or modify Turner's view of western settlement?** Does Turner's thesis reflect a mythic view of the West or real experiences?

SECONDARY SOURCE

1 Like the vast stretches of the West in which even Jedediah Smith occasionally got lost, Turner's frontier thesis is both alluring and deceptive. It is just as easy to be drawn into his argument as it is to lose one's way once there. Readers must be careful not to be ambushed by Turner's prose or by the simplicity of his thesis. They must be alert, inquisitive, and as interested in the small details of the trees as in the grand vision of the forest. As you read, therefore, notice the way Turner defines the frontier. Consider whether he sees it as a line of settlement, a type of society, a specific area or region, or a social process. Also be careful to note his evidence for the transforming power of the frontier.

Source: Excerpts from *Proceedings of the Forty-First Annual Meeting of the State Historical Society of Wisconsin* (Madison, Wis., 1894), pp. 79–112.

The Significance of the Frontier in American History (1893)

FREDERICK JACKSON TURNER

In a recent bulletin of the superintendent of the census for 1890 appear these significant words: "Up to and including 1880 the country had a frontier of settlement, but at present the unsettled area has been so broken into by isolated bodies of settlement that there can hardly be said to be a frontier line. In the discussion of its extent, its westward movement, etc., it cannot, therefore, any longer have a place in the census reports." This brief official statement marks the closing of a great historic movement. Up to our own day American history has been in a large degree the history of the colonization of the Great West. The existence of an area of free land, its continuous recession, and the advance of American settlement westward, explain American development. Behind institutions, behind constitutional forms and modifications, lie the vital forces that call these organs into life, and shape them to meet changing conditions. Now, the peculiarity of American institutions is the fact that they have been compelled to adapt themselves to the changes of an expanding people—to the changes involved in crossing a continent, in winning a wilderness, and in developing at each area of this progress out of the primitive economic and political conditions of the frontier into the complexity of city life. . . . Thus American development has exhibited not merely advance along a single line, but a return to primitive conditions on a continually advancing frontier line, and a new development for that area. American social development has been continually beginning over again on the frontier. This perennial rebirth, this fluidity of American life, this expansion westward with its new opportunities, its continuous touch with the simplicity of primitive society, furnish the forces dominating American character. The true point of view in the history of this nation is not the Atlantic coast, it is the Great West. . . .

In this advance, the frontier is the outer edge of the wave—the meeting point between savagery and civilization. Much has been written about the frontier from the point of view of border warfare and the chase, but as a field for the serious study of the economist and the historian it has been neglected.

What is the frontier? It is not the European frontier—a fortified boundary line running through dense populations. The most significant thing about it is, that it lies at the hither edge of free land. In the census reports it is treated as the margin of that settlement which has a density of two or more to the square mile. The term is a classic one, and for our purpose does not need sharp definition. . . .

. . . Now, the frontier is the line of most rapid and effective Americanization. The wilderness masters the colonist. It finds him a European in dress, industries, tools, modes of travel, and thought. It takes him from the railroad car and puts him in the birch canoe. It strips off the garments of civilization, and arrays him in the hunting shirt and the moccasin. It puts him in the log cabin of the Cherokee and the Iroquois, and runs an Indian palisade around him. Before long he has gone to planting Indian corn and plowing with a sharp stick; he shouts the war cry and takes the scalp in orthodox Indian fashion. In short, at the frontier the environment is at first too strong for the man. He must accept the conditions which it furnishes, or perish, and so he fits himself into the Indian clearings and follows the Indian trails. Little by little he transforms the wilderness, but the outcome is not the old Europe, . . . The fact is, that here is a new product that is American. At first, the frontier was the Atlantic coast. It was the frontier of Europe in a very real sense. Moving westward, the frontier became more and more American. *As successive terminal moraines result from successive glaciations, so each frontier leaves its traces behind it, and when it becomes a settled area the region still partakes of the frontier characteristics.* Thus the advance of the frontier has meant a steady movement away from the influence of Europe, a steady growth of independence on American lines. And to study this advance, the men who grew up under these conditions, and the political, economic and social results of it, is to study the really American part of our history. . . .

The Frontier Furnishes a Field for Comparative Study of Social Development

. . . The United States lies like a huge page in the history of society. Line by line as we read from west to east we find the record of social evolution. It begins with the Indian and the hunter; it goes on to tell of the disintegration of savagery by the entrance of the trader, the path-finder of civilization; we read the annals of the pastoral stage in ranch life; the exploitation of the soil by the raising of unrotated crops of corn and wheat in sparsely settled farming communities; the intensive culture of the denser farm settlement; and finally the manufacturing organization with city and factory system. This page is familiar to the student of census statistics, but how little of it has been used by our historians. Each of these areas has had an influence in our economic and political history; the evolution of each into a higher stage has worked political transformations.

Composite Nationality

First, we note that the frontier promoted the formation of a composite nationality for the American people. The coast was preponderantly English, but the later tides of continental immigration flowed across to the free lands. This was the case from the early colonial days. The Scotch-Irish and the Palatine Germans, or "Pennsylvania Dutch," furnished the stock of the colonial frontier. With these people were also the free indentured servants, or redemptioners, who at the expiration of their time of service passed to the frontier. Governor Spottswood of Virginia writes in 1717, "The inhabitants of our frontiers are composed generally of such as have been transported hither as servants, and, being out of their time, settle themselves where land is to be taken up and that will produce the necessarys of life with little labour." Very generally these redemptioners were of non-English stock. In the crucible of the frontier the immigrants were Americanized, liberated and fused into a mixed race, English in neither nationality or characteristics. The process has gone on from the early days to our own. . . .

National Tendencies of the Frontier

It is safe to say that the legislation with regard to land, tariff, and internal improvements—the American system of the nationalizing Whig party—was conditioned on frontier ideas and needs. But it was not merely in legislative action that the frontier worked against the sectionalism of the coast. The economic and social characteristics of the frontier worked against sectionalism. The men of the frontier had closer resemblances to the Middle region than to either of the other sections. Pennsylvania had been the seed-plot of frontier emigration, and, although she passed on her settlers along the Great Valley into the west of Virginia and the Carolinas, yet the industrial society of these Southern frontiersmen was always more like that of the Middle region than like that of the tide-water portion of the South, which later came to spread its industrial type throughout the South.

The Middle region, entered by New York harbor, was an open door to all Europe. The tide-water part of the South represented typical Englishmen, modified by a warm climate and servile labor, and living in baronial fashion on great plantations; New England stood for a special English movement— Puritanism. The Middle region was less English than the other sections. It had a wide mixture of nationalities, a varied society, the mixed town and county system of local government, a varied economic life, many religious sects. In short it was a region mediating between New England and the South, and the East and the West. It represented that composite nationality which the contemporary United States exhibits, that juxtaposition of non-English groups, occupying a valley or a little settlement, and presenting reflections of the map of Europe in their variety. It was democratic and non-sectional, if not national; "easy, tolerant and contented;" rooted strongly in material prosperity. It was typical of the modern United States. It was least sectional, not only because it lay between North and South, but also because with no barriers to shut out its frontiers from its settled region, and with a system of connecting waterways, the Middle region mediated between East and West as well as between North and South. Thus it became the typically American region. Even the New Englander, who was shut out from the frontier by the Middle region, tarrying in New York or Pennsylvania on his westward march, lost the acuteness of his sectionalism on the way. . . .

It was this nationalizing tendency of the West that transformed the democracy of Jefferson into the national republicanism of Monroe and the democracy of Andrew Jackson. The West of the War of 1812, the West of Clay, and Benton, and Harrison, and Andrew Jackson, shut off by the Middle states and the mountains from the coast sections, had a solidarity of its own with national tendencies. On the tide of the Father of Waters, North and South met and mingled into a nation. Interstate migration went steadily on—a process of cross-fertilization of ideas and institutions. . . .

Growth of Democracy

But the most important effect of the frontier has been in the promotion of democracy here and in Europe. As has been pointed out, the frontier is productive of individualism. Complex society is precipitated by the wilderness into a kind of primitive organization based on the family. The tendency is anti-social. It produces antipathy to control, and particularly to any direct control. The tax-gatherer is viewed as a representative of oppression. Professor [Herbert L.l Osgood, in an able article, has pointed out that the frontier conditions prevalent in the colonies are important factors in the explanation of the American revolution, where individual liberty was sometimes confused with absence of all effective government. The same conditions aid in explaining the difficulty of instituting a strong government in the period of the confederacy. The frontier individualism has from the beginning promoted democracy.

The frontier states that came into the Union in the first quarter of a century of its existence came in with democratic suffrage provisions, and had reactive effects of the highest importance upon the older states whose people were being attracted there. It was *western* New York that forced an extension of suffrage in the constitutional convention of that state in 1820, and it was *western* Virginia that compelled the tide-water region to put a more liberal suffrage provision in the constitution framed in 1830, and to give to the frontier region a more nearly proportionate representation with the tide-water aristocracy. The rise of democracy as an effective force in the nation came in with western preponderance under Jackson and William Henry Harrison, and it meant the triumph of the frontier—with all of its good and with all of its evil elements. An interesting illustration of the tone of frontier democracy in 1830 comes from the . . . debates in the Virginia convention.* . . . A representative from western Virginia declared: "But, sir, it is not the increase of population in the West which this gentleman ought to fear. It is the energy which the mountain breeze and western habits impart to those emigrants. They are regenerated, politically I mean, sir. They soon become *working politicians;* and the difference, sir, between a *talking* and a *working* politician is immense. The

*To revise the state constitution in 1829–1830.

Old Dominion has long been celebrated for producing great orators; the ablest metaphysicians in policy; men that can split hairs in all abstruse questions of political economy. But at home, or when they return from congress, they have negroes to fan them asleep. But a Pennsylvania, a New York, an Ohio, or a western Virginia statesman, though far inferior in logic, metaphysics and rhetoric to an old Virginia statesman, has this advantage, that when he returns home he takes off his coat and takes hold of the plough. This gives him bone and muscle, sir, and preserves his republican principles pure and uncontaminated."

So long as free land exists, the opportunity for a conpetency [sic] exists, and economic power secures political power. But the democracy born of free land, strong in selfishness and individualism, intolerant of administrative experience and education, and pressing individual liberty beyond its proper bounds, has its dangers as well as its benefits. Individualism in America has allowed a laxity in regard to governmental affairs which has rendered possible the spoils system, and all the manifest evils that follow from the lack of a highly developed civic spirit. In this connection may be noted also the influence of frontier conditions in permitting lax business honor, inflated paper currency and wild-cat banking. The colonial and revolutionary frontier was the region whence emanated many of the worst forms of an evil currency. The West in the War of 1812 repeated the phenomenon on the frontier of that day, while the speculation and wild-cat banking of the period of the crisis of 1837 occurred on the new frontier belt of the next tier of states. Thus each one of the periods of lax financial integrity coincides with periods when a new set of frontier communities had arisen, and coincides in area with these successive frontiers for the most part. The recent Populist agitation is a case in point. Many a state that now declines any connection with the tenets of the Populists, itself adhered to such ideas in an earlier stage of the development of the state. A primitive society can hardly be expected to show the intelligent appreciation of the complexity of business interests in a developed society. The continual recurrence of these areas of paper-money agitation is another evidence that the frontier can be isolated and studied as a factor in American history of the highest importance. . . .

Intellectual Traits

From the conditions of frontier life came intellectual traits of profound importance. The works of travellers along each frontier from colonial days onward describe for each certain traits, and these traits have, while softening down, still persisted as survivals in the place of their origin, even when a higher social organization succeeded. The result is that to the frontier the American intellect owes its striking characteristics. That coarseness and strength combined with acuteness and inquisitiveness, that practical, inventive turn of mind, quick to find expedients, that masterful grasp of material things, lacking in the artistic but powerful to effect great ends, that restless, nervous energy, that dominant individualism, working for good and for evil, and withal that buoyancy and exuberance which comes with freedom,—these are traits of the frontier, or traits called out elsewhere because of the existence of the frontier. Since the days when the fleet of Columbus sailed into the waters of the New World, America has been another name for opportunity, and the people of the United States have taken their tone from the incessant expansion which has not only been open but has even been forced upon them. He would be a rash prophet who should assert that the expansive character of American life has now entirely ceased. Movement has been its dominant fact, and, unless this training has no effect upon a people, the American intellect will continually demand a wider field for its exercise. But never again will such gifts of free land offer themselves. For a moment at the frontier the bonds of custom are broken, and unrestraint is triumphant. There is not *tabula rasa*. The stubborn American environment is there with its imperious summons to accept its conditions; the inherited ways of doing things are also there; and yet, in spite of environment, and in spite of custom, each frontier did indeed furnish a new field of opportunity, a gate of escape from the bondage of the past; and freshness, and confidence, and scorn of older society, impatience of its restraints and its ideas, and indifference to its lessons, have accompanied the frontier. What the Mediterranean Sea was to the Greeks, breaking the bond of custom, offering new experiences, calling out new institutions and activities, that, and more, the ever retreating frontier has been to the United States directly, and to the nations of Europe more remotely. And now, four centuries from the discovery of America, at the end of a hundred years of life under the Constitution, the frontier has gone, and with its going has closed the first period of American history.

PRIMARY SOURCES

The primary sources in this chapter relate to Americans' frontier experience in the first half of the nineteenth century. Settlers had moved from the Ohio of Jedediah Smith's youth early in the century to the Pacific coast by midcentury. These sources reflect the experiences of different groups in the West and therefore may reveal a variety of perspectives.

Fur Trappers in the Far West

In "The Significance of the Frontier in American History," Turner wrote that "the wilderness masters the colonist. It finds him a European in dress, industries, tools, modes of travel, and thought. . . . It strips off the garments of civilization, and arrays him in the hunting shirt and the moccasin." When Turner wrote those words, he may have had in mind scenes captured by Alfred Jacob Miller, an American artist who ventured into the Rocky Mountains and the Far West in 1837. From hundreds of sketches of trappers who, said Miller, "lead the van in the march of civilization," he later painted numerous watercolors.[3] But the West was also a fertile ground for business enterprise. By the first decades of the nineteenth century fur-trading companies had already established a pattern that would be followed by later railroad, mining, and timber companies. Control and direction of these enterprises lay with capitalists and managers outside the region. Is it more important that fur trappers dressed in "hunting shirt and . . . moccasin" or that they usually took orders from company officials in the East?

2 | Sketch of Trappers (1837)
ALFRED JACOB MILLER

Source: The Walters Art Gallery, Baltimore. acct. #37.1940.29.

3   N. J. Wyeth's Instructions for Robert Evans at the Fort Hall Trading Post (1834)

Fort Hall July 31st, 1834 as a gent. and Partner of the Columbia River Fishing and Trading Co I leave you the following instructions for your government during the time you may remain in charge of Fort Hall:

1st   You will remain untill you are relieved by another superintendent, or untill the expiration of your time of service with the Co unless you are obliged to evacuate by starvation or hostility of the Indians in either of which cases you will endeavor to cash what goods you are obliged to leave securely.

2nd   In trading you will adhere to the Tariff which is annexed and on no account deviate therefrom and you will give no credit to any one.

3rd   You will give no supplies to any of your men unless the Co are $20 in their debt by the acts which have been handed you, you will be able to ascertain when this is the case.

4th   You will have the animals left here guarded by one man in the day time and put into the Fort at night.

5th   You will keep one centry at night on duty untill your Fort is entirely finished and afterward and if any guard is found asleep you will note it in your Journal and for this and similar purposes you will keep a book in which you will enter all remarkable occurrences. . . .

Source: Clyde A. Milner II, *Major Problems in the History of the American West* (Lexington, Mass.: D. C. Heath and Co., 1989), p. 177.

4

George Caleb Bingham was a Missouri artist whose work often reflected political themes. A Whig representative in the Missouri General Assembly in the late 1840s, Bingham was no stranger to the political scenes he created in such paintings as *The Stump Orator.* As one St. Louis reporter enthused:

> It is not an attempt to caricature, but an effort to draw an unexaggerated representation of an assemblage which is familiar to every one in the west. The postures—the dress, as clean and neat as the humble means of western life will justify—the little knot of busy politicians around the finely dressed Demagogue, in the background—the idiotic expression of an unfortunate inebriate behind the speaker . . . give to the whole a merit, a richness and a beauty to which ordinary language cannot do justice.[4]

As you examine this painting, determine whether it reflects themes in Turner's frontier thesis.

Daguerreotype of *The Stump Orator* (1847)
GEORGE CALEB BINGHAM

Source: From the art collection of the Boatmen's National Bank of St. Louis.

The Indians' West

The pre-Civil War West was not an uninhabited land when settlers arrived. The following sources reveal information about white-Indian interaction. Keep in mind how a recognition of the Indian experience modifies Turner's thesis.

 Black Hawk was a Sauk Indian who in 1832 led an uprising of Sauk and Fox Indians in Illinois and Wisconsin. Facing famine, the Indians sought to reoccupy land they had previously abandoned. The Illinois militia, which included a young captain named Abraham Lincoln, was mobilized to remove the Indians. The result was the Black Hawk War. Later, the Sauk and Fox would be removed to Indian lands west of the Mississippi. Here Black Hawk discusses events leading to the war.

Autobiography (1833)
BLACK HAWK

During this summer, I happened at Rock Island, when a great chief arrived, (whom I had known as the great chief of Illinois, [governor Cole,] in company with another chief, who, I have been told, is a great writer, [judge Jas. Hall.] I called upon them and begged to explain to them the grievances under which me and my people were laboring, hoping that they could do something for us. The great chief, however, did not seem disposed to council with me. He said he was no longer the great chief of Illinois—that his children had selected another father in his stead, and that he now only ranked as they did. I was surprised at this talk, as I had always heard that he was a good, brave, and great chief. But the white people never appear to be satisfied. When they get a good father, they hold councils, (at the suggestion of some bad, ambitious man, who wants the place himself,) and conclude, among themselves, that this man, or some other equally ambitious, would make a better father than they have, and nine times out of ten they don't get as good a one again.

I insisted on explaining to these two chiefs the true situation of my people. They gave their assent: I rose and made a speech, in which I explained to them the treaty made by Quàsh-quà-me, and three of our braves, according to the manner the trader and others had explained it to me. I then told them that Quàsh-quà-me and his party *denied*, positively, having ever sold my village; and that, as I had never known them to *lie*, I was determined to keep it in possession.

I told them that the white people had already entered our village, *burnt our lodges, destroyed our fences, ploughed up our corn, and beat our people:* that they had brought *whisky* into our country, *made our people drunk,* and taken from them their *horses, guns,* and *traps;* and that I had borne all this injury, without suffering any of my braves to raise a hand against the whites.

My object in holding this council, was to get the opinion of these two chiefs, as to the best course for me to pursue. I had appealed in vain, time after time, to our agent, who regularly represented our situation to the great chief at St.

Source: Donald Jackson, ed., *Black Hawk: An Autobiography* (Urbana: University of Illinois Press, 1964), pp. 102–104.

Louis, whose duty it was to call upon our Great Father to have justice done to us; but instead of this, we are told *that the white people want our country, and we must leave it to them!*

I did not think it possible that our Great Father wished us to leave our village, where we had lived so long, and where the bones of so many of our people had been laid. The great chief said that, as he was no longer a chief, he could do nothing for us; and felt sorry that it was not in his power to aid us—nor did he know how to advise us. Neither of them could do any thing for us; but both evidently appeared very sorry. It would give me great pleasure, at all times, to take these two chiefs by the hand.

That fall I paid a visit to the agent, before we started to our hunting grounds, to hear if he had any good news for me. He had news! He said that the land on which our village stood was now ordered to be sold to individuals; and that, when sold, *our right* to remain, by treaty, would be at an end, and that if we returned next spring, we would be *forced* to remove!

We learned during the winter, that *part* of the lands where our village stood had been sold to individuals, and that the *trader* at Rock Island had bought the greater part that had been sold. The reason was now plain to me, why *he* urged us to remove. His object, we thought, was to get our lands. We held several councils that winter to determine what we should do, and resolved, in one of them, to return to our village in the spring, as usual; and concluded, that if we were removed by force, that the *trader,* agent, and others, must be the cause; and that, if found guilty of having us driven from our village, they should be *killed!* The trader stood foremost on this list. He had purchased the land on which my lodge stood, and that of our *grave yard* also! Ne-a-pope promised to kill him, the agent, interpreter, the great chief at St. Louis, the war chief at fort Armstrong, Rock Island, and Ke-o-kuck—these being the principal persons to blame for endeavoring to remove us.

---

6   This print was based on a painting that had been copied from a portrait by a member of Major Stephen H. Long's expedition through Minnesota in 1823. When Long first met Waneta, he wore a very different style of dress. "The chief's dress," noted Long, "presented a mixture of European and aboriginal costume: He wore moccasins and leggings of splendid scarlet cloth, a blue breech cloth, a fine shirt of printed muslin, over this a frock coat made of fine blue cloth with scarlet facings, somewhat similar to the underdress uniform coat of a Prussian officer."[5]

Waneta, a Yanktonai (ca. 1823)

Source: From David Penney, *Art of the American Indian Frontier.* Courtesy Harvard College Library.

Reports from the West

Immigrants and travelers in the West often left revealing evidence about conditions there. As you read and examine these sources, note how the observations they make and the experiences they relate support or modify Turner's thesis.

Barlien was a Norwegian immigrant who wrote this letter home.

On Settling in Missouri (1839)
HANS BARLIEN

All kinds of people from all nations of the world live together here like brothers and sisters; and in spite of the fact that there are no garrisons of soldiers, police, and the like, you never hear anything about theft, begging, or any noticeable ill will between neighbors. To me everybody is good, kind, and accommodating. Nobody here can take anything away from you by force; but he can do this by cunning, power of money, and forestallment. This I hope to prevent on our claims by the help of Congress and so, in time, to succeed in uniting the Norwegians who are still here.

Source: Letter of April 23, 1839, from Theodore C. Blegen, *Land of Their Choice: The Immigrants Write Home* (Minneapolis: University of Minnesota Press, 1955), p. 53.

This description was from Baird's guidebook for immigrants and travelers to the West.

View of the Valley of the Mississippi (1832)
ROBERT BAIRD

The peculiarities . . . of character, which may be said to distinguish the population of the West, are all created by the peculiar circumstances in which the people have been placed in that new world. They are,

1. *A spirit of adventurous enterprise:* a willingness to go through any hardship or danger to accomplish an object. It was the spirit of enterprise which led to

Source: Robert Baird, *View of the Valley of the Mississippi: or the Emigrant's and Traveller's Guide to the West* (1832).

the settlement of that country. The western people think nothing of making a long journey, of encountering fatigue, and of enduring every species of hardship. The great highways of the west—its long rivers—are familiar to very many of them, who have been led by trade to visit remote parts of the valley.

2. *Independence of thought and action.*—They have felt the influence of this principle from their childhood. Men who can endure any thing: that have lived almost without restraint, free as the mountain air, or as the deer and the buffalo of their forests—and who know that they are Americans all—will act out this principle during the whole of life. I do not mean that they have such an amount of it as to render them *really* regardless alike of the opinions and the feelings of everyone else. But I have seen many who have the virtue of independence greatly perverted or degenerated . . .

3. *An apparent roughness,* which some would deem *rudeness of manners.*

9 | Coronel came to California in 1834 and settled in Los Angeles. When gold was discovered in the Sierra foothills, *Californios* (Californians of Spanish descent) headed to the gold fields from as far away as San Diego. Coronel was among them. By 1849, when many other people had arrived in the mining camps, racial and ethnic conflict had flared up. Note Coronel's explanation for the hostility toward the Spanish.

Life in the Gold Fields (1849)
ANTONIO FRANCO CORONEL

. . . I arrived at the Placer Seco [about March, 1849] and began to work at a regular digging.

In this place there was already a numerous population of Chileans, Peruvians, Californians, Mexicans, and many Americans, Germans, etc. The camps were almost separated according to nationalities. All, some more, some less, were profiting from the fruit of their work. Presently news was circulated that it had been resolved to evict all of those who were not American citizens from the placers because it was believed that the foreigners did not have the right to exploit the placers.

One Sunday, [notices] appeared in writing in Los Pinos and in several places, that anyone who was not an American citizen must abandon the place within twenty-four hours and that he who did not comply would be obliged

Source: From Antonio Franco Coronel, "Casas de California," Ms., 1877 (BANC MSS C-D 61), the Bancroft Library, University of California, Berkeley. Reprinted by permission of the Brancroft Library.

to by force. This was supported by a gathering of armed men, ready to make that warning effective.

There was a considerable number of people of various nationalities who understood the order to leave—they decided to gather on a hill in order to be on the defensive in case of any attack. On the day in which the departure of the foreigners should take place, and for three or four more days, both forces remained prepared, but the thing did not go beyond cries, shots, and drunken men. Finally all fell calm and we returned to continue our work. Daily, though, the weakest were dislodged from their diggings by the strongest.

After this agitation had calmed down, a Frenchman named Don Augusto and a Spaniard named Luis were seized—persons with whom I had dealt and who appeared to me to be honorable and of fairly good upbringing. All who had known them had formed the same opinion as I, and this seizure caused great surprise. Some of the most prominent people met together and commissioned me to investigate the reason for these arrests. I went to an American I had known in Los Angeles, one Richard, who had been a cavalry sergeant—I asked him to look into it for me. He answered immediately that they had been accused by an Irish fellow (an old man) of having stolen from him four pounds of gold from the place where he had buried it. I gave an account of my constituents and then, without loss of time, five pounds of gold was gathered from among all of us to see if payment would set these prisoners free. I approached the leader, whose appearance was disagreeable and ferocious. Wanting to vindicate the two men, I presented my plan to him through an interpreter. I told him we knew them as good men who had sufficient resources of their own and no need to appropriate those of another. Nevertheless, I had here five pounds of gold, one more than the old Irishman said they had stolen from him. He took the five pounds of gold and told me that he would go to report to his group—that I should return in the afternoon, some two or three hours later. Before the hour he had indicated to me, we saw the movement of armed men, the major part under the influence of liquor. Afterward we saw a cart leave with our two unfortunates, their arms tied behind their backs. Two men guarded them from on top of the cart, which was followed by a large crowd, some on foot and others on horseback. On the cart there was an inscription, poorly written in charcoal or something similar, which said that whoever might intercede for them would suffer the same punishment. They reached an oak tree where the execution was to take place. When the ropes had been hung around their necks, they asked to write something to their families and to arrange their affairs. For having made this request, one of the men received a slap in the face. Then, suddenly, they moved the cart and the unlucky men were hanged.

This act horrified me and it had the same effect upon many others—in two days I raised camp and headed toward the northern placers.

The reason for most of the antipathy against the Spanish race was that the greater portion was composed of Sonorans who were men accustomed to prospecting and who consequently achieved quicker, richer results—such as the *Californios* had already attained by having arrived first and acquiring understanding of this same art. Those who came later [mainly Anglo Americans], were possessed by the terrible fever to obtain gold, but they did not get it because their diggings yielded but little or nothing, or because their work did not correspond to what they took out. Well, these men aspired to become rich in a minute and they could not resign themselves to view with patience the better fortune of others. Add to this fever that which the excessive use of liquor gives them. Add that generally among so many people of all nationalities there are a great number of lost people, capable of all conceivable crimes. The circumstance that there were no laws nor authorities who could protect the rights and lives of men gave to these men advantages over peaceful and honorable men. Properly speaking, there was no more law in those times than that of force, and finally, the good person, in his own defense, had to establish the law of retaliation.

10	There were more than 20,000 Chinese in the United States before the Civil War. This phrase book helped many of these *Gam Saan Haak* ("travelers to gold mountain") learn English. Published in 1875, it

clearly reflected the long experience of the Chinese in mining camps and elsewhere in the West. What do these phrases reveal about the experiences and hopes of the Chinese?

An English-Chinese Phrase Book (1875)

He took it from me by violence.
The men are striking for wages.
He claimed my mine.
When will the lease expire?
He cheated me out of my wages.
He was choked to death with a lasso, by a robber.
Can I sleep here tonight?
Have you any food for me?

Source: Ronald Takaki, *Strangers from a Different Shore: A History of Asian-Americans* (New York: Penguin Books, 1989), p. 128; originally from Wong Sam and Assistants, *An English-Chinese Phrase Book* (San Francisco, 1875), pp. 13, 14, 16, 18, 20, 22, 52, 56, 106, 108, 113, 122, 128, 155, 219, 232.

She is a good-for-nothing huzzy [sic].
The passage money is $50 from Hong Kong to California.
The steamer will leave to-morrow.
How long have you been in California?
She is my wife.
An unmarried man is called a bachelor.
I received a letter from China.
The United States have many immigrants.
The immigration will soon be stopped.

Women and the Frontier

Of course, women were very much a part of the frontier. As you examine the following sources, consider whether the frontier experience of women differed from that of male settlers and if it offered new opportunities for women or simply strengthened familiar roles.

11 | A Camp Meeting (n.d.)

Source: Library of Congress.

12 In 1856, Colt, her husband, and their two children moved to Kansas to join an experimental vegetarian colony. Her diary details some of the trials that they experienced there.

We Went to Kansas (1862)

MIRIAM DAVIS COLT

May 12th. Full of hope, as we leave the smoking embers of our camp-fire this morning. Expect tonight to arrive at our new home.

It begins to rain, rain, rain, like a shower; we move slowly on, from high prairie, around the deep ravine—are in sight of the timber that skirts the Neosho river. Have sent three men in advance to announce our coming; are looking for our Secretary, (Henry S. Clubb) with an escort to welcome us into the embryo city. If the booming of cannon is not heard at our approach, shall expect a salute from the firing of Sharp's rifles, certainly.

No escort is seen! no salute is heard! We move slowly and drippingly into town just at nightfall—feeling not a little nonplused on learning that our worthy, or unworthy Secretary was out walking in the rain with his dear wife. We leave our wagons and make our way to the large camp-fire. It is surrounded by men and women cooking their suppers—while others are busy close by, grinding their hominy in hand mills.

Look around, and see the grounds all around the camp-fire are covered with tents, in which the families are staying. Not a house is to be seen. In the large tent here is a cook stove—they have supper prepared for us; it consists of hominy, soft Johnny cake (or corn bread, as it is called here), stewed apple, and tea. We eat what is set before us, "asking no questions for conscience' sake."

The ladies tell us they are sorry to see us come to this place; which shows us that all is not right. Are too weary to question, but with hope depressed go to our lodgings, which we find around in the tents, and in our wagons. . . .

May 14th. Some improvements are being made in the "centre octagon" to-day. [*The octagon plan designated sixteen farms around a communal eight-sided building.*] My husband has put up some shelves on one side, by boring holes into the logs, putting in long and strong wooden pins, and laying on some of the "shakes" for shelves.

May 15th. A cold, drizzling rain. The prairie winds come whizzing in. Have hung up an Indian blanket at the door, but by putting trunks and even stones

Source: We Went to Kansas (1862), published by L. Ingalls and Co., reprinted by Readex Microprint Corporation (1966).

on to the end that drags, can hardly make it answer the purpose of a door. It is dark, gloomy, cheerless, uncomfortable and cold inside.

Have a fire out of doors to cook by; two crotches driven into the ground, with a round pole laid thereon, on which to hang our kettles and camp pails, stones laid up at the ends and back to make it as much as it can be in the form of a fireplace, so as to keep our fire, ashes and all, from blowing high and dry, when these fierce prairie winds blow. It is not very agreeable work, cooking out of doors in this windy, rainy weather, or when the scorching sun shines.

The bottoms of our dresses are burnt full of holes now, and they will soon be burnt off. If we stay here we must needs don the Bloomer costume. Our bill of fare is limited—hominy, Johnny cake, Graham pudding, some white bread, now and then stewed apple, a little rice, and tea occasionally for the old people. . . .

Father has got a broom stick, and is peeling a broom. He says, "I intend you shall keep this stone floor swept up clean."

May 22d. Members of the company . . . can claim and hold, by the preemption right, 240 acres of land—160 timber, and 80 prairie. My husband, his father, and sister L. are each claimants; they have accordingly located their claims side by side, making 720 acres of land belonging to our family. It is two miles east from the "centre octagon," and joining the Osage Indian lands. My husband says, the timber on our claim is fine; there are different kinds of walnut and oak . . . and that for several rods on the river is the prettiest bed of pebbles he ever saw, nice for walks. We intend, some time, to have walks made of them.

May 26th. Have been washing to-day, and dried our clothes right out in the burning hot sun. We dare not leave them out in the dewey nights, for fear of the Indians, who come thieving round—slying about—taking everything they can lay their hands on. . . . They are soon going two or three hundred miles west on their buffalo hunt, where they go twice a year, staying three months at a time. . . .

These [Osage] Indians are said to be friendly, but I cannot look at their painted visages without a shudder; and when they come around our cabin, I sit down and take Willie on my lap, and have Mema stand by my side, with my arm around her, for fear they may steal my children from me. They point to my boy and make signs that he is pretty. "Chintu-chinka," they call boy, and "che-me chinka," girl. . . .

May 28th. Took my children into our white-topped wagon, and went with my husband two miles, to his claim, to plant corn. A bright and lovely day came in with the rising sun, not a cloud in the heavens above. . . . Not a stump, fence, stone or log, to mar the beautiful picture. . . . We sat in the wagon, while my hopeful husband planted corn and garden seeds. After the ploughing, the planting is done by just cutting through the sod with an axe, and dropping in the seeds—no hoeing the first year; nothing more is to be done until the full yellow ears are gathered in the autumn time. . . .

After we had eaten our dinner in the wagon, we went and selected a site for our log cabin, a little way from the clear, stony-bottomed creek that flows through our claim. . . . My husband says we shall have an elegant building spot, and that he will build a neat little log cabin; that he will get the large flat stones from the creek that will cleave apart, for walks to the creek and around our cabin. . . . I do not like to hear the voice which whispers, "This never will be;" but still it will whisper.

Mormon Settlement in Salt Lake City (1847–1848)

It is impossible to discuss the settlement of the West without acknowledging the role played by the Latter-day Saints, or Mormons. When they entered the Salt Lake Valley in 1847, the Mormons immediately began laying plans for a city that reflected collective community action and a desire to live in an orderly society. It was a pattern of settlement that they would duplicate over a large portion of the West. As you examine these sources, ask yourself if the Mormons' approach to settlement conforms to Turner's thesis.

13 | Early View of Salt Lake City (1872)

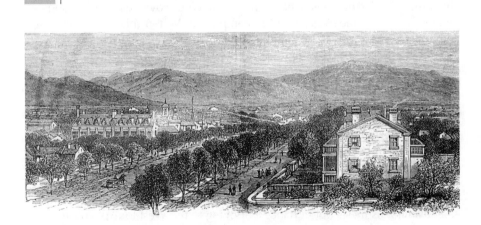

Source: Boston Athenaeum. From *Harper's Weekly,* January 27, 1872.

14 Brigham Young on Land Distribution (1848)

It is our intention to have the five acre lots next to the city accommodate the mechanics and artisans, the ten acres next, then the twenty acres, followed by the forty and eighty acre lots, where farmers can build and reside. All these lots will be enclosed in one common fence, which will be seventeen miles and fifty-three rods long, eight feet high; and to the end that every man may be satisfied with his lot and prevent any hardness that might occur by any method of dividing the land, we have proposed that it shall all be done by ballot, or casting lots, as Israel did in days of old.

Source: Leonard J. Arrington, *Great Basin Kingdom: An Economic History of the Latter-day Saints* (Lincoln: University of Nebraska Press, 1966), p. 52.

CONCLUSION

Turner's thesis was, if anything, grand. According to it, the frontier fostered such traits as independence, individuality, and self-reliance. At the same time, it also shaped the democratic character of the nation's political institutions. Indeed, Turner's essay was nothing less than an exploration of the unity of the American experience. Any historical argument that attributes so many effects to one grand cause is bound to attract critics.

In our time, many historians turn to the past with fewer nationalistic assumptions than Turner demonstrated, and they have uncovered a darker and less unified history of the West. Such contemporary Western historians as Patricia Limrick, Gerald Nash, and Donald Worster argue that the conquest of the West was often accompanied by oppression, exploitation, and environmental destruction. These "new Western historians" include in the story of Western settlement people who never appeared on Turner's frontier: women, blacks, Hispanics, Asians, and Indians. Doing so, they argue, reveals some of the flaws in Turner's conception of the frontier. It was not empty space into which Americans moved. Nor did settlers always enter it, as Turner's had, from somewhere back East. And they did not necessarily cast off their cultural baggage and develop new institutions and customs.

Thanks to the work of these historians, today the Western past looks much different than it did to Turner. Nonetheless, students of history make a mistake if they dismiss his thesis out of hand. In looking to the West to explain American development, Turner inspired generations of historians to reinterpret the frontier experience. He thus forced Americans to reconsider their past, just as Charles

Beard had done two decades later. After Beard, historians could not look at the Founding Fathers without thinking about economic interests. After Turner, they could not dismiss the West and pretend to understand American history. Nor could they define history merely as the actions of political elites, because Turner had found significance in the lives of millions of ordinary people. Beard himself declared that Turner's essay "was destined to have a more profound influence on thought about American history than any other essay or volume ever written on the subject."[6] Students of American history are thus indebted to Turner. Although his was not the last word on the West, what he had to say remains the starting point for understanding the significance of the frontier in American history.

FURTHER READING

Patricia Nelson Limerick, The Legacy of Conquest: The Unbroken Legacy of the American West (New York: W. W. Norton, 1987).

Cathy Luchetti and Carol Olwell, *Women of the West* (St. George, Utah: Antelope Island Press, 1982).

Gerald D. Nash, *Creating the West: Historical Interpretations 1890–1990* (Albuquerque: University of New Mexico Press, 1991).

Malcolm Rohrbough, *The Trans-Appalachian Frontier: Peoples, Societies, Institutions, 1775–1850* (New York: Oxford University Press, 1978).

Donald Worster, *Under Western Skies: Nature and History in the American West* (New York: Oxford University Press, 1992).

NOTES

1. Quoted in Richard Hofstadter, *The Progressive Historians* (New York: Alfred A. Knopf, 1968), p. 230.
2. Herbert Hoover, "American Individualism," *World's Work,* 43 (April 1922), 585.
3. Quoted in Alfred Jacob Miller, *The West of Alfred Jacob Miller* (Norman: University of Oklahoma Press, 1968), opposite plate 29.
4. Quoted in Nancy Rash, *The Painting and Politics of George Caleb Bingham* (New Haven: Yale University Press, 1991), p. 97.
5. Quoted in David W. Penney, *Art of the American Indian Frontier* (Seattle: University of Washington Press, 1992), p. 46.
6. Quoted in Hofstadter, *The Progressive Historians,* pp. 47–48.

CHAPTER | 9

HISTORY AS BIOGRAPHY:

HISTORIANS AND OLD HICKORY

This chapter's documents give a portrait of Andrew Jackson. The secondary source discusses the origins of his personality, and the primary sources offer more perspectives on the man and the times.

Secondary Source

1. Andrew Jackson and the Search for Vindication (1976), JAMES C. CURTIS

Primary Sources

2. Jackson on His Experiences During the Revolution (n.d.)
3. Andrew Jackson to Charles Henry Dickinson (1806)
4. Andrew Jackson to Rachel Jackson (1813)
5. List of Taxable Property (ca. 1792–1797)
6. Andrew Jackson to Rachel Jackson (1811)
7. The New Hermitage (1856)
8. Andrew Jackson to William Blount (1812)
9. Andrew Jackson to James Monroe (1817)
10. Andrew Jackson's Second Annual Message to Congress (1830)
11. Andrew Jackson (1828), ORRAMEL HINCKLEY THROOP
12. Address of the Republican General Committee of Young Men of the City and County of New York (1828)
13. Andrew Jackson's Nullification Proclamation (1832)

When Andrew Jackson was inaugurated, a huge crowd filled the streets and avenues leading to the Capitol. Restrained only by a ship's cable, it surged two-thirds of the way up the steps leading to the portico. Senator Daniel Webster declared that even he had never seen such a crowd. When General Jackson appeared between the portico's columns, the throng roared. "Never can I forget the spectacle," noted another observer, "nor the electrifying moment when the eager, expectant eyes of that vast and motley multitude caught sight . . . of their adored leader."[1] When Jackson stood and looked out over the crowd, the roar grew louder still.

The din continued during the ten-minute inaugural speech. When he finished, President Jackson pushed through the mob to a carriage waiting to take him to the White House. There another crowd nearly crushed him as he tried to shake well-wishers' hands. By the time Old Hickory fled to a nearby hotel, the guests were into the refreshments. They grabbed food and drink from the waiters, stomped in mud-covered boots on satin-covered chairs, broke China and glassware, and spilled pails of liquor on the carpet. "The mob . . . poured in in one uninterrupted stream of mud and filth," said one congressman. "What a scene did we witness!" said another guest, who was horrified by "a rabble, a mob, of boys, negros, [sic] women, children, scrambling, fighting, romping."[2]

Andrew Jackson's raucous inauguration in 1829 marked the beginning of the "age of Jackson," an era dominated by the policies and presence of Old Hickory. It is evidence of a powerful bond between Jackson and many of his countrymen. In this chapter we meet the man who stood above the inaugural crowd just as he towered above his peers in power and influence. We consider what his life reveals about the nameless people in the crowd below. And well we should. The man we encounter here decisively defeated the British at New Orleans in a battle that transformed a disastrous war into a magnificent triumph in most Americans' minds. He helped destroy the Creek and Seminole nations and later, as president, forced the Cherokees onto their tragic "Trail of Tears." Singlehandedly, he destroyed the Second Bank of the United States and faced down the South Carolina nullifiers. He also helped turn party politics into a game of spoils for the winners. Indeed, there are few better subjects for considering the individual's role in history than this man who gave his name to his age.

SETTING

Frontier dueler, hero of the Battle of New Orleans, Indian fighter, veteran of several vitriolic political campaigns, and enemy of "special privilege," Andrew

Jackson was no stranger to conflict or controversy. The scholars who have attempted to explain what his rise reveals about American society are equally combative. In the early twentieth century, historians argued that Jackson's triumph grew naturally from the democratization of American society. Frederick Jackson Turner was one of the first historians to associate Jackson with democratic trends in the early nineteenth century. To Turner, Jackson's election to the presidency represented the triumph of the West over a more conservative and less democratic East. A generation later, some historians countered that Jackson's career reflected instead a deep clash between economic groups. Arthur Schlesinger, Jr., for instance, said Jackson led a movement "to control the power of the capitalistic groups, mainly Eastern, for the benefit of noncapitalist groups, farmers and laboring men, East, West, and South."[3] In the 1950s, historian Richard Hofstadter argued that Jackson's victory actually represented the triumph of capitalism. Jackson's antimonopoly rhetoric, he said, was "closely linked to the ambitions of the small capitalist" in the expanding commercial market economy of the early nineteenth century.[4]

About the same time, historian Marvin Meyers challenged Hofstadter's view, maintaining that Jackson's age was characterized by a desire to *escape* an increasingly competitive and individualistic society. Jackson and his supporters, he said, longed for "a chaste republican order," where "the seductions of risk and novelty, greed and extravagance, rapid motion and complex dealings" could be resisted.[5] Still later, other researchers challenged the view that Old Hickory and his Democratic Party were the champions of democratic reforms. They questioned, for instance, how much support Jackson had among the working class. More recently, Michael Rogin and other historians who have examined Jackson's treatment of the Indians also dispute the democratic character of his policies.

Often lost in discussions about the age of Jackson are Old Hickory himself and the role he played in shaping his age. Partly, that is because modern historians reject the "great man" view of the past. In the nineteenth century, many historians looked to the past for heroic deeds and inspiration. They assumed that a few extraordinary individuals molded their times. Writer Thomas Carlyle said that "the History of the world is but the Biography of great men."[6] Although historians today continue to write biographies, it is not often with this "great man" view. Today, they study individual lives in search of understanding, not heroes. They do not believe that people stand outside their societies and impose their greatness on history. Historians now acknowledge the extent to which individuals are influenced by their times and circumstances. Still, when we consider Andrew Jackson, we must also wonder about one person's exceptional ability to influence events.

INVESTIGATION

Today, sober students of history who have the benefit of hindsight can see Andrew Jackson more clearly than did the drunken Inaugural Day revelers. You are thus in a better position to assess his influence and to answer the central question of this chapter: How did Andrew Jackson's background and personality influence the course of the nation? To answer this main question, however, you must also address several others:

1. **What were Jackson's most important personality traits?** What evidence does the essay by historian James Curtis (Source 1) present to establish Jackson's personality? Is it convincing? Is it supported by the primary sources?

2. **How did Jackson's personality shape his views about such issues as Indian removal and corruption in government, according to the essay?** Does the essay convincingly demonstrate this influence? Do the primary sources offer evidence that Jackson's positions were influenced by his personality?

3. **What important developments in American society made Jackson so appealing to many Americans?** What did his background and personality have to do with his widespread appeal, according to the essay? What clues do the primary sources offer about the reasons for Jackson's appeal?

Reading the section in your textbook on Andrew Jackson and his administration will provide you with useful background before you begin. Note whether your textbook has an argument about the relationship between Jackson's personality or background and his stands on issues.

SECONDARY SOURCE

1 ▎ James Curtis's biography of Jackson focuses on the influence of Old Hickory's personality on important decisions that affected the nation's past. It also explores why many Americans found him such an appealing figure. As you read this excerpt, keep in mind that biographers often know more about their subjects' adult lives than their early years. Sometimes, therefore, they are tempted to read the record backward by assuming that behavior can be projected back to a subject's childhood. In addition, they are often forced to speculate about the impact of childhood experiences on their subjects' unconscious motives. Pay particular attention to the evidence for Jackson's personality and how it influenced his stands on such issues as government corruption and Indian removal. Is the evidence convincing?

Andrew Jackson and the Search for Vindication (1976)
JAMES C. CURTIS

His soldiers called him Old Hickory, thus commending him to the ages. In the rhetoric of presidential politics, few titles are so vivid, so suggestive of vigor and action. Strength, toughness, physical courage, perseverance—these are qualities we associate with Andrew Jackson and have come to expect in both his martial and presidential successors. Indeed, Jackson ranks among the greatest of American generals and as the first modern chief executive. Always his image is one of action, decisiveness, and determination.

Andrew Jackson was more than a symbol; he was a vital force. As the force was rarely at rest, so the man was rarely at peace. Beneath the aggressiveness, the boldness, the quick temper, lay deep uncertainties rooted in his precarious back country upbringing and in events that left him an orphan at the age of fourteen. Throughout life he felt a need to prove himself, to triumph over enemies he believed were assaulting his reputation. Even in victory, he never felt victorious. The more his reputation grew, the more he feared that some conspiracy, some cabal was working to diminish his standing with the people.

Confronted by death at an early age, Andrew Jackson spent his life trying to prove his right to survival. This quest profoundly influenced his own destiny and that of the nation. Jackson's personal correspondence reveals an intense inner turmoil. . . . To overlook these feelings is to miss the essence of the man and the basis for his popular appeal. . . .

All accounts of Andrew Jackson's youth mention his wildness, yet few explain the cause, except to attribute it to the Scotch-Irish temperament and penchant for violent outdoor activity. High spirits were normal, especially in such an undisciplined environment, but the boy's behavior reached extremes. He entered everything with almost reckless abandon. He was the "most mischievous of youngsters thereabouts," recalled an old slave woman on the Crawford plantation. Perhaps he had to be, simply to gain attention in a large family in which he was the youngest. Notoriety he received, but little discipline. Doubtless his mother tried to control the excessive behavior, but her own circumstances made guidance difficult.* Scotch-Irish society assigned females household chores and field work, reserving to males the important decisions affecting the economic destiny of their offspring. Even after her sister died, Elizabeth was not formal mistress of her own house.

*Jackson's mother was widowed before Andrew was born. She went to live with her sister, Jane Crawford.

Andrew no doubt recognized his mother's subservient role and found it unworthy of imitation.

Nor could Mr. Humphries, the local schoolmaster, transform the young hellion. He taught Andrew to read and write, but little more. Throughout a long, famous career, Jackson misused the English language: his grammar was uncertain, his sentences incomplete, and his spelling atrocious. Considering his lack of formal education and the incoherent prose of some of his contemporaries, he did not fare too badly. He expressed himself directly, at times too directly. He mangled words but seldom minced them. As president he had the good sense to submit most of his public writing to the criticism of friends, who improved the style but seldom altered the content. The Carolina back country did not provide leisure or incentive for a contemplative life, and Jackson never developed a love of books or of abstract ideas. He had a practical mind and when young seemed totally preoccupied with finding his place among his peers. . . .

Although fond of mimicry and crude levity, Andrew was not a particularly happy youngster. He was often cantankerous and extremely defensive. In part this sensitivity had physical origins. He was never robust and early in life suffered a serious skin disease known as the "big itch," which no doubt added to his irascibility. Until he reached adulthood, he tended to slobber, a very embarrassing impediment about which he would tolerate no comment. He was extremely sensitive to criticism in general and would try to punish anyone who ridiculed him, no matter how slight the offense. He had an ugly temper, was full of anger that he could not control, and lost no opportunity to vent his aggressions. He thrived on conflict, yet even when victorious never allowed himself to feel triumphant. He continually needed to prove himself. In short, he was a violent and unpredictable youngster—a most difficult but lively companion.

Time might have smoothed the rough edges, but just as he reached adolescence, Andrew was plunged into the horror and confusion of war. . . .

In the spring of 1781, acting on information supplied by a Waxhaw loyalist, British troops captured a number of young militiamen, including Andrew and his brother Robert. Now a helpless witness to the looting and pillage, Andrew was further humiliated when a British officer demanded that he play the role of servant. When Andrew refused to clean the officer's boots, he narrowly missed being decapitated. The sword blow left a deep scar, as did the other events of his captivity.

Andrew had no idea how long he would be imprisoned or what his ultimate fate might be. Confined to a second-floor room of the district jail at Camden, South Carolina, he received no medical attention and little food. Smallpox broke out shortly after he arrived, threatening to devastate the prisoners. He escaped after a few weeks, thanks to the boldness of his mother who successfully pleaded with British commanders to release her sons in exchange for

English soldiers. By the time he left Camden, Andrew was seriously ill with a raging fever. He walked behind his brother Robert, who was so sick from the smallpox that he had to be tied on a horse. Within two days of their liberation Robert was dead. Andrew took little notice as he was delirious with fever. His mother nursed him as best she could, but she had many obligations. Two of Andrew's cousins lay sick on a British prison ship off Charleston. Having cared for so many strangers, she could not refuse the appeal of relatives. She left her feverish son in bed and set off for Charleston. She never returned. Fever took her life as it took so many during the war. The once proud soldier boy was now an orphan.

The tragedy left deep scars on Andrew Jackson's personality. The loss of his brother Hugh had first caused him to confront the possibility of death at an early age. His mother and remaining brother had calmed the fears. Now they too were suddenly gone, leaving him no protection against the awful finality of death. Fever shielded him for a time, but it could not stay the inevitable agony of introspection. No record of his exact thoughts exists, but his subsequent behavior suggests that he was consumed with anger and guilt. Perhaps he felt responsible for his mother's death, thinking that she had contracted his sickness. He had every reason to resent her decision to comfort two cousins while a son lay suffering. If so, her death must have made him feel doubly guilty for having harbored such thoughts. Certainly he wondered why he had been spared while his whole family had perished. Worse still, he had no way to resolve these feelings. Fate denied his mother a public funeral, thus preventing the comfort of ceremonial mourning. Her body never returned to the Waxhaws but lay in an unmarked grave in Charleston. . . .

For the rest of his life, Andrew Jackson tried to resolve the awful anxieties of this adolescent trauma. Like many other survivors he made martyrs of the dead. "She was as gentle as a dove and as brave as a lioness," he said of his mother three decades later. By idealizing his childhood and honoring his mother's errand of mercy, Jackson attempted to profit from his sorrow. "The memory of my mother and her teachings were after all the only capital I had to start my life with." He convinced himself that he had been spared to create the kind of life that she had always cherished: a life of honor, a life of courage, a life of order. In such a full life there would be no room for fear of death. . . .

. . . Alone and angry, Andrew Jackson could not express his anger directly for in doing so he would undermine the image of his mother as martyr, an image vital to his own peace of mind. "If ever you have to vindicate your feelings or defend your honor, do it calmly," she had counseled shortly before leaving for Charleston. "If angry at first, wait till your anger cools before you proceed." Jackson rarely let his wrath cool, but he justified it to himself by projecting his own unacceptable emotions outward onto someone, something. There were always suitable scapegoats: the Indians, the British, the Bank. Believing himself under attack, Jackson felt exonerated for striking back. The battle joined, he could then renew his mission, triumph over the terrible fears that haunted him, and thereby reassert his right to survive.

Contradictions always bothered Andrew Jackson, who prized order as much as he valued control. He found the government's Indian policy devoid of both. He objected primarily to the historic practice of treating Indian tribes as foreign nations. Calling the arrangement an "absurdity," Jackson argued that "Indians are subjects of the United States" and urged that they be brought under congressional control. Although paying lip service to the idea of civilization, the intent of Jackson's policy was to destroy tribal structure, replacing it with the "fostering care" of the central government, which would then "prescribe their bounds at will." Without such control, the "real Indians, the natives of the forest" would fall prey to the "designing half breeds and renegade white men who have taken refuge in their country." "For it is too true," he believed, "that avarice and fear are the predominant passions that govern an Indian."

Similar feelings guided Jackson's policies as a treaty negotiator. He urged the government to bring ceded Indian lands "into the market" and have them "populated." Only white settlement could bring adequate defense to an area that "for thirty years" had been the "den of murderers." In 1816, Jackson succeeded in having his former cavalry commander, John Coffee, appointed to survey conquered Creek lands and settle the conflicting claims that arose following the war. Like so many colonial surveyors before him, Coffee turned public service to private profit, becoming one of the largest land owners and speculators in Alabama. The names of Overton, Donelson, and Lewis also appeared in the land registers. For himself, Jackson claimed very little; he bought a small estate for his ward, Andrew J. Hutchings, but the plantation never proved particularly profitable and Jackson sold it within a decade. He realized more from the sale of Indian lands in western Tennessee, but by comparison with the huge land grabs of the day, Jackson's own speculations were modest. Nevertheless, the general's negotiations served the wealthy speculators, as the profits of his friends clearly reveal.

Avarice did not shape Jackson's policies nearly so much as did his fear of disorder. It was an old fear, one that had haunted him since adolescence, one given harrowing dimension by the Indian attacks and resulting social instability in the Cumberland. Military authority enabled him to conquer that fear by striking at the root of disorder. In quick succession, he had destroyed the "murderers," seized their territory, and prescribed limits to future Indian aggression. He did not sicken at the carnage nor quaver at the awful finality of death. He felt justified in destroying those who threatened society, and he believed that their death would bring a new social order in which white and Indian could coexist. By surrounding the Indians with "an industrious and virtuous population you set them good examples, their manners habits and customs will be imbibed and adopted." . . .

. . . Jackson's Indian conquests opened up huge tracts of fertile land in the deep South, land that would soon give rise to an entrenched cotton culture and slavery. Tidewater planters fretted about the loss of population; they were unable to stop the flow. New Englanders voiced similar concerns about the massive migrations that left towns deserted, pulpits vacant. They, too, were powerless. Cities grew and multiplied, threatening comfortable, agrarian self-images. Immigrants began to arrive in ever-increasing numbers, some joining in the journey west, others contributing to the burgeoning urban population.

With the first faint rumblings of expansion, people began to search for remedies to ease their discomfort. Religious revivals renewed faith and suggested new mechanisms for acting on general concerns. Missionary societies flourished in the first quarter of the nineteenth century, offering the distraught faithful an opportunity to ennoble themselves at home by supporting God's work abroad. By the time the first missions were firmly established in the Sandwich Islands, a host of reform societies had sprung up, each trying to cope with the symptoms of national unrest. Convert the heathen, institutionalize the insane, remove the Indians, protect the Sabbath, reform the drunkard, deport the blacks: through these crusades, Americans sought to regain control over their society. Like the forces of change, these institutional remedies were frenzied and uncoordinated. All this activity took place in an atmosphere of intense introspection; old heroes were summoned to pass on reassurances that the nation was not deserting its revolutionary heritage. . . .

. . . Jackson had come forward at precisely the right time. The congressional nominating machinery was falling apart, having been badly damaged by the conflicting aspirations of four prominent Washington figures: Secretary of War John C. Calhoun, Secretary of State John Quincy Adams, Secretary of the Treasury William H. Crawford, and House Speaker Henry Clay. Popular disapproval completed what excessive ambition had begun; to a citizenry increasingly attracted by democratic rhetoric, the caucus became a symbol of vested interests and aristocracy. With the central party structure in disarray, local newspapers and state legislatures made their own evaluations of a candidate's fitness. All this was to Jackson's advantage. To the South he was slaveholder; to the Scotch Irish of Pennsylvania he was kin; to the frontiersmen of the Southwest he was protector; to former Federalists he was forgiving spoilsman; to all he was military hero.

Jackson benefited by the collapse of men as well as machinery. After the general's impressive showing in Pennsylvania's nominating convention of 1823, Calhoun withdrew. A stroke nearly cost Crawford his life. He remained in seclusion in his Georgia home, his health shattered, his strength ebbing, his forces leaderless. As senator, Jackson tried to seclude himself but for different reasons. He was determined to stand "entirely aloof from the intriguers and caucus mongers" in Washington, fearing that his reputation might be contaminated by this "unclean procedure." He would "become the perfect philosopher" and disappoint those "whose minds were prepared to see me with a Tomahawk in one hand, and a scalping knife in the other." Jackson disclaimed any real desire to be president but looked forward to the election nevertheless. By displaying himself as a civilized, austere, and dignified gentleman, he would put down the slanders once and for all. The candidate desperately wanted such vindication. "I court it from the nation." . . .

The people shared Jackson's sense of injury and resented the secrecy shrouding the caucus. They naturally sympathized with a man who had no ties to such a closed, elitist system, a man whose fame rested upon martial feats, not partisan maneuvers. Given widespread public discontent, even Jackson's tiffs with congressional committees became political assets. They proved his determination not to submit to the cabal, just as many voters refused to bend to the political dictates of the caucus. In the fall balloting in 1824, Jackson received nearly a third more popular votes than John Quincy Adams and triple the totals of Crawford and Clay. Still, Old Hickory lacked a majority of the electoral votes, and the contest was thrown into the House of Representatives. . . .

Jackson was hardly philosophical in defeat. He came to the House vote armed with a rationalization: only corruption could thwart the people's will. "If party or intrigue should prevail and exclude me, I shall retire to my comfortable farm with great pleasure." This studied indifference vanished once the ballots were counted. "Demagogues barter them as sheep," Jackson said of the voters the day after Adams's triumph. Then came a Godsend! In a move he would later publicly regret, Henry Clay accepted the president-elect's offer to become secretary of state, confirming Jackson's worst suspicions and providing ample grist for the campaign mill. . . .

To the public, Andrew Jackson was now both hero and victim. Clay's appointment seemed to confirm what Jackson's supporters had long been saying: corruption dominated the highest levels of government. This sense of outrage coincided with broader concerns for the nation's well-being. Unprecedented westward migration, a large influx of immigrants, economic boom, financial collapse, slave expansion, and slave rebellion upset the rhythm of American life. State politicians reacted as best they could, devising programs to settle new land, regulate financial growth, guard against failure, and protect the institution of slavery. Although they expected little in the way of national legislation, these leaders hoped the central government would not frustrate their efforts to achieve stability. Instead, the intrigues of the Washington community increased the confusion, as did President Adams, who proposed an ambitious program of public works that seemed destined to heighten interstate rivalry and further sectional discord.

Jackson promised relief, not by legislative act or executive program, but by removing the major source of decay: governmental corruption. He vowed to slay King Caucus, remove its proponents, and end its hold over the central government. Troubled and dismayed, eager and ambitious, the people responded to this appeal by renewed support for the state organizations that were mobilizing to carry forward the Jackson crusade. Fervor and spirit the new alliance had; structure and sophistication it lacked. . . .

. . . Voters might wonder where Andrew Jackson stood on the tariff and internal improvements, but they were never allowed to forget his stand at New Orleans. . . .

Uncomfortable though it was, Jackson played the role of Cincinnatus* and played it well. His state supporters promised the electorate a return to simple government, presided over by a benevolent hero who had agreed to leave the retirement of his agrarian retreat to combat the forces of corruption. By avoiding any discussion of how Jackson might wage this war, by stressing instead his advanced age and political innocence, Democratic strategists neatly sidestepped the inherent dilemma in Old Hickory's candidacy: How could a president serve the cause of reform and limited government at the same time?

The voters were too preoccupied to worry about this dilemma. Upset by social, economic, and political change, a substantial segment of the American electorate applauded the promise of an end to corruption and a return to the "Arcadian past." In celebrating the miracle of New Orleans, the voters recalled more than military heroism; they remembered the order that it had preserved.

*The Roman soldier-statesman who left his farm to save the republic.

PRIMARY SOURCES

The primary sources in this chapter reflect Jackson's personality and his stands on various issues. As you consider these sources, determine whether they support the conclusions in Curtis's essay (Source 1) about Jackson's personality and the basis of his widespread appeal.

Jackson's Personality

Some of Jackson's personality traits show through clearly in his writings. The following description of his early life, as well as letters to associates and to his wife Rachel, reveal something about his personality. What labels would you apply to Jackson?

 2 This description was probably written late in life.

Jackson on His Experiences During the Revolution (n.d.)

"When we were taken prisoners we were thrown into jail in Camden with about 250 others. My brother, couisin and myself, as Soon as our relationship was known, were separated from each other. No attention whatever was paid to the wounds or to the comfort of the prisoners, and the small pox having broken out among them, for the want of proper care, many fell victims to it. I frequently heard them groaning in the agonies of death and no regard was paid to them. Before our exchange took place I also had become infected with the contagion. Having only two horses in our company when we left Camden, and my brother, on account of weakness caused by a severe bowel complaint and the wound he had received on his head, being obliged to be held on the horse, and my mother riding the other, I was compelled to walk the whole way. The distance to the nearest house to Camden where we stopped that night was forty five miles and the enemy having taken my shoes and jacket I had to trudge along barefooted. The fury of a violent storm of rain to which we were exposed for several hours before we reached the end of our journey caused the small pox to strike in and consequently the next day I was dangerously ill. No attention having been given to my brothers wound or to his illness until after his release, two days subsequent to it he expired. As soon as my recruiting health would permit, my mother hastened to Charleston to administer to the comfort of two of her nephews, Wm. & Jas Crawford then prisoners at this place. On her return She died about three miles from Charleston. When my mother left home I staid with my Uncle Major Crawford. Captain Galbraith in charge of Comissary Stores, ammunition &c. for the American Army, was then staying with my Uncle, and being of a very proud and haughty disposition, for some reason, I forget now what, he threatened to chastise me. I immediately, answered, 'that I had arrived at the age to know my rights, and although weak and feeble from disease, I had courage to defend them, and if he attempted anying of that kind I would most assuredly Send him to the other world.'

Source: Excerpted from Sam B. Smith and Harriet Chappell Owsley, *The Papers of Andrew Jackson,* University of Tennessee Press, 1980. Reprinted by permission.

3   Dickinson was reputed to be the best shot in Tennessee. Unfortunately, while drunk he made some irreverent remarks about Rachel Jackson, and Old Hickory killed him in a duel.

Andrew Jackson to Charles Henry Dickinson (1806)

May 23rd. 1806.

Sir.

Your conduct and expressions relative to me of late have been of such a nature and so insulting that requires, and shall have, my notice—Insults may be given by men, of such a kind, that they must be noticed, and the author treated with the respects due a gentleman, altho (as in the present instance) he does not merit it—You have, to disturb my quiet, industriously excited Thomas Swann to quarrel with me, which involved the peace and harmony of society for a while—You on the tenth of January wrote me a very insulting letter, left this country and caused this letter to be delivered after you had been gone some days; and securing yourself in safety from the contempt I held you in, have a piece now in the press, more replete with blackguard abuse, than any of your other productions; and are pleased to state that you would have noticed me in a different way than through the press, but my cowardice would have found a pretext to evade that satisfaction, if it had been called for &c &c. I hope sir your courage will be an ample security to me, that I will obtain speedily that satisfaction due me for the insults offered—and in the way my friend, who hands you this, will point out—He waits upon you, for that purpose, and with your friend, will enter into immediate arrangements for this purpose—I am &c.

Andrew Jackson

Source: Excerpted from Sam B. Smith and Harriet Chappell Owsley, *The Papers of Andrew Jackson,* University of Tennessee Press, 1980. Reprinted by permission.

4   In December 1813, Jackson was engaged in the Creek Campaign. He was waiting for reinforcements at Fort Strother in the Mississippi Territory, the heart of the Creek nation.

Andrew Jackson to Rachel Jackson (1813)

Head quarters Fort Strother
Decbr 29th. 1813. ½ past 11 oclock at night

My love

. . . I am fearfull when I get supplies up, which I am making every exertion to do I shall have no men to fight with The shamefull desertion from their posts of the Volunteer Infantry—The Violated Pledge of the cavalry & mounted infantry under their own proper signatures, and the apathy displayed in the interior of the state by the fireside Patriotts will sink the reputation of our State—and I weep for its fall—and with it the reputation of the once brave and patriotic Volunteers—who a few privations, sunk from the highest elevation of patriots—to mere, wining, complaining, sedioners and mutineers—to keep whom from open acts of mutiny I have been compelled to point my cannon against, with a lighted match to destroy them—This was a grating moment of my life—I felt the pangs of an affectionate parent, compelled from duty, to chastise his child—to prevent him from destruction & disgrace and it being his duty he shrunk not from it—even when he knew death might ensue—This was a painfull moment, but it is still more painfull, to hear of their disorderly, and disgracefull conduct on their return—had I have been with them this should not have happened . . . There abandonment of the service may destroy the campaign and leave our frontier again exposed to the Tomhawk of the ruthless savage—. . . .

Andrew Jackson

Source: Excerpted from Sam B. Smith and Harriet Chappell Owsley, *The Papers of Andrew Jackson,* University of Tennessee Press, 1980. Reprinted by permission.

Andrew Jackson, Man on the Make

Frederick Jackson Turner said that the ideal of frontier society was the self-made man. The sources provide evidence of the ways Jackson advanced himself. Do his actions embody the frontier ideal? Why might it have been especially popular in his day?

5 Jackson had arrived in Tennessee from North Carolina with few possessions in 1788.

List of Taxable Property (ca. 1792–1797)

A List of the Taxable property of Andrew Jackson (viz) three hundred and

thirty acres of land in Jones Bend	330
Six hundred & forty acres on harpeth	640
Six hundred & forty on Spring Creek	640

	Poles[†]
Eight Negroes includin one of Saml. Donelson*	
in my Possession, Sampson	8
Two white Poles myself & Saml. Donelson	2

Andw. Jackson

*Samuel Donelson (c1759–1803), a brother of Rachel, was Jackson's partner in a short-lived mercantile business in 1795.
[†]Polls were adult males, free or slave, upon whom a head tax of $12\frac{1}{2}$¢ was levied.

Source: Excerpted from Sam B. Smith and Harriet Chappell Owsley, *The Papers of Andrew Jackson* (Knoxville: University of Tennessee Press, 1980), I, 34. Reprinted by permission.

6   ## Andrew Jackson to Rachel Jackson (1811)

Natchez Decbr 17th. 1811.

My Love—

on last evening I reached this place after a detention of two days at Mr A[braham] Greens near Gibson Port by the loss of my horses—on tomorrow I shall set out from here homewards, on the Biopierre I expect to be detained Some days preparing the negroes for the wilderness My trusty friend John Hutchings, on the recpt of my letter had come down to this place recd. all the negroes on hand and had carried them up to his farm—I have Just seen Mr. [Horace] Green last evening this morning he was to have Seen me, but as yet, he has not appeared as to the State of the business I can give you no account—untill I have a Settlement with him—or have an account of the appropriation

Source: Excerpted from Sam B. Smith and Harriet Chappell Owsley, *The Papers of Andrew Jackson,* University of Tennessee Press, 1980. Reprinted by permission.

of the amount of sales from him I shall bring home with me from twelve to Twenty—I hope to be able to sell some of them on the way at good prices—but many of them I Shall be obliged to bring home and as most of that number will be females I leave you to point out to Mr [John] Fields* where to have the house built for them— . . . —believe me to be your affectionate Husband.

Andrew Jackson

*Fields was an overseer at the Hermitage from about 1811 to at least 1815, with a brief interruption in 1813.

 The Hermitage, Jackson's home outside Nashville, was built in 1818 on property he purchased and moved to in 1804. It was extensively remodeled in 1831.

The New Hermitage (1856)

Source: Library of Congress, Prints and Photographs Division.

Andrew Jackson and the Indians

As a Westerner, Jackson often experienced conflict with the Indians. Note what these sources reveal about his attitudes toward the Indians and consider whether they support Curtis's assertion that Jackson's Indian policies reflected his personality traits. How do his views compare to Thomas Jefferson's? Would Jackson's attitudes have been popular with many Americans?

 ## 8 | Andrew Jackson to William Blount* (1812)

Hermitage June 5th. 1812

Dear sir,

I have this moment returned from the State of Georgia. My heart bleeds within me at hearing of the wanton massacre of our women and children by a party of Creeks since I left home.

With infinite regret I learned that Genl. Johnson at the head of 500 men was in the neighborhood of this massacre, at the time of its perpetration, and yet omitted to send a detachment against these marauders or to follow them himself, with his whole force. Thus far they have escaped with impunity carrying off an unfortunate woman along with them. But this cruel outrage must not go unrevengd. The assassins of Women and Children must be punishd.

Now Sir the object of *Tecumpsies* visit to the creek nation is unfolding to us. That incendiary, the emissary of the *Prophet,* who is himself the tool of England, has caused our frontier to be stained with blood, and our peacefull citizens to fly in terror from their once happy abodes.

The sooner we strike, the less resistance we shall have to overcome; and a terrible vengeance inflicted at once upon one tribe may have its effect upon all others.

Even the wretches upon the wabash might take some warning from such a lesson. We must therefore march to the heart of the Creek Nation: a competent force can be raised at the shortest notice; for the spirit of the whole people is on fire. They burn to carry fire and sword to the heart of the Creek Nation, and to learn these wretches in their own Towns and villages what it is to massacre

*Blount was a Tennessee politician and land speculator.
Source: Excerpted from Sam B. Smith and Harriet Chappell Owsley, *The Papers of Andrew Jackson,* University of Tennessee Press, 1980. Reprinted by permission.

Women and Children at a moment of profound peace. I wait therefore for your Orders! Give me permission to procure provisions and munitions of war, and I pledge myself for the ballance. Twenty five hundred brave men from the 2nd Division will be ready on the first signal to visit the Creek towns, and bring them to terms without the aid of presents. . . . I have the honour to be with great consideration yours Respectfully

Andrew Jackson

9 | Monroe had just become president. Jackson had recently been involved in treaty negotiations with the Cherokees and Chickasaws.

Andrew Jackson to James Monroe (1817)

Head Qrs. D. of the South
Nashville 4th. March 1817

Sir

I have waited with anxious solicitude for the period to arrive, when I could congratulate my Country and myself on your being placed into the Presidential chair of this rising Republic. . . . I have long viewed treaties with the Indians an absurdity not to be reconciled to the principles of our Government. The Indians are the subjects of the United States, inhabiting its territory and acknowledging its sovereignty, then is it not absurd for the sovereign to negotiate by treaty with the subject—I have always thought, that Congress had as much right to regulate by acts of Legislation all Indian concerns as they had of Territories; there is only this difference, that the inhabitants of Territories, are Citizens of the United States and entitled to all the rights thereof, the Indians are Subjects and entitled to their protection and fostering care; the proper guardian of this protection and fostering care is the Legislature of the Union—I would therefore contend that the Legislature of the Union have the right to prescribe their bounds at pleasure, and provide for their wants and whenever the safety, interest, or defence of the country should render it necessary for the Government of the United States to occupy and possess any part of the Territory, used by them for hunting, that they have the right to take it and dispose of it.

Source: Excerpted from Sam B. Smith and Harriet Chappell Owsley, *The Papers of Andrew Jackson,* University of Tennessee Press, 1980. Reprinted by permission.

10 Andrew Jackson's Second Annual Message to Congress (1830)

It gives me pleasure to announce to Congress that the benevolent policy of the government, steadily pursued for nearly thirty years, in relation to the removal of the Indians beyond the white settlements is approaching to a happy consummation. Two important tribes have accepted the provision made for their removal at the last session of Congress, and it is believed that their example will induce the remaining tribes also to seek the same obvious advantages.

The consequences of a speedy removal will be important to the United States, to individual States, and to the Indians themselves. The pecuniary advantages which it promises to the government are the least of its recommendations. It puts an end to all possible danger of collision between the authorities of the General and State governments on account of the Indians. It will place a dense and civilized population in large tracts of country now occupied by a few savage hunters. By opening the whole territory between Tennessee on the north and Louisiana on the south to the settlement of the whites it will incalculably strengthen the southwestern frontier and render the adjacent States strong enough to repel future invasions without remote aid. It will relieve the whole State of Mississippi and the western part of Alabama of Indian occupancy, and enable those States to advance rapidly in population, wealth, and power. It will separate the Indians from immediate contact with settlements of whites; free them from the power of the States; enable them to pursue happiness in their own way and under their own rude institutions; will retard the progress of decay, which is lessening their numbers, and perhaps cause them gradually, under the protection of the Government and through the influence of good counsels, to cast off their savage habits and become an interesting, civilized, and Christian community. These consequences, some of them so certain and the rest so probable, make the complete execution of the plan sanctioned by Congress at their last session an object of much solicitude.

Toward the aborigines of the country no one can indulge a more friendly feeling than myself, or would go further in attempting to reclaim them from their wandering habits and make them a happy, prosperous people. I have endeavored to impress upon them my own solemn convictions of the duties and powers of the General Government in relation to the State authorities. For the justice of the laws passed by the States within the scope of their reserved powers they are not responsible to this Government. As individuals

Source: Andrew Jackson, Second Annual Message, December 6, 1830, in James D. Richardson, *A Compilation of the Messages and Papers of the Presidents* (New York: Bureau of National Literature, n.d.), 3: pp. 1082–1085.

we may entertain and express our opinions of their acts, but as a Government we have as little right to control them as we have to prescribe laws for other nations. . . .

Humanity has often wept over the fate of the aborigines of this country, and Philanthropy has been long busily employed in devising means to avert it, but its progress has never for a moment been arrested, and one by one have many powerful tribes disappeared from the earth. . . . What good man would prefer a country covered with forests and ranged by a few thousand savages to our extensive Republic, studded with cities, towns, and prosperous farms, embellished with all the improvements which art can devise or industry execute, occupied by more than 12,000,000 happy people, and filled with all the blessings of liberty, civilization, and religion?

The present policy of the Government is but a continuation of the same progressive change by a milder process. The tribes which occupied the countries now constituting the Eastern States were annihilated or have melted away to make room for the whites. The waves of population and civilization are rolling to the westward, and we now propose to acquire the countries occupied by the red men of the South and West by a fair exchange, and, at the expense of the United States, to send them to a land where their existence may be prolonged and perhaps made perpetual. Doubtless it will be painful to leave the graves of their fathers; but what do they more than our ancestors did or than our children are now doing? To better their condition in an unknown land our forefathers left all that was dear in earthly objects. Our children by thousands yearly leave the land of their birth to seek new homes in distant regions. . . .

And is it supposed that the wandering savage has a stronger attachment to his home than the settled, civilized Christian? Is it more afflicting to him to leave the graves of his fathers than it is to our brothers and children? Rightly considered, the policy of the General government toward the red man is not only liberal, but generous. He is unwilling to submit to the laws of the States and mingle with their population. To save him from this alternative, or perhaps utter annihilation, the General Government kindly offers him a new home, and proposes to pay the whole expense of his removal and settlement.

 11 Andrew Jackson's actions and his image were very familiar to Americans by 1828. He may have been the most painted of all presidents, and his likeness could be seen on tavern signs and in parlors throughout the land. Old Hickory was tall and lean and possessed a penetrating gaze, but appearance alone does not explain the demand for his image. Rather, the way Jackson was portrayed may provide clues to his popularity. Commenting on the engraving below, one newspaper said that "most, if not all of the portraits heretofore published, have represented him as a military character." This image, it went on, presents Jackson "as a civilian, both in employment and costume, a character which he has deservedly acquired as that of the citizen soldier."[7] Note the scholarly setting as well as the rolled document with the inscription "Plan—8th of January 1815" in Jackson's hand. Compare this portrayal with that of John Quincy Adams in Source 12. Does this engraving support the claim of Curtis's essay (Source 1) that Jackson took advantage of the Cincinnatus image?

Andrew Jackson (1828)
ORRAMEL HINCKLEY THROOP

Source: Baltimore Museum of Art; gift of Aaron Strauss and Lillie Strauss Foundation, Inc., BMA 1958. 184.5.

During the 1828 campaign, Jackson supporters distributed campaign literature and made speeches designed to burnish the image of their man and tarnish that of the opponent. Note how John Quincy Adams and Jackson are portrayed in this address. (Even though the name *Republican* was still in use, most of Jackson's supporters called themselves Democrats.)

Address of the Republican General Committee of Young Men of the City and County of New York (1828)

That Mr. Adams is possessed of *learning* . . . we are willing to admit. We are not ignorant that he has received a college education—that he has been a professor of rhetoric . . . He may be a philosopher, a lawyer, an elegant scholar, and a poet, too, forsooth (we know he wrote doggerel verses upon Mr. Jefferson,) and yet the nation may be little better off for all these endowments and accomplishments. That he is *learned* we are willing to admit; but his *wisdom* we take leave to question . . . We confess our attachment to the homely doctrine; thus happily expressed by the great Englis[h] poet:—

> That not to know of things remote
> 'From use, obscure and subtle, but to know
> 'That which before us lies in daily life,
> 'Is the prime wisdom.'

That wisdom we believe Gen. Jackson possesses in an eminent degree.

Source: Address (New York, 1828), p. 41.

After South Carolina passed an Ordinance of Nullification in 1832, Jackson moved decisively to put down the state's defiance of the federal tariff. As you read this excerpt from his proclamation, note whether it reflects any of Jackson's personality traits.

Andrew Jackson's Nullification Proclamation (1832)

This, then, is the position in which we stand: A small majority of the citizens of one State in the Union have elected delegates to a State convention; that convention has ordained that all the revenue laws of the United States must be repealed, or that they are no longer a member of the Union. The governor of that State has recommended to the legislature the raising of an army to carry the secession into effect, and that he may be empowered to give clearances to

Source: State Papers on Nullification (Boston, 1834), pp. 29–31.

vessels in the name of the State. No act of violent opposition to the laws has yet been committed, but such a state of things is hourly apprehended. And it is the intent of this instrument to *proclaim,* not only that the duty imposed on me by the Constitution "to take care that the laws be faithfully executed" shall be performed to the extent of the powers already vested in me by law, or of such others as the wisdom of Congress shall devise and intrust to me for that purpose, but to warn the citizens of South Carolina who have been deluded into an opposition to the laws of the danger they will incur by obedience to the illegal and disorganizing ordinance of the convention; to exhort those who have refused to support it to persevere in their determination to uphold the Constitution and laws of their country; and to point out to all the perilous situation into which the good people of that State have been led, and that the course they are urged to pursue is one of ruin and disgrace to the very State whose rights they affect to support.

Fellow-citizens of my native State, let me not only admonish you, as the First Magistrate of our common country, not to incur the penalty of its laws, but use the influence that a father would over his children whom he saw rushing to certain ruin. In that paternal language, with that paternal feeling, let me tell you, my countrymen, that you are deluded by men who are either deceived themselves or wish to deceive you. Mark under what pretenses you have been led on to the brink of insurrection and treason on which you stand. . . .

The laws of the United States must be executed. I have no discretionary power on the subject; my duty is emphatically pronounced in the Constitution. Those who told you that you might peaceably prevent their execution deceived you; they could not have been deceived themselves. They know that a forcible opposition could alone prevent the execution of the laws, and they know that such opposition must be repelled. Their object is disunion. But be not deceived by names. Disunion by armed force is *treason.* Are you really ready to incur its guilt? If you are, on the heads of the instigators of the act be the dreadful consequences; on their heads be the dishonor, but on yours may fall the punishment. On your unhappy State will inevitably fall all the evils of the conflict you force upon the Government of your country. . . .

CONCLUSION

As we saw in the previous chapter, historians for a long time defined history as "past politics." They focused on mostly white, male political and military leaders like Andrew Jackson. Biography was perfectly suited to this approach to the past. Here personality and character rather than vast impersonal forces could determine the outcome of history. Indeed, if Jackson's life reveals anything, it is that one individual can influence history. Although it is often difficult to do, understanding one personality can thus be a good way to learn about the past. Old Hickory's life is a reminder that historians who attempt to understand even an era "of the common man" can do so through the life of one extraordinary person.

Still, even the most influential people are constrained by powerful political, economic, social, and cultural forces beyond their control. Thus historians, even biographers, cannot ignore ordinary people who, in many if not always obvious ways, limit the actions of the prominent and powerful. That is one reason why many historians today focus on the lives of obscure, poor, or seemingly powerless people. As we will see in the next chapter, such a "bottom-up" approach to history yields a very different perspective on the past.

FURTHER READING

James Barber, *Old Hickory: A Life Sketch of Andrew Jackson* (Washington, D.C.: National Portrait Gallery, Smithsonian Institution, 1990).

John A. Garraty, *The Nature of Biography* (New York: Alfred A. Knopf, 1957).

Robert V. Remini, *Andrew Jackson* (New York: Twayne Publishers, 1966).

Michael Paul Rogin, *Fathers and Children: Andrew Jackson and the Subjugation of the American Indian* (New York: Alfred A. Knopf, 1975).

John William Ward, *Andrew Jackson: Symbol for an Age* (New York: Oxford University Press, 1955).

NOTES

1. Quoted in Robert V. Remini, *The Election of Andrew Jackson* (Philadelphia: J. B. Lippincott, 1963), p. 200.
2. Quoted in Robert V. Remini, *Andrew Jackson and the Course of American Freedom, 1822–1832* (New York: Harper & Row, 1981), p. 178.
3. Quoted in Charles Sellers, "Andrew Jackson Versus the Historians," in *American Themes: Essays in Historiography,* ed. Frank Otto Gatel and Allen Weinstein (New York: Oxford University Press, 1968), p. 143.
4. Quoted in ibid., p. 144.
5. Quoted in ibid., p. 147.
6. Quoted in Edward Hallett Carr, *What Is History?* (New York: Alfred A. Knopf, 1962), p. 68.
7. Quoted in James G. Barber, *Andrew Jackson: A Portrait Study* (Seattle: University of Washington Press, 1991), p. 96.

CHAPTER | 10

History "From the Bottom Up":

Historians and Slavery

The sources in this chapter—an essay drawing from a slaveholder's memoirs and various primary sources—present evidence on slave life in the antebellum South.

Secondary Source

1. Community, Culture, and Conflict on an Antebellum Plantation (1980), DREW GILPIN FAUST

Primary Sources

2. Leaves from a Slave's Journal of Life (1842), LEWIS CLARK
3. Harry McMillan, Interviewed by the American Freedmen's Inquiry Commission (1863)
4. Charity Bowery (1847–1848)
5. Uncle Ben (1910)
6. Sarah Fitzpatrick (1938)
7. A Slave's Letter to His Former Master (1844)
8. "Lynchburg Negro Dance," an Artist's View of Slavery (1853)
9. A Slave Spiritual (ca. 1863)
10. Brer Rabbit Outsmarts Brer Fox
11. A Slave Child's Doll (ca. 1850)
12. A Plantation Plan (ca. 1857)

*L*ike many planters, the lord of the magnificent Cumberland Valley estate saw himself as a kind slave master. The owner of nearly one hundred slaves instructed his overseer "to treat them with great humanity, feed and cloath them well, and work them in moderation." "My negroes," he declared, "shall be treated humanely."[1] Yet this plantation master sometimes whipped and chained his slaves. When he believed his wife's maid was "guilty of a great deal of impudence," he ordered her whipped with perhaps as many as fifty lashes. He had even less patience with runaways. When four of his slaves escaped and were later captured, he put two of them in shackles until he could sell or exchange them. On another occasion, he offered fifty dollars for the capture of a fugitive and "ten dollars for every hundred lashes any person will give him to the amount of three hundred."[2]

This "humane" planter who whipped and chained his slaves was Andrew Jackson. Old Hickory illustrates the contradictions of slavery and the self-deception the institution induced. "Kind" masters often meted out frightening punishment. They condemned their chattel as "lazy," never realizing that it was irrational for slaves to work diligently. They did not see in the faces of slave children the clear evidence of their own sexual liaisons in the slave quarters. Nor did they really know their slaves, certainly not as well as their slaves had to know them. As one former slave put it, "The only weapon of self defence [*sic*] I would use successfully, was that of deception."[3]

If slavery blinded slaveholders to its harsh realities, historians have also suffered from nearsightedness when examining the peculiar institution. Through much of the twentieth century most historians were not interested in the bottom of society. Andrew Jackson's life mattered; those of his slaves did not. Yet we cannot comprehend America's past without understanding slavery. And that is impossible without knowing slavery's impact on slaves. So in this chapter we look at history "from the bottom up." We examine the lives slaves led within an institution filled with contradictions, deception, and self-deception.

SETTING

Like slave masters, historians often saw what they wanted to when they looked at slave life. Early twentieth-century historian Ulrich B. Phillips, for instance, studied the lives of slaves as a Southerner sympathetic to the slaveholder. His observations about slaves and their interaction with masters were tainted by racist assumptions. Indeed, Phillips concluded that slavery was a paternalistic institution that trained Africans in the ways of a superior white civilization. When views about the status of blacks in American society began to change, so did assessments about slavery and its impact on African Americans. In 1956 historian Kenneth Stampp published *The Peculiar Institution,* a direct assault on Phillips's view of slavery. Where Phillips saw slavery as benevolent, Stampp characterized it as harsh and oppressive. In his study *Slavery* (1959), Stanley Elkins went further, arguing that the trauma of enslavement had obliterated slaves' African cultural roots. Moreover, Elkins attempted to show that slaves retained little power to shape their own personalities, so emotionally devastating was bondage. Applying modern theories of social psychology, Elkins asserted that many slaves came to assume their masters' view of them as inferior and dependent "Sambos."

Phillips, Elkins, and Stampp shared an assumption that blacks were molded by white masters. Phillips saw slaves as beneficiaries of slavery; Stampp and Elkins saw them as helpless victims. As African Americans fought for civil rights and even black separation in the 1960s, other historians began to question whether slaves had been passive victims of white domination. Elkins's thesis came in for particular attack, even though it had challenged Phillips's paternalistic view. Many critics found incorrect and offensive Elkins's characterization of black slaves as helpless, childlike "Sambos." In such books as John Blassingame's *The Slave Community* (1972), Eugene Genovese's *Roll, Jordan, Roll* (1974), and Herbert Gutman's *The Black Family in Slavery and Freedom* (1976), historians began to examine slavery from the slaves' point of view. They discovered a resilient culture in the slave quarters and portrayed blacks not as passive objects but as people who maintained a separate culture and shaped their own lives.

More recently, other historians have criticized Blassingame, Genovese, Gutman, and other modern scholars for ignoring or distorting the role of women in slave society. They argue that these historians were so intent on negating the Sambo image of the black male that they usually reduced the slave woman's role to insignificance or, in the words of one, sometimes "impos[ed] the Victorian model of domesticity and maternity on the pattern of black female slave life."[4] In the last decade, such students of slavery as Deborah Gray White, Jacqueline Jones, and Elizabeth Fox-Genovese have explored the world of the female slave. They have discovered that slave women had different roles than men and that the male supremacy of the plantation house was not necessarily to be found in the slave quarters. As Deborah Gray White concluded, "they were not submissive, subordinate, or prudish and . . . they were not expected to be so."[5]

Such revelations, whether about male or female slaves, have not come easily. Because literacy was withheld from slaves by law, they rarely left written records. So historians have relied on such nontraditional sources as songs, folklore, slave narratives, and even material objects to reconstruct life in the slave quarters. Although these sources are sometimes difficult to interpret, they offer big rewards. Thanks to fresh assumptions about their sources and subjects, historians now understand more fully the impact of the peculiar institution on slaves and the slaves' impact on their society.

INVESTIGATION

By its very nature, of course, slavery was oppressive. Yet historians have not stopped at that obvious conclusion. Although they acknowledge great variety in slaves' circumstances, historians have come to conclusions about all aspects of the peculiar institution, from the profitability of plantations to the culture of slaves. Your main goal in this chapter is to answer another question that historians have asked about slavery: What was life like for plantation slaves in the decades before the Civil War? That is a very broad question. In formulating an answer to it, therefore, you will need to address several related questions:

1. **In what ways were slaves able to shape their own world on James Hammond's Silver Bluff plantation, according to Source 1?** What evidence does the essay offer for a separate culture among slaves? What role did religion play?

2. **To what extent were Hammond's slaves able to resist the oppression of slavery?** Was the plantation an all-powerful institution that made slaves helpless and passive, or did slaves have opportunities to exercise power?

3. **Do the primary sources support or contradict the essay's conclusions about the nature of plantation slavery?** What do they reveal about the pleasures and suffering that slaves experienced? How did female slaves' experiences differ from those of their male counterparts?

4. **What were the most important factors affecting the slave experience?** Was the relationship between Hammond and his slaves typical?

Read the sections in your textbook on antebellum slavery for additional background before you begin, paying particular attention to its conclusions about the nature of plantation slavery.

SECONDARY SOURCE

 Historian Drew Gilpin Faust's essay on the relationship between master and slaves on James Henry Hammond's South Carolina plantation is based on Hammond's extensive plantation records. Although Faust bases her discussion about planter-slave relations on documents produced by a white master, they reveal a great deal about slave autonomy and power and the existence of a separate slave community on the plantation. With the primary sources, you will be able to evaluate Faust's findings with evidence from other slaves and plantations. As you read this selection, note how Hammond attempted to assert mastery over his slaves and whether psychological manipulation or physical punishment was more important in his efforts to achieve control. Also pay attention to the ways Hammond's slaves tried to undermine his efforts to dominate them. Finally, note what Hammond's slaves did at the end of the Civil War, and Faust's explanation for their behavior.

Community, Culture, and Conflict on an Antebellum Plantation (1980)

DREW GILPIN FAUST

A dozen miles south of Augusta, Georgia, the Savannah River curves gently, creating two bends that were known to ante-bellum steamboat captains as Stingy Venus and Hog Crawl Round. Nearby, on the South Carolina shore, a cliff abruptly rises almost thirty feet above the water. Mineral deposits in the soil give the promontory a metallic tinge, and the bank and the plantation of which it was part came as early as colonial times to be called Silver Bluff.

In 1831, an opportune marriage placed this property in the hands of twenty-four-year-old James Henry Hammond. An upwardly mobile lawyer, erstwile schoolmaster and newspaper editor, the young Carolinian had achieved through matrimony the status the Old South accorded to planters alone. When he arrived to take possession of his estate, he found and carefully listed in his diary 10,800 acres of land, a dwelling, assorted household effects, and 147 bondsmen. But along with these valued acquisitions, he was to receive a challenge he had not anticipated. As he sought to exert his mastery over the labor force on which the prosperity of his undertaking depended, he was to discover that his task entailed more than simply directing 147 individual lives. Hammond had to dominate a complex social order already in existence on the plantation and to struggle for the next three decades to control what he called a "system of roguery" amongst his slaves.

Hammond astutely recognized that black life on his plantation was structured and organized as a "system," the very existence of which seemed

Source: Excerpted from Drew Gilpin Faust, "Culture, Conflict, and Community: The Meaning of Power on an Antebellum Plantation," *Journal of Social History,* 14, No. 1 (Fall 1980), pp. 83–87, 90–94. Reprinted by permission.

necessarily a challenge to his absolute control—and therefore, as he perceived it, a kind of "roguery." Because Hammond's mastery over his bondsmen depended upon his success at undermining slave society and culture, he established a carefully designed plan of physical and psychological domination in hopes of destroying the foundations of black solidarity. Until he relinquished management of the estate to his sons in the late 1850s, Hammond kept extraordinarily detailed records. Including daily entries concerning the treatment, work patterns, and vital statistics of his slaves, they reveal a striking portrait of slave culture and resistance and of the highly structured efforts Hammond took to overpower it. . . . While Hammond sought to assert both dominance and legitimacy, the slaves at Silver Bluff strove to maintain networks of communication and community as the bases of their personal and cultural autonomy. This struggle, which constantly tested the ingenuity and strength of both the owner and his slaves, touched everything from religion to work routines to health, and even determined the complex pattern of unauthorized absences from the plantation. . . .

The desire to control black religious life led Hammond to endeavor to replace independent black worship with devotions entirely under white direction. At first he tried to compel slaves into white churches simply by making black ones unavailable, and even sought to prevent his neighbors from permitting black churches on their own lands. But soon he took positive steps to provide the kind of religious environment he deemed appropriate for his slaves. For a number of years he hired itinerant ministers for Sunday afternoon slave services. By 1845, however, Hammond had constructed a Methodist Church for his plantation and named it St. Catherine's after his wife.

The piety of the Hammond slaves became a source of admiration even to visitors. A house guest on the plantation in the 1860s found the services at St. Catherine's "solemn and impressive," a tribute, she felt, to Hammond's beneficent control over his slaves. "There was a little company of white people," she recalled, "the flower of centuries of civilization, among hundreds of blacks but yesterday . . . in savagery, now peaceful, contented, respectful and comprehending the worship of God. . . . By reason of Senator Hammond's wise discipline," the visitor assured her readers, there was no evidence of "religious excesses," the usual "mixture of hysteria and conversion" that she believed characterized most black religion. These slaves, it appeared to an outsider, had abandoned religious ecstasy for the reverential passivity prescribed for them by white cultural norms.

Hammond had taken great pains to establish just such white standards amongst his slaves, and the visitor's description of the behavior he succeeded in eliciting from his bondsmen would undoubtedly have pleased him. But even Hammond recognized that the decorous behavior of his slaves within the walls of St. Catherine's was but an outward compliance with his directives.

He seemed unable to eradicate black religious expression, evidences of which appeared to him like tips of an iceberg indicating an underlying pattern of independent belief and worship that persisted among his slaves. Twenty years after his original decision to eliminate the slave church, Hammond recorded in his plantation diary, "Have ordered all church meetings to be broken up except at the Church with a white preacher." Hammond's slaves had over the preceding decades tested their master's initial resolve, quietly asserting their right to their own religious life in face of his attempt to deny it to them. . . .

The struggle for power manifested in the conflict over religious autonomy was paralleled in other areas of slave life on the Hammond domain. Just as Hammond sought from the time of his arrival in 1831 to control religious behavior, so too he desired to supervise work patterns more closely. "When I first began to plant," he later reminisced, "I found my people in very bad subjection from the long want of a master and it required of me a year of severity which cost me infinite pain." The slaves, accustomed to a far less rigorous system of management, resented his attempts and tried to undermine his drive for efficiency. "The negroes are trying me," Hammond remarked in his diary on more than one occasion during the early months of his tenure. In response, he was firm, recording frequent floggings of slaves who refused to comply with his will. When several bondsmen sought to extend the Christmas holiday by declining to return to work as scheduled, Hammond was unyielding, forcing them back to the fields and whipping them as well.

As the weeks passed, the instances of beatings and overt insubordination noted in plantation records diminished; a more subtle form of conflict emerged. Over the next decade, this struggle over work patterns at Silver Bluff fixed on the issue of task versus gang labor. The slaves clearly preferred the independent management of their time offered by the task system, while Hammond feared the autonomy it provided the bondsmen. . . .

Although at this time Hammond succeeded in establishing the gang as the predominant form of labor at Silver Bluff, the victory was apparently neither final nor total. Indeed, it may simply have served to regularize the pattern of poorly performed work Hammond had viewed as a form of resistance to the gang system. He continued to record hoeing that ignored weeds, picking that passed over bulging cotton bolls, and cultivating that destroyed both mule and plough. But eventually the slaves here too won a compromise. By 1850, Hammond was referring once again in his correspondence and in his plantation diary to task work, although he complained bitterly about continuing poor performance and the frequent departure of many bondsmen from the fields as early as midafternoon.

Hammond seemed not so much to master as to manipulate his slaves, offering a system not just of punishments, but of positive inducements, ranging from picking contests to single out the most diligent hands, to occasional rituals of rewards for all, such as Christmas holidays; rations of sugar, tobacco and coffee; midsummer barbecues; or even the pipes sent all adult slaves from Europe when Hammond departed on the Grand Tour. The slaves were more than just passive recipients of these sporadic benefits; they in turn manipulated their master for those payments and privileges they had come to see as their due. Hammond complained that his bondsmen's demands led him against his will to countenance a slave force "too well fed & otherwise well treated," but he nevertheless could not entirely resist their claims. When after a particularly poor record of work by slaves in the fall of 1847 Hammond sought to shorten the usual Christmas holiday, he ruefully recorded on December 26 that he had been "persuaded out of my decision by the Negroes."

Hammond and his slaves arrived at a sort of accommodation on the issue of work. But in this process, Hammond had to adjust his desires and expectations as significantly as did his bondsmen. His abstract notions of order and absolute control were never to be fully realized. He and his slaves reached a truce that permitted a level of production acceptable to Hammond and a level of endeavor tolerable to his slaves. . . .

For some Silver Bluff residents, however, there could be no such compromise. Instead of seeking indirectly to avoid the domination inherent to slavery, these individuals confronted it, turning to arson and escape as overt expressions of their rebelliousness. Throughout the period of his management, Hammond referred to mysterious fires that would break out in the gin house on one occasion, the mill house or the plantation hospital the next. While these depredations could not be linked to specific individuals and only minimally affected the operation of the plantation, running away offered the angry slave a potentially more effective means of immediate resistance to the master's control. Between 1831 and 1855, Hammond recorded fifty-three attempts at escape by his bondsmen. Because he was sometimes absent from the plantation for months at a time during these decades, serving in political office or travelling in Europe, it seems unlikely that this list is complete. Nevertheless, Hammond's slave records provide sufficient information about the personal attributes of the runaways, the circumstances of their departure, the length of their absence and the nature of their family ties to demonstrate the meaning and significance of the action within the wider context of plantation life.

The most striking—and depressing—fact about Silver Bluff's runaways is that Hammond records no instance of a successful escape. A total of thirty-seven different slaves were listed as endeavoring to leave the plantation. Thirty-five percent of these were repeaters, although no slave was recorded as making more than three attempts. Newly purchased slaves who made several efforts to escape were often sold; those with long-term ties to the Silver Bluff community eventually abandoned the endeavor. . . .

While the decision to run away might appear to be a rejection of the ties of black community as well as the chains of bondage, the way in which escape functioned at Silver Bluff shows it usually to have operated somewhat differently. Because there were no runaways who achieved permanent freedom and because most escapees did not get far, they remained in a very real sense a part of the slave community they had seemingly fled. Forty-three percent of the runaways at the Bluff left with others. The small proportion—sixteen percent of the total—of females were almost without exception running with husbands or joining spouses who had already departed. Once slaves escaped, they succeeded in remaining at large an average of forty-nine days. Sixty-five percent were captured and the rest returned voluntarily. The distribution of compulsory and elective returns over the calendar year reveals that harsh weather was a significant factor in persuading slaves to give themselves up. Seventy-seven percent of those returning in the winter months did so voluntarily, while in the spring and summer eighty percent were brought back against their will. Weather and workload made summer the runaway season, and fifty-eight percent of all escape attempts occurred in June, July, and August.

While certain individuals—notably young males, particularly those without family ties—were most likely to become runaways, the slave community as a whole provided these individuals with assistance and support. Hammond himself recognized that runaways often went no farther than the nearby Savannah River swamps, where they survived on food provided by those remaining at home. The ties between the escapees and the community were sufficiently strong that Hammond endeavored to force runaways to return by disciplining the rest of the slave force. On at least one occasion Hammond determined to stop the meat allowance of the entire plantation until the runaways came in. In another instance, he severely flogged four slaves harboring two runaways, hoping thereby to break the personal and communal bonds that made prolonged absences possible. . . .

In the initial part of his tenure at the Bluff, Hammond recorded efforts to round up runaway slaves by means of extensive searches through the swamps on horseback or with packs of dogs. After the first decade, however, he made little mention of such vigorous measures and seems for the most part simply to have waited for his escapees to be captured by neighbors, turn up in nearby jails, or return home. In order to encourage voluntary surrender, Hammond announced a policy of punishment for runaways that allotted ten lashes for each day absent to those recaptured by force and three lashes per day to those returning of their own will. The establishment of this standardized rule integrated the problem of runaways into the system of rewards and punishments at Silver Bluff and rendered it an aspect of the understanding existing between master and slaves. Since no one escaped permanently, such a rule served to set forth the cost of unauthorized absence and encouraged those who had left in irrational rage to return as soon as their tempers had cooled. When the respected fifty-three-year-old driver John Shubrick was flogged for drunkenness, he fled in fury and mortification, but within a week was back exercising his customary responsibility in plantation affairs. . . .

While runaways disrupted routine and challenged Hammond's system of management, his greatest anxieties about loss of control arose from the fear that slave dissatisfaction would be exploited by external forces to threaten the fine balance of concession and oppression he had established. From the beginning of his tenure at the Bluff, he sought to isolate his bondsmen from outside influences, prohibiting their trading in local stores, selling produce to neighbors, marrying off the plantation or interacting too closely with hands on the steamboats that refuelled at the Bluff landing. Despite such efforts, however, Hammond perceived during the 1840s and 1850s an ever-growing threat to his power arising from challenges levelled at the peculiar institution as a whole. To Hammond's horror, it seemed impossible to keep information about growing abolition sentiment from the slaves. Such knowledge, Hammond feared, might provide the bondsmen with additional bases for ideological autonomy and greater motivation to resist his control. . . .

At the beginning of the war, Hammond was uncertain about the sympathies of his slaves. In 1861, he noted that they appeared "anxious," but remarked "Cant tell which side." As the fighting grew closer, with the firing of large guns near the coast audible at Silver Bluff, Hammond began to sense growing disloyalty among his slaves, and to confront intensifying problems of control. "Negroes demoralized greatly. Stealing right and left," he recorded in 1863. By the middle of that year, it seemed certain that the slaves expected "some great change." Despite his efforts, they seemed at all times "well apprised" of war news, sinking into "heavy gloom" at any Union reverse. Hammond observed the appearance of "a peculiar furtive glance with which they regard me & a hanging off from me that I do not like." They seemed to "shut up their faces & cease their cheerful greetings." Hammond felt the war had rendered his control tenuous, and he believed that even though his slaves sought to appear "passive . . . the roar of a single cannon of the Federal's would make them frantic—savage cutthroats and incendiaries."

Hammond never witnessed the Union conquest of the South or the emancipation of his slaves, for he died in November of 1864. Despite his dire prophecies, however, the people of Silver Bluff did not rise in revolution against those who had oppressed them for so long. Unlike many slaves elsewhere who fled during the war itself, the Hammond bondsmen did not depart even when freedom was proclaimed. "We have not lost many negroes," Hammond's widow complained in September 1865 as she worried about having too many mouths to feed. "I wish we could get clear of many of the useless ones."

Given the turbulent nature of the interaction between Hammond and his slaves in the antebellum years, it would be misguided to regard the blacks' decision to remain on the plantation as evidence either of docility or of indifference about freedom. Instead, it might better be understood as final testimony to the importance of that solidarity we have seen among bondsmen on the Hammond estate. These blacks were more concerned to continue together as a group than to flee Hammond's domination. In the preoccupation with the undeniable importance of the master-slave relationship, historians may have failed fully to recognize how for many bondsmen, the positive meaning of the web of slave interrelationships was a more central influence than were the oppressive intrusions of the power of the master. Silver Bluff had been home to many of these slaves before Hammond ever arrived; the community had preceded him, and now it had outlived him. Its maintenance and autonomy were of the highest priority to its members, keeping them at Silver Bluff even when any single freedman's desire for personal liberty might have best been realized in flight. The values central to this cultural group were more closely associated with the forces of tradition and community than with an individualistic revolutionary romanticism. . . .

. . . These freedmen saw themselves and their aspirations defined less by the oppressions of slavery than by the positive accomplishments of autonomous black community that they had achieved even under the domain of the peculiar institution.

PRIMARY SOURCES

Most of the sources in this chapter were produced by slaves or former slaves. Such documents are very helpful to historians who want to know what slavery was like. As you evaluate them, consider what evidence they provide for a separate slave culture and about slaves' opportunities to resist or escape the oppression of slavery.

 Clark, a former slave, delivered this speech in 1842. It was recorded by abolitionist Lydia Maria Child and published in the *National Anti-Slavery Standard*. As you read it, consider whether Clark's sympathetic Brooklyn, New York audience might have influenced what he said.

Leaves from a Slave's Journal of Life (1842)
LEWIS CLARK

"There was a widower in Kentucky, who took one of his women slaves into the house. She told her master one day that seven of the young girls had poked fun at her for the way she was living. This raised his *ambition*. 'I'll teach 'em to make fun!' said he. So he sent the woman away, and ordered the young girls to come to him, one by one." (An ill-mannered and gross laughter, among the boys of the audience, here seemed to embarrass him.) "Perhaps I had better not try to tell this story," he continued; "for I cannot tell it as it was; though surely it is more shameful to have such things *done,* than it is to *tell* of 'em. He got mad with the girls, because they complained to their mothers; but he didn't like to punish 'em for that, for fear it would make a talk. So he ordered 'em to go out into the field to do work that was too hard for 'em. Six of 'em said they couldn't do it; but the mother of the seventh, guessing what it was for, told her to go, and do the best she could. The other six was every one of 'em tied up naked, and flogged, for disobeying orders. Now, who would like to be a slave, even if there was nothing bad about it but such treatment of his sisters and daughters? But there's a worse thing yet about slavery; the worst thing in the whole lot; though it's all bad, from the butt end to the *pint.* I mean the *patter-rollers* (patrols.) . . . If a slave don't open his door to them at any time of night they break it down. They steal his money if they can find it, and act just as they please with his wives and daughters. If a husband dares to say a word, or even look as if he wasn't quite satisfied, they tie him up and give him thirty-nine lashes. If there's any likely young girls in a slave's hut, they're mighty apt to have business there, especially if they think any colored young man takes a fancy to any of 'em. Maybe he'll get a pass from his master, and go to see the young girl for a few hours. The patter-rollers break in and find him there. They'll abuse the girl as bad as they can, a purpose to provoke him. If he looks cross, they give him a flogging, tear up his pass, turn him out of doors, and then take him up and whip him for being out without a pass. If the slave says they tore it up, they swear he lies; and nine times out of ten the master won't come out agin 'em; for they say it won't *do* to let the niggers suppose they may complain of the patter-rollers; they must be taught that it's their business to obey 'em in everything; and the patter-roller knows that very well. Oh, how often I've seen the poor girls sob and cry, when there's been such goings on! Maybe you think, because they're slaves, they an't got no feeling and no shame? A woman's being a slave, don't stop her having genteel ideas; that is, according to their way, and as far as they can. They know they

Source: National Anti-Slavery Standard, October 20, 1842.

must submit to their masters; besides, their masters, maybe, dress 'em up, and make 'em little presents, and give 'em more privileges, while the whim lasts; but that an't like having a parcel of low, dirty, swearing, drunk patter-rollers let loose among 'em, like so many hogs. This breaks down their spirits dreadfully, and makes 'em wish they was dead.

"Now who among you would like to have your wives, and daughters, and sisters, in such a situation? This is what every slave in all these States is exposed to.—Yet folks go from these parts down to Kentucky, and come back, and say the slaves have enough to eat and drink, and they are very happy, and they wouldn't mind it much to be slaves themselves. I'd like to have 'em try it; it would teach 'em a little more than they know now.

Slave Interviews

Many former slaves were interviewed during and after the Civil War. Some of these interviews appeared in newspapers and magazines. In addition, the American Freedmen's Inquiry Commission, established in 1863, gathered testimony from numerous former slaves. Former bondsmen were also interviewed by scholars in the early twentieth century. In the 1930s, for instance, Works Progress Administration interviewers recorded the testimony of former slaves. As you read these interviews, note what they reveal about the treatment of slaves, the threat to families under slavery, and the female slave experience.

3   Harry McMillan, Interviewed by the American Freedmen's Inquiry Commission (1863)

I am about 40 years of age, and was born in Georgia but came to Beaufort when a small boy. I was owned by General Eustis and lived upon his plantation.

Q. Tell me about the tasks colored men had to do?

A. In old secesh times each man had to do two tasks, which are 42 rows or half an acre, in "breaking" the land, and in "listing" each person had to do a task and a half. In planting every hand had to do an acre a day; in hoeing your first hoeing where you hoe flat was two tasks, and your second hoeing, which is done across the beds, was also two tasks. After going through those two operations you had a third which was two and a half tasks, when you had to go over the cotton to thin out the plants leaving two in each hill.

Q. How many hours a day did you work?

Source: John Blassingame, ed., *Slave Testimony: Two Centuries of Letters, Speeches, Interviews, and Autobiographies* (Baton Rouge: Louisiana State University Press, 1977), pp. 379–380. (Originally from American Freedmen's Inquiry Commission Interviews [1863])

A. Under the old secesh times every morning till night—beginning at daylight and continuing till 5 or 6 at night.

Q. But you stopped for your meals?

A. You had to get your victuals standing at your hoe; you cooked it over night yourself or else an old woman was assigned to cook for all the hands, and she or your children brought the food to the field.

Q. You never sat down and look your food together as families?

A. No, sir; never had time for it.

Q. The women had the same day's work as the men; but suppose a woman was in the family way was her task less?

A. No, sir; most of times she had to do the same work. Sometimes the wife of the planter learned the condition of the woman and said to her husband you must cut down her day's work. Sometimes the women had their children in the field.

4 | Charity Bowery (1847–1848)

Interviewed, 1847–1848. New York.
   by Lydia Maria Child

Age: sixty-five
b. 1782. North Carolina
Enslaved: North Carolina
House servant

The following story was told me by an aged colored woman in New York. I shall endeavor to relate it precisely in her own words, so oft repeated that they are tolerably impressed on my memory. Some confusion of names, dates, and incidents, I may very naturally make. I profess only to give "the pith and marrow" of Charity's story, deprived of the highly dramatic effect it received from her swelling emotions, earnest looks and changing tones.

"I am about sixty-five years old. I was born on an estate called Pembroke, about three miles from Edenton, North Carolina. My master was very kind to his slaves. If an overseer whipped them, he turned him away. . . .

"Sixteen children I've had, first and last, and twelve I've nursed for my mistress. From the time my first baby was born, I always set my heart upon buying freedom for some of my children. I thought it was of more consequence to them than to me; for I was old and used to being a slave. But mistress McKinley wouldn't let me have my children. One after another—one after another—she sold 'em away from me. Oh, how *many* times that woman broke my heart!"

Source: Emancipation, April 5, 1848.

Here her voice choked, and the tears began to flow. She wiped them quickly with the corner of her apron, and continued: "I tried every way I could to lay up a copper, to buy my children, but I found it pretty hard; for mistress kept me at work all the time. It was 'Charity! Charity, Charity!' from morning till night. Charity do this or that.

"I used to do the washings of the family; and large washings they were. The public road run right by my little hut, and I thought to myself, while I stood there at the wash-tub, I might just as well as not be earning something to buy my children. So I set up a little oyster-board, and when anybody came along that wanted a few oysters and a cracker, I left my wash-tub and waited upon them. When I got a little money laid up, I went to my mistress and tried to buy one of my children. She knew not how long my heart had been set upon it, and how hard I had worked for it. But she wouldn't let me have one! So I went to work again; and I set up late o'night, in hopes I could earn enough to tempt her. When I had two hundred dollars I went to her again; but she thought she could find a better market, and she wouldn't me have one. At last, what do you think that woman did? She sold me and five of my children to the speculators! Oh, how I *did* feel when I heard my children was sold to the speculators!"

5 | Uncle Ben (1910)

Interviewed, 1910. Alabama.   Enslaved: Alabama, Texas,
    by Mary White Ovington   N.C.

"Yes, we was worked hard in those days, we sure was. You think, maybe, people done have a rest on Sunday? I done never see it. Half-time work on Sunday pullin' fodder in the field for the mules an' cows. Then Sunday mornin' we'd build fences for the cattle, old fashion' bridge fences, we calls 'em. The women too was worked terrible. You see the railroad yonder? Women helped grade that railroad. Other times they'd plow in the field an' when night come they mus' spin two cuts o' cotton. Don't matter how tired they might be, they mus' spin their two cuts or in the morning they'd be whipt. That's what I's tellin' you.

"There were terrible persecution then. I's seen men with fly blows. You don't know what that mean, perhaps? Fly blows is what we calls the meat when it turns to maggots. They'd whip a man until he's so warm the blood creep thru his shirt, an' the flies 'ud come. Workin' out in the fiel' all the time,

Source: Independent, 48 (May 26, 1910), pp. 1131–1136.

bendin' over the hoe, an' the flies suckin' the blood. Some men wouldn't stan' it. They'd take to the woods, an' then the dogs 'ud ketch 'em. After that they'd be chained, an' you'd hear rattling like they was chained logs. When night comes, there by deir bed there'd be a staple. The overseer'd come along an' lock the chain to the staple so they couldn't get away. In the mornin' the overseer let 'em out. They done put 'em, too, in screw boxes, what you call presses. When they put down the foller-block, then the nigger was tight. It was out-o-doors an' he was like to freeze. They chain him in the graveyard, too, keep him there all the night to skeer him. Oh, I knows what I's talking about, yes ma'am. Now an' den you can ketch some ole person who knows, who bear witness like hallelujah meeting, to what I say. . . .

 6 | ## Sarah Fitzpatrick (1938)

Interviewed, 1938. Alabama.
   by Thomas Campbell

Age: ninety
b. 1847. Alabama
Enslaved: Alabama
House servant

In dem times "Niggers" had'ta hav'va a pass to go to church too. White fo'ks axed you whut church ya' wan'na go to an' dey issue ya a pass, write on dere de name ob de church an' de name ob de pu'son an' de time to git back home. Co'se when "Niggers" went to church wid deir white fo'ks dey didn't haf'ta have no pass. Ya'see, us "Niggers" had our meetin' in de white fo'ks Baptist Church in de town o' Tuskegee. Dere's a place up in de loft dere now dat dey built fer de "Nigger" slaves to 'tend church wid de white fo'ks. White preacher he preach to de white fo'ks an' when he git thu' wid dem he preach some to de "Niggers". Tell'em to mind deir Marster an' b'have deyself an' dey'll go to Hebben when dey die. Dey come 'round an' tell us to pray, git 'ligion, dat wuz on Sun'dy, but dey'ed beat de life out'cha de next day ef ya didn't walk de chalk line. Our white fo'ks made us go to church an' Sun'dy School too. Dey made us read de Catechism. G'ess de re'son fo' dat wuz, dey tho't it made us min' dem bedder. "Niggers" commence'ta wanna go to church by de'selves, even ef dey had'ta meet in de white church. So white fo'ks have deir service in de mornin' an' "Niggers" have deirs in de evenin', a'ter dey clean up, wash de dishes, an' look a'ter ever'thing. Den de white fo'ks come back at night an' have deir Church Service. Ya'see "Niggers" lack'ta shout a whole lot an' wid de white fo'ks al'round'em, dey couldn't shout jes' lack dey want to. . . .

Source: Thomas Monroe Campbell Papers, Files of the Tuskegee Department of Records and Research, Hollis Burke Frissell Library, Tuskegee University.

Mos' all de "Niggers" use'ta steal in Slav'ry time, co'se 'bout all dey stole f'om dey Marster 'n Mistrus wuz sum'in t'eat, steal hogs 'n kill'um an' clean'um at night den dey dig a pit an' put'um 'way in de woods, den dey go back dere an' git some uv'it when dey want it, an' cook it. Som'times de white fo'ks ketch'em wid it an' beat'em. Didn't have no cook stove in dem times. Som' uv'em cook out doors, some uv'em in fi'place. Any "Nigger" would steal when he didn't get 'nuff t'eat. Ya'fam'ly didn't git but three an' haf' pounds uv meat, one an' er haf' pecks uv meal a week, dat wont e'nuff, so "Niggers" jes' had'ta steal. He didn't steal nothing' but sump'in t'eat dough. Co'se ma' white fo'ks wux high class, deir house gals didn't have no right to steal 'cause ma' mistrus tel' us anythin' we want, don't take it, but ax' fer it. Ef we wanna wear piece of her jewry we ax' her fer it an' she let us wear it, to church som'time. She leave money 'roun an' udder val'able things an' we didn't bodder it. Dey taught us not to take things. I knowed whar ma' marster kep' his money box: he kep'it right out in de sec'e'tary. He nuver did bodder 'bout lockin' it up fo'm us. We jes' didn't bodder his money. Durin' de war de white fo'ks sunt all de cot'on dey could get to de war . . . . "Niggers" didn't think dat stealin' wuz so bad in dem times. Fak' is dey didn't call it stealin', dey called it takin'. Dey say, "I ain't takin' fo'm nobody but ma' mistrus an' Marster, an' I'm doin' dat 'cause I'se hongry." "Niggers" use'ta steal cot'on an' anything dey could sell to 'nudder white man. Co'se dats whut de whites taught'em.

7 | Henry Bibb, the author of this letter, escaped from slavery in 1840. He campaigned for the Liberty Party in 1844 and 1845 and, after the passage of the Fugitive Slave Law in 1850, moved to Canada. Note what this letter reveals about Bibb's treatment and his feelings toward his former master.

A Slave's Letter to His Former Master (1844)

Detroit, March 23d, 1844

William Gatewood

Dear Sir:—I am happy to inform you that you are not mistaken in the man whom you sold as property, and received pay for as such. But I thank God that

Source: Henry Bibb, *Narrative of the Life and Adventures of Henry Bibb, an American Slave* (New York, 1849).

I am not property now, but am regarded as a man like yourself, and although I live far north, I am enjoying a comfortable living by my own industry. If you should ever chance to be traveling this way, and will call on me, I will use you better than you did me while you held me as a slave. Think not that I have any malice against you, for the cruel treatment which you inflicted on me while I was in your power. As it was the custom of your country, to treat your fellow men as you did me and my little family, I can freely forgive you.

I wish to be remembered in love to my aged mother, and friends; please tell her that if we should never meet again in this life, my prayer shall be to God that we may meet in Heaven, where parting shall be no more.

You wish to be remembered to King and Jack. I am pleased, sir, to inform you that they are both here, well, and doing well. They are both living in Canada West. They are now the owners of better farms than the men who once owned them.

You may perhaps think hard of us for running away from slavery, but as to myself, I have but one apology to make for it, which is this: I have only to regret that I did not start at an earlier period. I might have been free long before I was. But you had it in your power to have kept me there much longer than you did. I think it is very probable that I should have been a toiling slave on your plantation today, if you had treated me differently.

To be compelled to stand by and see you whip and slash my wife without mercy, when I could afford her no protection, not even by offering myself to suffer the lash in her place, was more than I felt it to be the duty of a slave husband to endure, while the way was open to Canada. My infant child was also frequently flogged by Mrs. Gatewood, for crying, until its skin was bruised literally purple. This kind of treatment was what drove me from home and family, to seek a better home for them. But I am willing to forget the past. I should be pleased to hear from you again, on the reception of this, and should also be very happy to correspond with you often, if it should be agreeable to yourself. I subscribe myself a friend to the oppressed, and Liberty forever.

Henry Bibb
Windsor, Sept. 23, 1852

8 Sometimes art captured scenes from slavery. At a dance in Virginia, one artist saw slaves playing musical instruments of both European origin (the fiddle) and African origin (the banjo and the bones). As you examine this picture, determine what it reveals about slave culture and plantation life.

"Lynchburg Negro Dance," an Artist's View of Slavery (1853)

Source: Abby Aldrich Rockefeller Folk Art Center, Williamsburg, VA. acct. #78.301.1.

9 | Although masters often used religion to teach obedience to their slaves, the slaves often derived other lessons from what they were taught. As you read this spiritual, ask yourself how religion helped sustain a slave culture. What lessons did slaves take from the Bible?

A Slave Spiritual (ca. 1863)

THE SHIP OF ZION.

"Dis de good ole ship o' Zion,
  Dis de good ole ship o' Zion,
  Dis de good ole ship o' Zion,
      And she's makin' for de Promise Land.

Source: Atlantic Monthly, June 1867, pp. 685–694.

She hab angels for de sailors. (*Thrice.*)
    And she's, &c.
And how you know dey's angels? (*Thrice.*)
    And she's, &c.
Good Lord, shall I be de one? (*Thrice.*)
    And she's, &c.

"Dat ship is out a-sailin', sailin', sailin',
    And she's, &c.
She's a-sailin' mighty steady, steady, steady,
    And she's, &c.
She'll neither reel nor totter, totter, totter,
    And she's, &c.
She's a-sailing' away cold Jordan, Jordan, Jordan,
    And she's, &c.
King Jesus is de captain, captain, captain,
    And she's makin' for de Promise Land."

10	Brer (Brother) Rabbit was a familiar figure to slaves. As in African folk tales, slave stories assigned human qualities to animals. What traits allow Brer Rabbit to survive against a much stronger Brer Fox? What

might these animal characters have stood for?

Brer Rabbit Outsmarts Brer Fox

De fox had a way goin' to de man hawg-pen an' eatin' up all his hawg. So de people didn' know how to ketch de fox. An' so de rabbit was goin' along one Sunday mornin'. Say was goin' to church. Ber Fox singin', "Good-mornin', Ber Rabbit!" Ber Rabbit singin', "Good-mornin', Ber Fox!" Say, "Whey you goin'?" Say, "I'm goin' to church." Ber Fox say, "Dis is my time. I'm hungry dis mornin'. I'm goin' to ketch you."—"O Ber Fox! leave me off dis mornin'! I will sen' you to a man house where he got a penful of pretty little pig, an' you will get yer brakefus' fill. Ef you don' believe me, you can tie me here, an' you can go down to de house, an' I'll stay here until you come back." So Ber Fox tie him. When he wen' down to de house, de man had about fifty head of houn'-dawg. An' de man tu'n de houn'-dawg loose on him. An' de fox made de long run right by Ber Rabbit. Ber Fox say, "O Ber Rabbit! dose is no brakefus', dose is a pile of houn'-dawg."—"Yes, you was goin' to eat me, but dey will eat you for your brakefus' and supper to-night." An' so dey did. Dey cut [caught] de fox. An'

Source: Elsie Clews Parsons, *Foke-Lore of the Sea Islands of South Carolina, Memoirs of the American Folk-Lore Society* (Cambridge, Mass.), XVI, 26–27, 66–67.

Ber Rabbit give to de dawgs, "Gawd bless yer soul! dat what enemy get for meddlin' Gawd's people when dey goin' to church." Said, "I was goin' to school all my life an' learn every letter in de book but *d*, an' D was death, an' death was de en' of Ber Fox."

Artifacts from Slavery

Like other kinds of evidence, physical artifacts can tell historians much about what life was like for slaves. What does this evidence suggest about the opportunities for a separate existence in the slave quarters?

  This doll was found in the attic walls of a North Carolina plantation.

A Slave Child's Doll (ca. 1850)

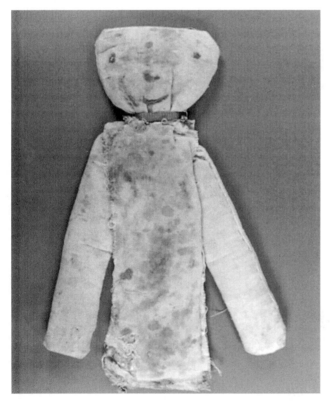

Source: Historic Stagville, NC Department of Cultural Resources.

12 Bellegrove, a plantation built in 1857 in Louisiana, had twenty double cabins for slaves and a dormitory for 150 laborers.

A Plantation Plan (ca. 1857)

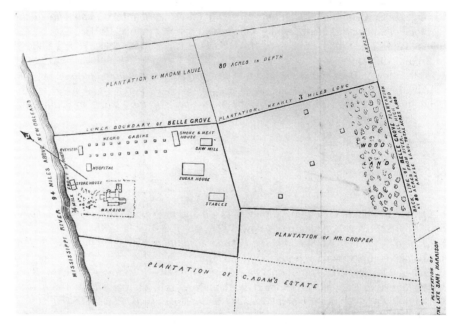

Source: The Historic New Orleans Collection, acct. #1970.13.1.

CONCLUSION

The abolitionist Frederick Douglass, himself a runaway slave, made a point illustrated by this chapter. A free man, said Douglass, "cannot see things in the same light with the slave, because he does not, and cannot, look from the same point from which the slave does."[6] The study of slavery demonstrates the need to write history from several vantage points. That lesson applies to many topics in history. In the next chapter, you will have the opportunity to assess historians' conclusions about female abolitionists. Although most of these women were far removed from the experience of slavery, they also illustrate Douglass's argument. Female abolitionists did not look at their antislavery activity "from the same point" as their male counterparts, and historians who ignore that fact will miss much of abolitionism's meaning. Like conclusions about slavery, judgments about the impact of antislavery agitation depend heavily on whom historians listen to in the past.

FURTHER READING

John W. Blassingame, *The Slave Community: Plantation Life in the Antebellum South,* rev. ed. (New York: Oxford University Press, 1979).

John W. Blassingame, *Slave Testimony: Two Centuries of Letters, Speeches, Interviews, and Autobiographies* (Baton Rouge: Louisiana State University Press, 1977).

Edward D. C. Campbell, Jr., *Before Freedom Came: African-American Life in the Antebellum South* (Charlottesville: University Press of Virginia, 1991).

Eugene Genovese, *Roll, Jordan, Roll: The World the Slaves Made* (New York: Pantheon Books, 1974).

Kenneth Stampp, *The Peculiar Institution: Slavery in the Ante-Bellum South* (New York: Alfred A. Knopf, 1956).

Deborah Gray White, *Ar'n't I a Woman? Female Slaves in the Plantation South* (New York: W. W. Norton, 1985).

NOTES

1. Quoted in Robert V. Remini, *Andrew Jackson and the Course of American Empire, 1767–1821* (New York: Harper & Row, 1977), pp. 133–134.
2. Quoted in Kenneth M. Stampp, *The Peculiar Institution: Slavery in the Ante-Bellum South* (New York: Vintage Books, 1956), p. 188.
3. Gilbert Osofsky, ed., *Puttin' on Ole Massa: The Slave Narratives of Henry Bibb, William Wells Brown, and Solomon Northup* (New York: Harper & Row, 1969), p. 9.
4. Deborah Gray White, *Ar'n't I a Woman? Female Slaves in the Plantation South* (New York: W.W. Norton, 1985), p. 21.
5. Ibid., p. 22.
6. Quoted in John Blassingame, ed., *Slave Testimony: Two Centuries of Letters, Speeches, Interviews, and Autobiographies* (Baton Rouge: Louisiana State University Press, 1977), p. lxv.

CHAPTER | 11

THE EMERGENCE OF AN IDEOLOGY:

ANTISLAVERY AND THE BOUNDS OF WOMANHOOD

This chapter presents two secondary sources on women abolitionists and several primary sources by and on women abolitionists. These documents help one reconsider the importance of this women's movement.

Secondary Sources

1. "Am I Not a Woman and a Sister?" Abolitionist Beginnings of Nineteenth-Century Feminism (1979), BLANCHE GLASSMAN HERSH
2. Gender and Class in the Boston Female Anti-Slavery Society (1993), DEBRA GOLD HANSEN

Primary Sources

3. An Anti-Abolitionist Cartoon (ca. 1835)
4. Letter to Catherine Beecher (1836), ANGELINA GRIMKÉ
5. Women Petition Congress to Abolish Slavery (1834)
6. The Secretary of the Boston Female Anti-Slavery Society Responds to Critics (1836)
7. The Times That Try Men's Souls (1837), MARIA WESTON CHAPMAN
8. A'n't I a Woman? (1851), SOJOURNER TRUTH

Women abolitionists in the early 1800s often drew angry crowds. At one meeting when William Lloyd Garrison arrived to address the Boston Female Anti-Slavery Society, a mob crowded the stairs and shouted at the abolitionist agitator. Garrison quickly slipped out, but the women continued their meeting. Soon thereafter Mayor Theodore Lyman ordered the abolitionists to go home; asking them if they wished "to see a scene of bloodshed and confusion." The women refused to adjourn and accused Lyman's friends of instigating the mob. "If this is the last bulwark of freedom," president Mary S. Parker declared, "we may as well die here as anywhere."[1] Anti-Slavery Society founder Maria Chapman reported later that when they finally relented and marched out of the hall arm in arm, they "emerged into the open daylight [and] there went up a roar of rage and contempt."[2]

By the 1830s abolitionist women stirred the "rage and contempt" of many Americans who believed antislavery agitation would split the union. But the heated emotions of anti-abolitionist mobs were stoked by more than fears for the union. Because most white Americans did not accept African Americans as equals, the sight of whites and blacks mingling freely was an affront. And many Americans also found female abolitionists outrageous because a woman's proper sphere was the home. These women were involved in affairs better left to men; proper "ladies" never discussed politics or addressed "mixed" crowds of men and women. By breaking these taboos, female abolitionists gave people a powerful reason to ridicule them. As the Boston *Commercial Gazette* put it, the Boston Female Antislavery Society women could be "more usefully and profitably employed at home" rather than "preaching on a subject about which they know no more than the man in the moon."[3]

By the 1840s, such attacks as well as discrimination by male abolitionists had given rise to a vocal women's rights movement. Led by Lydia Maria Child, Maria Weston, and other female abolitionists, women's rights advocates questioned their inequality and compared their status to the bondage of slaves. By 1848, delegates at a women's rights convention at Seneca Falls, New York, were demanding the right to vote and protesting such injustices as the exclusion of women from professions and the forfeiture by married women of control over their own property. They were led by abolitionists Lucretia Mott and Elizabeth Cady Stanton.

Abolitionism's relationship to a remarkably modern women's rights movement thus appears clear-cut. Abolitionist activity led many women to the realization that they needed to fight not only for the rights of slaves but also for their own rights. Yet the impact of abolitionism on women demonstrates why historians must be wary of simple explanations and sweeping generalizations, for its effect was not as obvious as it may seem.

SETTING

Few figures in the American past inspired more emotion than abolitionists, and few people have elicited more controversy among historians. Contemporaries of the abolitionists saw them as either villains or heroes. So too have many historians. In the early twentieth century, historians sympathetic to the white South often looked at antislavery crusaders as fanatics bent on disrupting the Union. By the 1960s, however, they began to reassess abolitionists. Changing views about slavery and protests against segregation and the Vietnam War led many historians to the more sympathetic conclusion, that these earlier agitators were trying to get America to live up to its ideals.

Assessments of female abolitionists have also changed over time. Through much of the twentieth century historians considered women's involvement in abolitionism important only because it split the antislavery movement. As women began to speak out against slavery, abolitionists fought bitterly over the proper role of women in the movement and over the wisdom of taking up the cause of women's rights. William Lloyd Garrison, Maria Chapman, Abby Kelley, and other female abolitionists argued that the liberation of women and slaves was inseparable. Meanwhile, such antislavery leaders as Lewis Tappan and James G. Birney insisted that fighting for women's rights was unwise because it eroded support for abolitionism. For a long time historians agreed. The demand for women's rights was proof of abolitionists' rigidity and fanaticism. As Gilbert H. Barnes put it in *The Anti-Slavery Impulse* (1933), "Over the cause of women's rights [the Garrisonians] cast the same odium of narrow fanaticism and brawling intolerance which had cursed the antislavery agitation from its beginning."[4]

By the 1960s, however, a growing women's rights movement encouraged some, mostly female, historians to reassess the split among abolitionists caused by the "woman question." In *Means and Ends in American Abolitionism* (1967), Aileen S. Kraditor noted that earlier historians often "ridicule[d] that minority of abolitionists who advocated women's rights for having tacked an 'extraneous' issue onto the antislavery movement."[5] At the same time, she observed, they condemned early twentieth-century suffragist leaders for failing to demand black voting rights, a move that would have split the suffrage movement into northern and southern factions and thus delayed the passage of the women's suffrage amendment. Their respective reactions, Kraditor concluded, revealed that historians had little respect for gender equality.

As historians reexamined abolitionism with new assumptions, they began to reassess the role of women in the antislavery movement. They found far greater participation by women than historians had previously realized. They also concluded that women antislavery advocates were important not just because they provoked a split within abolitionist ranks. These female abolitionists also confronted and challenged the boundaries of their "proper sphere." Today, therefore, historians study these crusaders both to understand their role in ending slavery and to discover women's place in nineteenth-century society.

INVESTIGATION

What was the impact of thousands of women involved in the antislavery crusade? Of course, one answer would be secession, the Civil War, and the abolition of slavery. A second response would point to women themselves. Thus historians ask another question about female abolitionism: In trying to liberate slaves, in what ways did women also liberate themselves? To help you formulate an answer to that question, this chapter contains a small set of primary sources and two historians' arguments (Sources 1 and 2). The two essays have different perspectives on women's abolitionist activity and thus do not come to the same conclusions about it. A good analysis of this chapter's main question will use the primary and secondary sources to address the following questions:

1. **How do the two authors' arguments about the impact of abolitionist activity on antebellum feminism differ?** Do they agree about the female abolitionists' ideas regarding gender equality? To what extent are their conclusions influenced by the women they examine?

2. **Why did abolitionism not affect all women the same way?** Why did some of them advocate equality in the public sphere and some embrace other ideals? What important factors influenced their views about gender equality?

3. **What evidence do the primary sources offer to indicate that female abolitionists' views about gender were influenced by their antislavery activity?** Do the primary sources reveal that the assumption of a unique female sphere was widespread? To what extent do female abolitionists' arguments against slavery rely upon it?

4. **What changes in their own lives did female abolitionists achieve?** What factors limited their ability to change women's position in nineteenth-century society?

The sections on abolitionism and the antebellum women's rights movement in your textbook will provide useful background for this assignment. As you read, note what kind of connection your textbook makes between these two movements.

SECONDARY SOURCES

1 In this selection, historian Blanche Glassman Hersh discusses the involvement of women in the antislavery crusade and its impact on their thinking about equality. She argues that antislavery activity led directly to a women's rights movement. Note Hersh's evidence that women's work in the abolitionist crusade was a "feminist consciousness-raising experience." Also pay attention to her argument about women antislavery crusaders' views regarding gender equality. You can then compare it to the argument about their views in the second selection.

"Am I Not a Woman and a Sister?" Abolitionist Beginnings of Nineteenth-Century Feminism (1979)
BLANCHE GLASSMAN HERSH

Nineteenth-century feminists talked of "the slavery of sex" in describing married women's legal subservience to their husbands and, in a broader sense, the imprisonment of all women within the traditional concept of woman's proper sphere. This phrase had a double connotation: it suggested not only the parallel position of woman and slave, a principal theme of nineteenth-century feminist rhetoric, but also the close historical link between abolitionism and feminism. All the women who were the first to speak out and to organize for woman's rights were abolitionists, as were the men who supported them. Feminism grew naturally out of antislavery because the abolitionists' argument for human rights transcended both sex and color, and because the obstacles that women faced made their efforts to work against slavery a feminist consciousness-raising experience. . . .

By venturing into the male domain of antislavery work, the feminist-abolitionist women also became the cutting edge for the creation of new social roles for women. In defending woman's domestic role but demanding that she have equal access to a broader sphere, they foreshadowed the basic tone of nineteenth-century feminism. By expanding their own spheres to include the dual roles of wife-mother and reformer, they provided models for other women eager to free themselves from old patterns in order to exert an influence on the world about them. By marrying men who were also feminist-abolitionists and willing to apply the doctrine of human rights to their own unions, they became partners in relatively egalitarian marriages that afforded them the freedom to pursue their goals. Though not completely resolving the female dilemma of balancing family and work outside the home, they suggested important patterns and possibilities for the future. By modifying their society's definition of woman's sphere in important ways, they set the example for a new type of woman who was both a private and a public person. . . .

. . . The controversy over the "woman question," . . . came to a head in the late 1830s. Although these events have been detailed in antislavery studies, they need to be reexamined here from a new perspective. For abolitionism, the internal dispute over women's role in the movement was a serious, divisive blow. This same controversy, however, sparked an increased feminist consciousness and the beginnings of an important and continuing debate over woman's rights, and also led to an expanded role for women in the radical wing of the movement.

In the early 1830s, women were still content to play a subordinate role in antislavery, but their activities were given new impetus with [William Lloyd] Garrison's arrival on the scene. One of his goals was to arouse American women to indignation and sympathy for the cause. . . . The early issues of his *Liberator* contained a "Ladies Department" headed by a picture of a kneeling slave woman in chains and the entreaty "Am I Not A Woman And A Sister?" In the text he implored his female readers to take note of the one million enslaved women "exposed to all the violence of lust and passion—and treated with more indelicacy and cruelty than cattle," and urged them to work for immediate emancipation.

Garrison's appeal struck a responsive note in at least a few New England women who became his staunch supporters. The abolitionist cause would change their lives drastically and move them from positions of status and respectability to places among the social outcasts and martyrs of their society. They in turn would, in the next decade, transform the traditional auxiliary role of women in antislavery into a more active, independent force. . . .

By 1837, there were intimations that abolitionist women were feeling hampered in the auxiliary role assigned to them. Their first attempt at national organization, the Anti-Slavery Convention of American Women, met in May of that year with about one hundred delegates from ten states attending the three-day meeting. Lucretia Mott, in recalling the mood of the group, noted that one of their first resolutions proclaimed that it was time for "woman to act in the sphere which Providence had assigned her, and no longer to rest satisfied with the circumscribed limits in which corrupt custom and a perverted application of the Scriptures had encircled her." Mary S. Parker of Boston, president of the convention and sister of Unitarian minister and reformer Theodore Parker, was authorized to send a circular to all female antislavery societies of the country. In it she urged action on current petitions and gave the women some feminist advice. They should follow their own consciences, she said, not the will of their husbands. . . .

The question of woman's proper role in the antislavery movement was finally raised publicly later in 1837. The woman's rights issue was never quiescent thereafter. The central figures in the first stage of the controversy were Angelina and Sarah Grimké. Reared in an aristocratic, slaveholding South Carolina family (they would remain anomalies in the New England-dominated movement), they had moved to Philadelphia in the 1820s. Looking for something that would give their lives meaning, they found this sense of purpose first in Quakerism and, more lastingly, in antislavery work. . . .

In 1836, Angelina Grimké came to public attention by writing *An Appeal to the Christian Women of the South* in which she urged her southern sisters to use their influence with husbands and brothers to act against slavery. In explaining her bold action she wrote: "God has shown me what I can do . . . to speak to them in such tones that they *must* hear me, and through me, the voice of justice and humanity." She followed this *Appeal* with an eloquent address to the convention of antislavery women in 1837, challenging the "Women of the Nominally Free States" to break their own bonds to aid those of their sex in slavery. Published as a pamphlet by the convention, it served to enhance the reputation of both sisters among the abolitionists. Following this convention, they were invited to address the Boston Female Anti-Slavery Society. They were especially desirable as speakers because of their unique experience with slavery. They went on from there to speak to other women's groups in the area. Prim and plain in their Quaker bonnets, they impressed their audiences with their intense devotion to their cause. In addition, Angelina was becoming known as an eloquent orator. For all of these reasons, they attracted large numbers of men as well as women to their lectures. Churches and meeting halls were filled to overflowing. They found themselves addressing mixed audiences, a situation which even abolitionist women had not faced before. Even staunch antislavery people had doubts about the wisdom of defying convention to this extreme.

The Grimkés' speaking tour, which lasted about six months and included over sixty New England towns, was successful in gaining attention for the cause. It also brought down upon them the wrath of the orthodox clergy of Massachusetts. The General Association of Congregationalist Ministers issued an edict to all its member churches, in effect condemning the Grimkés—without specifically mentioning them—for the unfeminine act of addressing "promiscuous" or mixed audiences.

The pastoral letter attacking the Grimkés triggered the first extended public controversy over woman's rights because it spoke directly to the question of her proper sphere, an issue that would dominate the nineteenth-century movement. Its language clearly revealed the boundaries of acceptable female behavior in 1837. Citing the New Testament as its authority, the letter emphasized that woman's power lay in her dependence. Likening her to a vine "whose strength and beauty is to lean upon the trellis-work," it warned that the vine which "thinks to assume the independence and the over-shadowing nature of the elm" would not only cease to bear fruit, but "fall in shame and dishonor into the dust." The character of the woman who "assumes the place and tone of man as public reformer . . . becomes unnatural."

This was a harsh public attack on the Grimkés and a warning to other women who might dare to venture outside their prescribed sphere. . . .

. . . What began in 1837 as a confrontation with forces which were antiabolitionist as well as antifeminist, became an internecine conflict that lasted from 1838 to 1840 and eventually contributed to the division of the entire abolitionist movement.

The focal point of this controversy was the right of women to vote and participate in the business of the "male" antislavery societies. The final division in the movement came in 1840 when Abby Kelley was appointed to a committee of the American Anti-Slavery Society—Whittier called her "the bomb-shell that *exploded* the society." Garrison and his supporters defended her, while their opponents in the organization demanded her resignation. Kelley refused to resign and, like the Grimkés, defended her position on the ground that men and women had the same moral rights and duties. The impasse over her appointment split the national society. The group of New York abolitionists who opposed her—the Garrisonians called them "New Organization Men"—seceded to form a second organization. . . .

. . . In the 1830s there was as yet no woman's rights "movement"—this would begin in the next decade with lecturers, newspapers, political campaigns, and the first conventions. Significant beginnings had been made during these early years, however, and the important bond between abolitionism and feminism had been forged. The two movements were linked in crucial ways: by the antislavery events and controversies which proved to be feminist consciousness-raising experiences, by the feminist-abolitionist people whose leadership spanned both movements, and by the belief in human rights which provided the ideological underpinning for both causes.

The controversy over woman's role in antislavery had been the important catalyst in moving a few independent-minded abolitionist women to take action in defense of woman's rights. Stirred to a realization of their own enslavement in "woman's sphere," feminism became for them a necessary adjunct to abolitionism. Abby Kelley expressed this best when she noted in 1838 that women had good cause to be grateful to the slave "for the benefit we have received to *ourselves* in working for *him*." "In striving to strike his irons off," she continued, "we found most surely that *we* were manacled *ourselves*." In order to free the slaves, they were forced to move to free themselves.

Abolitionism also bequeathed to feminism the basic philosophy which sustained all radical reform, the idea that all good causes are linked together. Maria Weston Chapman expressed it clearly in one of her reports: "Truth is like a strong cable." The belief in fundamental principles, she wrote, would lead inevitably to the emancipation of *all* people from bondage, not only slaves but "women from the subjugation of men" and people oppressed by poverty, religion, and government—in short, emancipation "of the whole earth from sin and suffering." It was with this belief that the women who began their antislavery work with the plea "Am I not a woman and a sister?" went on to speak in the name of a sisterhood which included not only slave women but all women.

2   In this selection, historian Debra Gold Hansen examines an ideological split within the Boston Female Anti-Slavery Society. Pay attention to Hansen's argument about the social causes of this ideological division and about the ways two separate ideologies liberated women from traditional definitions of their proper sphere. Then determine whether the two essays agree about antislavery's impact on women's awareness of their oppression. Would you modify the first essay's conclusion that antislavery activity was a "feminist consciousness-raising experience"?

Gender and Class in the Boston Female Anti-Slavery Society (1993)
DEBRA GOLD HANSEN

During its brief history, the Boston Female Anti-Slavery Society progressed from a modest charity to one of the most notorious, if not most influential, women's organizations in the country. Yet at its pinnacle of fame and prominence the organization virtually ceased to function as a unified group. By 1838 the Boston Female Anti-Slavery Society had become, in reality, two organizations whose concerns and priorities were not only different from but wholly unacceptable to each other. Moreover, each faction accused the other of creating the dissension and discord that had culminated in the society's destruction. . . .

. . . The women in the Boston Female Anti-Slavery Society were a diverse lot, representing the old and the new, tradition and change. The society included many women from the city's established and wealthy merchant and professional class, which historically had assumed moral and financial responsibility for the needy. Joining with them were individuals belonging to the city's rising middle class, wives of proprietors, clerks, and skilled artisans who, in a number of instances, would amass fortunes rivaling that of the

Source: Reprinted from *Strained Sisterhood: Gender and Class in the Boston Female Anti-Slavery Society* by Debra Gold Hansen (Amherst: University of Massachusetts Press, 1993). Copyright © 1993 by the University of Massachusetts Press.

Brahmins. Prosperous African Americans also participated in the organization as part of their effort to uplift the local black community. The society included a number of employed women, many of whom were part of the massive migration to Boston that began in the 1830s. But, unlike the majority of female newcomers who became poorly paid seamstresses and domestics, the women in abolition carved out new employment opportunities as teachers, boarding-house operators, writers, editors, lecturers, and social workers. In terms of religious affiliation, most members were Congregational and Baptist, but the society also included a significant number of Unitarians and Quakers, as well as a scattering of Universalists, Methodists, Episcopalians, and African Baptists. . . .

In religious affiliation, white, middle-class women in the Boston Female Anti-Slavery Society, like the Parkers and Balls,* were almost entirely Congregationalist and Baptist. In fact, of the members whose religious affiliation is known, all but two Baptists and fifty-three of the sixty-two Congregationalists voted with the Parker-Ball faction. As evangelicals, they were alarmed at the radicals' repudiation of religious authority, "filled with horror," to quote Anne Weston, that some of their sisters were no longer "under the watch and care of any minister." At one point, word passed among the society that Maria Chapman had never been converted, leading many evangelicals to wonder "whether any thing she [Chapman] can possibly do in the Society will be blessed to the cause." To this Chapman dryly remarked, "If the slaves' condition be the *tragedy* of human life, surely these things are the *farce*." . . .

In appearance, personal habits and leisure activities, white middle-class reformers continued to encourage morality and restraint and denounced many of the popular diversions of the day: Smoking, for example, was condemned as a "dirty habit"; cigars led to insanity. Because "in the Bible we read nothing about the two sexes dancing together and spending whole nights in rioting and sin," dancing was denounced as "but a step this side of debauchery and infamy." Theatergoing, too, excited "the lower feelings of our nature" and threatened to "kindle the fires of illicit passion," and Boston confectioneries encouraged individuals to spend free time in "unprofitable conversation" and "vicious and unnatural indulgence," both of which led directly to the "house of debauchery." . . .

Implicit in the middle-class critique of the "fashionable dissipation and extravagance of the present age" was a rejection of the prerogatives and authority of Boston's aristocracy. Using licentiousness as a code for excess, immorality, and corruption, women such as abolitionist-turned-moral reformer Susan Frost denounced those "in high places" who considered themselves "beyond the reach of human laws." . . .

Elite women abolitionists, on the other hand, continued to operate within traditional forms of status and power. Though women, they were accustomed

---

*Lucy and Mary Parker and Lucy and Martha Ball.

to established means of social and political action, and their abolition tactics emulated male models like petitioning, lecturing, publishing editorials and tracts, and initiating legal suits. Unlike middle-class women in the Boston Female Anti-Slavery Society, whose benevolent activities were carried out under the aegis of local churches and female charities, elites availed themselves of established upper-class networks, using customary social forms like visiting and parties to further the abolition cause. Relying on traditional modes of authority, Chapman and her supporters had assumed that support for their reform agenda by the middle class would be forthcoming. They were unprepared for the repudiation of their program and the subsequent independent action taken by Mary Parker, the Balls, and others of the Boston Female Anti-Slavery Society middle class. . . .

By 1839 radical elites in the Boston Female Anti-Slavery Society would not be satisfied with less than an official role within male abolition societies, each person ready, as Anne Weston said, "to man or rather *woman* her point to the last." In their view it was an "immoral custom" and an "unutterable wrong" to continue to disguise women's power within the antislavery movement. To limit women's participation to "that subservient capacity" of auxiliary had the effect of excluding them "except as beasts of burden." Henceforth, Chapman declared, women would no longer act "slavishly by permission, but freely by inward determination." . . .

According to the evangelical middle class . . . white women's assigned station entailed submitting to male authority, limiting their sphere of action to the private world of home and family, denying personal talents or interests save those that impinged upon the household, and doing so cheerfully and willingly. As Martha Ball once wrote, "Marriage is to woman at once the happiest and the saddest event of her life." However, evangelical women were not unaffected by the feminist stirrings of their colleagues, and feminist language and ideas frequently found their way into evangelicals' writings. Moreover, by developing what one activist termed an "enlightened scriptural" definition of womanhood, evangelicals modified some of the more oppressive strictures regarding woman's sphere.

For one thing, evangelicals made it clear that they did not equate female domesticity with female inferiority. As one woman wrote, "Difference in character and condition does not necessarily imply inferiority." The duties of both sexes, agreed another, were "assigned by the Creator without superiority conferred on the one or degradation imposed on the other." This separate-but-equal philosophy enabled Congregational and Baptist women simultaneously to uphold the ideal of male authority and advocate a limited version of women's rights. These reformers sought to "elevate woman as a moral and intellectual being" as a way of fulfilling her domestic responsibilities, not to make "a farmer or politician of her." Thus the typical argument ran: "I am not so much for elevating woman *out* of her present sphere, as for elevating her *in it.*" . . .

Having elevated women's status and power within the home and promoted gender solidarity without, white evangelicals proceeded to use these ideals to encourage women's participation in the social and political movements of the day. These women believed they had an important role to play in urban public life precisely because of the unique sensibilities of their sex. "There is a distinction in the nature of woman's power and man's power in the promotion of the same great objects," argued the *Friend of Virtue*. The magazine urged every woman to make use of "those peculiarities" which comprised "the very elements of her strength" to better glorify God and benefit mankind. As the women of the Massachusetts Female Emancipation Society declared:

> If woman has nothing to do with politics, then she has nothing to do with the rising generation; then she has no duty to her husband—none to her neighbor—in fine, none to the world. . . . We cannot live without exerting a *direct* influence on the destiny of our country, and how important is it that we understand its policy and give our proportion of effort to increase its stability.

As a result of this appreciation for women's political potential, many evangelical women joined their radical sisters in becoming members of the New England Anti-Slavery Society and the Massachusetts Anti-Slavery Society when these organizations admitted women for the first time.

Regardless of their advocacy of women's duty to be socially aware and politically active and their initial interest in joining male societies, middle-class reformers were still loath to abandon their female-only societies or renounce their customary role in the movement. . . . Ultimately, they preferred to organize their charities as they did their households, with each sex having important but separate roles to play. Evangelical women endorsed Lewis Tappan's assertions that "women have equal rights with men." As the New York evangelical explained: "They have a right to form societies of women only. Men have the same right." Within their female-only organizations, women were able to retain control over their operations and thus maintain relative independence. . . .

White upper-class women in the Boston Female Anti-Slavery Society resisted the social and personal constraints imposed upon them by the evangelicals' doctrine of separate spheres. . . .

In rejecting the white middle-class ideology of woman's sphere, upper-class abolitionists believed that the rights and duties of females and males were the same. "In all spiritual things, their functions are identical," argued Chapman in an 1837 circular to female antislavery societies in New England. "With respect to secondary pursuits—whether mercantile, mechanical, domestic or professional," she added, "the tools to whosoever can use them. All are alike bound to the free and strenuous exercise of such faculties as God has given them." . . .

The challenge of the woman question forced white upper- and middle-class Boston Female Anti-Slavery Society members to confront their feelings regarding women's sphere of action and articulate an ideology that would explain their participation in the political world. The evangelicals drew their ideology from Old Testament theology and traditional social arrangements. For the most part Congregationalists and Baptists, they upheld scriptural teachings regarding patriarchy and female submission and conceived of human society as divided into two discrete arenas of activity, the public male sphere and the private female sphere. As a result, they discouraged women's participation in many nondomestic activities, save those connected with church and charity. Within religious and benevolent organizations, evangelicals preferred the role of assistant rather than that of equal. Schooled in self-effacement and self-denial, they expected and accepted the age-old dominance of male household, religious, and political authorities. . . .

Wealthy women in the Boston Female Anti-Slavery Society also drew upon the cultural predispositions and prejudices of their class in formulating what they considered the rights and responsibilities of women in urban society. As socially committed Unitarians and Quakers, they rejected Old Testament lessons concerning sin, punishment, and submission to worldly authorities, arguing that the Bible had been misrepresented by self-seeking males in order to defend and perpetuate all forms of oppression. Each individual was accountable to God not man and therefore entitled to follow his or her personal, spiritual, and intellectual commission, regardless of strictures laid down by self-appointed rulers and judges. Anne Weston urged women not to let male criticism deter them from participation in liberation movements. "Will you allow these men who have been for years unmindful of their own most solemn duties to prescribe to you yours? Shall . . . they be esteemed by you as fit judges of the sphere you shall occupy?"

Upper-class abolitionists found so-called woman's sphere one of the primary sources of continued female subjugation. According to Chapman, asking women to remain within such circumscribed limits (and, she might have added, to restrict women to tasks better done by servants) was "the most insulting" request "to human nature of all." There were no differences between the sexes, wealthy radicals maintained, save for those created by improper socialization and education, and the time had come for women to assume their proper station as men's social and political equals. As Chapman once declared in connection with Abby Kelley, women would never attain their full potential until they "called no man master." . . .

Cultured, cosmopolitan, and irreverent, upper-class women sought to break the bonds of custom and religion and release repressed female potential. . . . [T]heirs was an ideology of liberation and personal fulfillment, as they called for the free expression of women's ideas and personalities regardless of tradition or cultural dictates concerning appropriate feminine decorum. . . . [T]he message of upper-class activists was geared toward New England's cultural and intellectual elite and largely ignored the concerns of lower- and middle-class women. . . .

Once freed from the domination of both males and upper-class females, middle-class women, upon leaving the Boston Female Anti-Slavery Society, increasingly committed themselves to what they considered to be their causes, women's causes: the orphan, the destitute minister, the prostitute, and so forth. Invoking their model of womanhood, they also felt justified in battling what they saw as crimes against women—enslavement and rape, seduction and adultery, and abandonment and abuse—all of which limited women's ability to fulfill prescribed roles. It was as women, then, that they had reached out to their enslaved African sisters, and it was as mothers that they had demanded that black females be restored to their rightful position at the center of their families.

Excluded by reason of class and gender from Boston's sociopolitical hierarchy, white middle-class women articulated a value system based not upon power, privilege, and personal success but upon morality, piety, and domesticity. They sought virtue not wealth, pleasure in self-control rather than in extravagance or self-indulgence. They hoped to secure status and respectability through upright Christian deportment, not through individual creativity or accomplishment. Middle-class women did not find their exclusion from public life or intellectual endeavor necessarily oppressive or demeaning, since they believed that women's roles and capabilities were entirely different from those of men. Although they acquiesced in the patriarchal organization of society and politics, believing that the separation of the sexes and the fulfillment of prescribed gender roles were the natural order of things, they considered their responsibilities to be different from, not inferior, to men's. . . .

The emergence of these two models of womanhood within the brief history of the Boston Female Anti-Slavery Society did not take place in a social vacuum. That women with a common conceptualization of gender roles also shared a similar socioeconomic and religious background suggests the extent to which ideology is socially constructed. Moreover, the dialog between these upper- and middle-class groups helped determine the shape their different models would take and, perhaps, made them more inflexible than they otherwise might have been. Unfortunately, the bitterness and intolerance out of which these ideologies emerged helped create an unnecessarily rigid dichotomy between the belief in gender equality and the assumption of gender difference. This dichotomy plagued the woman's movement throughout the nineteenth century, and although the women who inherited and perpetuated these two models united briefly in 1914 for the final push for suffrage, the coalition disintegrated with the passage of the Nineteenth Amendment. This inability to incorporate different ideologies into a universal model of feminism continues today, even among feminist scholars and theorists, a testimony to the limits of women's solidarity based upon gender alone.

PRIMARY SOURCES

Most of the sources in this section were produced by female abolitionists. They reflect attitudes about gender in the decades before the Civil War and the effect of abolitionism on those attitudes. Look for evidence of how female abolitionists challenged prevailing definitions of gender.

3 | "For the sake of general emancipation try a little of that squeezing my dear Niobe, then you will look just like the white people," suggests Mr. Philander in this anti-abolitionist cartoon. Niobe refuses, responding that if she is to be free at all, she wishes to be so in "every respect." What does this cartoon suggest about female abolitionists' relationship to traditional morality?

An Anti-Abolitionist Cartoon (ca. 1835)

Source: New York Historical Society.

4   Angelina Grimké was an effective spokeswoman for abolitionism and one of the first female abolitionists to demand women's rights. As you read this appeal, consider what impact Grimké's abolitionism had on her view of gender differences.

Letter to Catherine Beecher (1836)
ANGELINA GRIMKÉ

The investigation of the rights of the slave has led me to a better understanding of my own. I have found the Anti-Slavery cause to be the high school of morals in our land—the school in which *human rights* are more fully investigated, and better understood and taught, than in any other. Here a great fundamental principle is uplifted and illuminated, and from this central light, rays innumerable stream all around. Human beings have *rights,* because they are *moral* beings: the rights of *all* men grow out of their moral nature; and as all men have the same moral nature, they have essentially the same rights. These rights may be wrested from the slave, but they cannot be alienated: his title to himself is as perfect *now,* as is that of Lyman Beecher: it is stamped on his moral being, and is, like it, imperishable. Now if rights are founded in the nature of our moral being, then the *mere circumstance of sex* does not give to man higher rights and responsibilities, than to woman. To suppose that it does, would be to deny the self-evident truth, that the "physical constitution is the mere instrument of the moral nature." To suppose that it does, would be to break up utterly the relations, of the two natures, and to reverse their functions, exalting the animal nature into a monarch, and humbling the moral into a slave; making the former a proprietor, and the latter its property. When human beings are regarded as *moral beings, sex,* instead of being enthroned upon the summit, administering upon rights and responsibilities, sinks into insignificance and nothingness. . . .

This regulation of duty by the mere circumstance of sex, rather than by the fundamental principle of moral being, has led to all that multifarious train of evils flowing out of the anti-christian doctrine of masculine and feminine virtues. By this doctrine, man has been converted into the warrior, and clothed with sternness, and those other kindred qualities, which in common estimation belong to his character as a *man;* whilst woman has been taught to lean upon an arm of flesh, to sit as a doll arrayed in "gold, and pearls, and costly array," to be admired for her personal charms, and caressed and humored like a spoiled child, or converted into a mere drudge to suit the convenience of her lord and master. . . .

Source: Women's Rights in the United States: A Documentary History, Winston E. Langley and Vivian C. Fox, Eds. Copyright © 1994 by Greenwood Press. Reproduced by permission of Greenwood Publishing Group, Inc., Westport, CT.

. . . I recognize no rights but *human* rights—I know nothing of men's rights and women's rights; for in Christ Jesus, there is neither male nor female. It is my solemn conviction, that, until this principle of equality is recognised and embodied in practice, the church can do nothing effectual for the permanent reformation of the world. Woman was the first transgressor, and the first victim of power. In all heathen nations, she has been the slave of man, and Christian nations have never acknowledged her rights. Nay more, no Christian denomination or Society has ever acknowledged them on the broad basis of humanity. I know that in some denominations, she is permitted to preach the gospel; not from a conviction of her rights, nor upon the ground of her equality as a *human being*, but of her equality in spiritual gifts—for we find that woman, even in these Societies, is allowed no voice in framing the Discipline by which she is to be governed. Now, I believe it is woman's right to have a voice in all the laws and regulations by which she is to be *governed*, whether in Church or State; and that the present arrangements of society, on these points, are *a violation of human rights, a rank usurpation of power,* a violent seizure and confiscation of what is sacredly and inalienably hers—thus inflicting upon woman outrageous wrongs, working mischief incalculable in the social circle, and in its influence on the world producing only evil, and that continually. *If* Ecclesiastical and Civil governments are ordained of God, *then* I contend that woman has just as much right to sit in solemn counsel in Conventions, Conferences, Associations and General Assemblies, as man—just as much right to sit upon the throne of England, or in the Presidential chair of the United States.

 5 Until it passed a so-called "gag rule" in 1836, Congress was flooded with thousands of antislavery petitions like the one below. Note the assumptions about the connection between gender and morality that are revealed in this petition. Would its appeal have been a particularly effective means to spread the antislavery message?

Women Petition Congress to Abolish Slavery (1834)

TO THE HON. THE SENATE AND HOUSE OF REPRESENTATIVES
OF THE U. STATES, IN CONGRESS ASSEMBLED:

Petition of the Ladies resident in _____ County, State of Ohio.

Fathers and Rulers of our Country:

Suffer us, we pray you, with the sympathies which we are constrained to feel as wives, as mothers, and as daughters, to plead with you in behalf of a

Source: Gilbert H. Barnes and Dwight L. Dumond, eds., *Letters of Theodore Dwight Weld, Angelina Grimké Weld and Sarah Grimké, 1822–1844* (New York: Appleton-Century-Crofts, Inc., 1934), I, 175–176.

long oppressed and deeply injured class of native Americans residing in that portion of our country which is under your exclusive control. We should poorly estimate the virtues which ought ever to distinguish your honorable body could we anticipate any other than a favorable hearing when our appeal is to men, to philanthropists, to patriots, to the legislators and guardians of a Christian people. We should be less than women, if the nameless and unnumbered wrongs of which the slaves of our sex are made the defenceless victims, did not fill us with horror and constrain us, in earnestness and agony of spirit to pray for their deliverance. By day and by night, their woes and wrongs rise up before us, throwing shades of mournful contrast over the joys of domestic life, and filling our hearts with sadness at the recollection of those whose hearths are desolate.

Nor do we forget, in the contemplation of their other sufferings, the intellectual and moral degradation to which they are doomed; how the soul formed for companionship with angels, is despoiled and brutified, and consigned to ignorance, pollution, and ruin.

Surely then, as the representatives of a people professedly christian, you will bear with us when we express our solemn apprehensions in the language of the patriotic Jefferson "we tremble for our country when we remember that God is just, and that his justice cannot sleep forever," and when in obedience to a divine command "we remember them who are in bonds as bound with them." Impelled by these sentiments, we solemnly purpose, the grace of God assisting, to importunate high Heaven with prayer, and our national Legislature with appeals, until this christian people abjure forever a traffic in the souls of men, and the groans of the oppressed no longer ascend to God from the dust where they now welter.

We do not ask your honorable body to transcend your constitutional powers, by legislating on the subject of slavery within the boundaries of any slaveholding State; but we do conjure you to abolish slavery in the District of Columbia where you exercise exclusive jurisdiction. In the name of humanity, justice, equal rights and impartial law, our country's weal, her honor and her cherished hopes we earnestly implore for this our humble petition, your favorable regard. If both in christian and in heathen lands, Kings have revoked their edicts, at the intercession of woman, surely we may hope that the Legislators of a free, enlightened and christian people will lend their ear to our appeals, when the only boon we crave is the restoration of rights unjustly wrested from the innocent and defenceless.—And as in duty bound your petitioners will ever pray. (T.D.W. 1834)

| NAMES | NAMES |

. . . . .

6 In 1836, Martha Ball of the Boston Female Anti-Slavery Society wrote this letter to the Boston *Courier* in response to attacks on the society by antiabolitionists. As you read it, consider whether it was possible for women to acknowledge a separate female sphere and yet demand women's rights.

The Secretary of the Boston Female Anti-Slavery Society Responds to Critics (1836)

. . . The cause of human freedom is our religion; the same taught by him who died on Calvary,—the great reformer, Christ. In it we will live—in it, if it must be so, we will die. We feel for those that are in bonds as bound with them. God's truth does not become threadbare, as certain gentlemen of respectability have heretofore asserted; but is found fraught with deeper meaning, as the history of the present age unrolls. We sit by our firesides and muse over our sleeping infants—not in vain. The sight of their helpless childhood reminds us of the great debt we incurred when we brought them into existence.

We must meet together, to strengthen ourselves to discharge our duty as the mothers of the next generation—as the wives and sisters of this. We cannot descend to bandy words with those who have no just sense of their own duty or ours, who dread lest the delicacies of the table should be neglected, who glory in the darning-needle, and whose talk is of the distaff. This is a crisis which demands of us not only mint, and annise,* and cummin, but also judgment, mercy, and faith; and God being our helper, none of these shall be required in vain at our hands. Our sons shall not blush for those who bore them.

The strong expression of public sentiment against antislavery men and women, at Faneuil Hall, is gravely assigned as a reason why our sentiments should not be strongly expressed. We draw an inference directly contrary. Certainly our right to express sentiments, and to uphold principles, which are contrary to public opinion, is undoubted. We deny the right of gentlemen to use violence. But we are abolitionists, and, as such, are bound by our principles to endure, unresistingly, the outrages with which we are threatened. . . .

---

*Anise is an herb with aromatic seeds.
Source: Report of the Boston Female Anti-Slavery Society (Boston: Boston Female Anti-Slavery Society, 1836), pp. 25–26; reprinted in *Anti-slavery Records and Pamphlets* (Westport, Conn.: Negro Universities Press, 1970).

 7 Maria Weston Chapman was a founder of the Boston Female Anti-Slavery Society. She wrote this poem in response to a letter written by Congregational church leaders attacking Angelina and Sarah Grimké for speaking against slavery before a male audience. Compare its tone to that of Martha Ball's response to antiabolitionists in the previous source.

The Times That Try Men's Souls (1837)
MARIA WESTON CHAPMAN

Confusion has seized us, and all things go wrong,
    The women have leaped from "their spheres,"
And, instead of fixed stars, shoot as comets along,
    And are setting the world by the ears!
In courses erratic they're wheeling through space,
In brainless confusion and meaningless chase.

In vain do our knowing ones try to compute
    Their return to the orbit designed;
They're glanced at a moment, then onward they shoot,
    And are neither "to hold nor to bind";
So freely they move in their chosen ellipse,
The "Lords of Creation" do fear an eclipse.

They've taken a notion to speak for themselves,
    And are wielding the tongue and the pen;
They've mounted the rostrum; the termagant* elves,
    And—oh horrid!—are talking to men!
With faces unblanched in our presence they come
To harangue us, they say, in behalf of the dumb.

They insist on their right to petition and pray,
    That St. Paul, in Corinthians, has given them rules
For appearing in public; despite what those say
    Whom we've trained to instruct them in schools;
But vain such instructions, if women may scan
And quote texts of Scripture to favor their plan.

Our grandmothers' learning consisted of yore
    In spreading their generous boards;
In twisting the distaff, or mopping the floor,
    And *obeying the will of their lords.*

*A boisterous, scolding female.
Source: Elizabeth Cady Stanton, Susan B. Anthony, and Matilda Joslyn Gage, *History of Woman Suffrage* (New York: Fowler and Wells, 1881), I, 82–83.

Now, misses may reason, and think, and debate,
Till unquestioned submission is quite out of date.
. . . .

Oh! shade of the prophet Mahomet, arise!
    Place woman again in "her sphere,"
And teach that her soul was not born for the skies,
    But to flutter a brief moment here.
This doctrine of Jesus, as preached up by Paul,
If embraced in its spirit, will ruin us all.

8 Sojourner Truth was the child of slaves who traveled throughout the North speaking against slavery. She delivered this speech at the Woman's Rights Convention at Akron, Ohio. Suffragist Frances D. Gage recorded the speech and the crowd's response to it. What does it reveal about the relationship between abolitionism and women's rights? Does Sojourner Truth acknowledge a separate female sphere?

A'n't I a Woman? (1851)
SOJOURNER TRUTH

. . . I rose and announced "Sojourner Truth," and begged the audience to keep silence for a few moments. The tumult subsided at once, and every eye was fixed on this almost Amazon form, which stood nearly six feet high, head erect, and eye piercing the upper air, like one in a dream. At her first word, there was a profound hush. She spoke in deep tones, which, though not loud, reached every ear in the house, and away through the throng at the doors and windows:—

"Well, chilern, whar dar is so much racket dar must be something out o' kilter. I tink dat 'twixt de niggers of de Souf and de women at de Norf all a talkin' 'bout rights, de white men will be in a fix pretty soon. But what's all dis here talkin' 'bout? Dat man ober dar say dat women needs to be helped into carriages, and lifted ober ditches, and to have de best place every whar. Nobody eber help me into carriages, or ober mud puddles, or gives me any best place [and raising herself to her full hight and her voice to a pitch like rolling thunder, she askedl, and a'n't I a woman? Look at me! Look at my arm! [And she bared her right arm to the shoulder, showing her tremen-

Source: Elizabeth Cady Stanton, Susan B. Anthony, and Matilda Joslyn Gage, *History of Woman Suffrage* (New York: Fowler and Wells, 1881), I, 115–117.

dous muscular power.] I have plowed, and planted, and gathered into barns, and no man could head me—and a'n't I a woman? I could work as much and eat as much as a man (when I could get it), and bear de lash as well—and a'n't I a woman? I have borne thirteen chilern and seen 'em mos' all sold off into slavery, and when I cried out with a mother's grief, none but Jesus heard—and a'n't I a woman? Den dey talks 'bout dis ting in de head—what dis dey call it?" "Intellect," whispered some one near. "Dat's it honey. What's dat got to do with women's rights or niggers' rights? If my cup won't hold but a pint and yourn holds a quart, wouldn't ye be mean not to let me have my little half-measure full?" And she pointed her significant finger and sent a keen glance at the minister who had made the argument. The cheering was long and loud.

"Den dat little man in black dar, he say women can't have as much rights as man, cause Christ want a woman. Whar did your Christ come from?" Rolling thunder could not have stilled that crowd as did those deep, wonderful tones, as she stood there with outstretched arms and eye of fire. Raising her voice still louder, she repeated, "Whar did your Christ come from? From God and a woman. Man had nothing to do with him." Oh! what a rebuke she gave the little man.

Turning again to another objector, she took up the defense of mother Eve. I cannot follow her through it all. It was pointed, and witty, and solemn, eliciting at almost every sentence deafening applause; and she ended by asserting that "if de fust woman God ever made was strong enough to turn the world upside down, all 'lone, dese togedder [and she glanced her eye over us], ought to be able to turn it back and get it right side up again, and now dey is asking to do it, de men better let em." Long-continued cheering. "Bleeged to ye for hearin' on me, and now ole Sojourner ha'n't got nothing more to say."

CONCLUSION

In 1910, American Historical Association president Frederick Jackson Turner called upon historians to "rework our history from the new points of view afforded by the present."[6] In heeding Turner's call, historians bring constant change to even thoroughly researched fields like abolition. Two generations ago, many historians had written off the antislavery crusade as a fertile field for further study. As one scholar put it, many researchers believed abolitionism "had been plowed, planted, cultivated, and harvested so thoroughly that there was not much left to learn about it."[7] Yet as this chapter demonstrates, historians should not be too quick to declare their fields barren. Few historians a half century ago were likely to acknowledge the role female abolitionists played in the antislavery movement. They were even more unlikely to study abolitionism to understand the position of women in antebellum America. Today historians realize that these women participated in an important debate about the meaning of gender in the early nineteenth century. Recent studies of abolitionism are thus excellent examples of the way "new points of view afforded by the present" have resulted in an abundant harvest from a seemingly worn-out field. In the next chapter, we will turn to another well-worked plot that has lost none of its ability to produce an abundant crop of fresh historical insights—the Civil War.

FURTHER READING

Gerda Lerner, *The Grimké Sisters of South Carolina: Rebels Against Slavery* (Boston: Houghton Mifflin, 1967).

Alma Lutz, *Crusade for Freedom: Women in the Antislavery Movement* (Boston: Beacon Press, 1968).

Keith Melder, *The Beginnings of Sisterhood: The American Women's Rights Movement, 1800–1850* (New York: Schocken Books, 1977).

Carol Thompson, "Women in the Anti-Slavery Movement," *Current History,* 70 (May 1976).

Wendy Hamand Venet, *Neither Bullets nor Ballots: Women Abolitionists and the Civil War* (Charlottesville: University Press of Virginia, 1991).

NOTES

1. Alma Lutz, *Crusade for Freedom: Women of the Antislavery Movement* (Boston: Beacon Press, 1968), p. 57.
2. *Report of the Boston Female Anti-Slavery Society* (Boston: Boston Female Anti-Slavery Society, 1836), p. 34.
3. Quoted in Lutz, *Crusade for Freedom,* p. 71.
4. Gilbert Hobbs Barnes, *The Anti-Slavery Impulse 1830–1844* (New York: Harcourt, Brace and World, 1964), p. 160.
5. Aileen S. Kraditor, *Means and Ends in American Abolitionism: Garrison and His Critics on Strategy and Tactics, 1834–1850* (New York: Random House, 1967), p. 40.
6. Quoted in Barton J. Bernstein, ed., *Towards a New Past: Dissenting Essays in American History* (New York: Vintage Books, 1969), p. v.
7. Quoted in Kraditor, *Means and Ends,* p. vii.

CHAPTER | 12

GRAND THEORY, GREAT BATTLES, AND HISTORICAL CAUSES: WHY SECESSION FAILED

The documents in this chapter address the question of why the North won the Civil War.

Secondary Sources

Primary Sources

*O*n July 3, 1863, Confederate general Robert E. Lee decided to attack the very center of the Union position at Gettysburg. The Confederates opened fire with 150 cannons from Seminary Ridge. The Union Army responded with eighty guns. One Union general said the Confederate barrage was "the heaviest artillery fire" he had ever known.[1] Yet it only pounded open ground behind the Union troops. When the fire finally died down and the smoke cleared, the Union soldiers looked over the fields and saw the enemy forming battle lines. "My brave boys were full of hope and confident of victory as I led them forth," said Confederate General George Pickett. Pickett's division would spearhead the attack of 10,500 men against the Federal position on Cemetery Ridge. The Union soldiers waited for the assault. "Every eye could see the enemy's legion, an overwhelming resistless tide of an ocean of armed men sweeping upon us!"[2]

At seven hundred yards, the Union artillery opened fire with devastating effect. Canisters (tin cans packed with slugs that created huge shotgunlike blasts) decimated the Confederate ranks. Witnesses saw body parts, rifles, and knapsacks hurled into the air. At least one soldier heard "a vast mournful roar" rise from the battlefield.[3] Undaunted, Pickett's men continued up Cemetery Ridge. Then the Union infantry opened fire. The Confederates stopped, returned fire, and resumed their advance. For a few moments the Confederate battle flag waved over Cemetery Ridge as the Confederates and Federals fired at nearly point-blank range. Then more Union troops swarmed in and the Confederates fell back. Within moments the battle was lost.

When the fighting was over, one Union general tried to ride over the field, but could not guide his horse through the dead and wounded soldiers. Pickett's charge had left 5,675 Confederate casualties and nearly 800 more captured. After three days of fighting at Gettysburg, 23,000 Union and nearly 20,500 Confederate soldiers were dead, wounded, captured, or missing. Lee took full responsibility. "All this has been my fault," he told his men after the futile charge.[4] Then he retreated back to Virginia, never to launch another assault so far into Union territory. In less than two years, Lee handed his sword to Ulysses S. Grant at Appomattox. The day after he surrendered, the Confederate general offered this explanation: "After four years of arduous service marked by unsurpassed courage and fortitude, the Army of Northern Virginia has been compelled to yield to overwhelming numbers and resources."[5]

More than 130 years later, historians continue to debate the reasons for the Confederacy's defeat. They have found them on Cemetery Ridge and other bloody battlefields. They have also found them in important developments on the home fronts of the North and South. Like Robert E. Lee after Pickett's charge, some historians argue that individual battles and military decisions were crucial to the outcome of the war. Like Lee after Appomattox, however, other historians have found the key to the Union's triumph in economic and other differences between the North and South. Which of Lee's explanations for defeat was more accurate? In this chapter we consider the role of factors both on and off the battlefield in explaining the Civil War's outcome.

SETTING

Each side had advantages at the outset of the Civil War. The Union had a much larger population, a growing factory system, and a superior transportation network. But Southerners needed only to defend their own territory to win. Historians who point to the superiority of Northern resources in explaining the triumph of the Union emphasize the "modern" nature of the Civil War. What counts in such wars is the ability to mobilize the entire society for a protracted struggle. Thus these historians maintain that the Union victory had more to do with home front morale than battlefield maneuvers. Other researchers see political leaders as the decisive factor. They point to Lincoln's political skills and his administration's ability to forestall foreign intervention in the conflict. They also emphasize Jefferson Davis's limitations as a political leader and his administration's inability to mobilize Southern resources. Other scholars cite additional factors far from the battlefield to explain the outcome of the Civil War, from the North's superior agricultural system to large numbers of slaves and other Union sympathizers in the South.

In these debates, it is easy to forget that the preservation of the Union was hardly a foregone conclusion at the beginning of the war. Indeed, the first two years of the war saw few Union victories on Eastern battlefields. Thus some scholars explain the Union's early reverses and its eventual victory on men and events closer to the field of battle. They argue that military commanders, including the respective commanders-in-chief, were crucial to the outcome of the war. Many military historians argue that Confederate commanders were often better tacticians and generally more aggressive than their Union counterparts. Yet they also maintain that some Union generals demonstrated better strategic sense in adjusting to total war. These historians point to numerous reasons for the differences between Confederate and Union commanders. Some cite the impact on each group of the Swiss military strategist Antoine Henri Jomini, the most important writer on warfare in the early nineteenth century. Others have argued that the different way Union and Confederate generals fought was due to ethnic and cultural differences. One scholar has even suggested that each side's perceptions of the other's fighting abilities determined the way the generals fought.

Students of the Civil War can be forgiven if they conclude that there are as many explanations for the outcome of the war as there are Civil War historians. Yet as numerous as these explanations are, they revolve around two basic questions. Historians want to know if the North won the Civil War because of its inherent strengths or if the South lost the war because of its internal weaknesses. And they want to know whether it was military events or developments far from the battlefield that better explain the war's outcome. Historians' answers to the first question determine their conclusions about the Civil War. Their answers to the second question, as we shall see, reflect their assumptions about history itself.

INVESTIGATION

In this chapter, we compare two arguments about the outcome of the Civil War. One historian emphasizes the Union's tremendous advantages and attempts to relate them to a grand theory to account for the North's victory. The other points to military turning points as the crucial factor in the defeat of the South. As you read and think about the primary and secondary sources in this chapter, your main assignment is this: Explain why the Civil War turned out as it did. In your explanation you should assess the two historians' arguments regarding the war's outcome and determine which one is more plausible. To do that, you need to determine whether factors far from the battlefield most influenced the outcome of the war or whether it can be better explained by focusing on commanders, campaigns, and battles. To complete this assignment, you should address the following questions:

1. **Do the historians argue that the South lost the Civil War or that the North won it?** Do they argue that the North's advantages or the South's weaknesses were more important? What is their most important evidence to answer that question?

2. **Was the outcome of the Civil War inevitable because it was determined by the balance of resources on each side?** What do the authors conclude? What do the primary sources reveal about that question?

3. **Cite the best examples of how developments on the home front affected events on the battlefield and of the way people or events on the battlefield affected developments on the home front. What problems do historians face in attempting to establish these connections?**

Before you do this assignment, be sure to read the appropriate chapters in your textbook. They will give you valuable background and even suggest additional factors to consider. Pay attention to your textbook's reasons for the outcome of the war. When you are finished, you can compare its interpretation to those in this chapter's essays.

SECONDARY SOURCES

1

In this selection, historian George Fredrickson assesses a number of interpretations about the outcome of the Civil War that emphasize the North's advantages. He also builds his own case for the triumph of the Union, a kind of grand synthesis or theory. Note why Fredrickson thinks explanations that emphasize the North's advantages are flawed. Also consider his argument that Southern military leaders were rigid and conservative and how it relates to his overall theory about the reason for the Union's triumph. Does Fredrickson find the answer to the North's victory on the battlefield or on the home front? Does he make a connection between the way each side fought the war and the respective home fronts? Finally, what role does slavery play in his analysis?

Blue over Gray: Sources of Success and Failure in the Civil War (1975)

GEORGE M. FREDRICKSON

Historians have expended vast amounts of time, energy, and ingenuity searching for the causes and consequences of the Civil War. Much less effort has been devoted to explaining the outcome of the war itself. Yet the question is obviously important. One only has to imagine how radically different the future of North America would have been had the South won its permanent independence. It is also possible that a full comparison of how the two sides responded to the ultimate test of war will shed reflex light on both the background and legacy of the conflict. If northern success and southern failure can be traced to significant differences in the two societies as they existed on the eve of the war, then we may have further reason for locating the origins of the war in the clash of divergent social systems and ideologies. If the relative strengths of the North in wartime were rooted in the character of its society, then the sources of northern victory would foreshadow, to some extent at least, the postwar development of a nation reunited under northern hegemony.

A number of plausible explanations of "why the North won" have been advanced. The problem with most of them is not that they are wrong but that they are partial or incomplete. . . .

Perhaps the most widely accepted explanation of why the North won and the South lost derives from the time-honored proposition that God is on the

Source: Excerpted with permission of Burgess International Group, Inc. from *A Nation Divided: Problems and Issues of the Civil War and Reconstruction,* edited by George M. Fredrickson. © 1975 by Burgess Publishing.

side of the heaviest battalions. The North's advantages in manpower, resources, and industrial capacity were clearly overwhelming. According to the
census of 1860, the Union, not counting the contested border states of Missouri
and Kentucky, had a population of approximately 20,275,000. The Confederacy, on the other hand, had a white population of only about 5,500,000. If we
include the 3,654,000 blacks, the total population of the eleven Confederate
states adds up to slightly more than 9,000,000. Even if we consider the black
population an asset to the Confederacy in carrying on a war for the preservation of slavery, the North still ends up with a more than two-to-one advantage
in population. There was an even greater differential in readily available
manpower of military age; the northern advantage in this respect was well in
excess of three-to-one. In industrial capacity, the Union had an enormous edge.
In 1860, the North had approximately 110,000 manufacturing establishments
manned by about 1,300,000 workers, while the South had only 18,000 establishments with 110,000 workers. Thus for every southern industrial worker the
North had a factory or workshop! Finally, in railroad mileage, so crucial to the
logistics of the Civil War, the North possessed over seventy percent of the
nation's total of 31,256 miles.

With such a decisive edge in manpower, industrial plant, and transportation
facilities, how, it might well be asked, could the North possibly have lost? Yet
history shows many examples of the physically weaker side winning, especially in wars of national independence. The achievement of Dutch independence from Spain in the seventeenth century, the colonists' success in the
American Revolution, and many "wars of national liberation" in the twentieth
century, including the Algerian revolution and the long struggle for Vietnam-
ese self-determination, provide examples of how the physically weaker side
can prevail. . . .

Recognizing the insufficiency of a crude economic or demographic explanation, some historians have sought psychological reasons for the Confederate
defeat. It has been argued that the South "whipped itself" because it did not
believe strongly enough in its cause. While the North could allegedly call on
the full fervor of American nationalism and antislavery idealism, the South
was saddled with the morally dubious enterprise of defending slavery and
was engaged in breaking up a union of hallowed origin for which many
southerners still had a lingering reverence. It has even been suggested that
large numbers of loyal Confederates had a subconscious desire to lose the war.
The northern victory is therefore ascribed to the fact that the North had a better
cause and thus higher morale; the breakdown in the South's will to win is seen
as the consequence of a deep ambivalence about the validity of the whole
Confederate enterprise.

This thesis is highly speculative and not easily reconciled with the overall
pattern of pro-Confederate sentiment and activity. It would seem to underes-
timate or even to belittle the willingness of large numbers of southerners to
fight and die for the Confederacy. No northerner who fought the "Rebs" at

places such as Shiloh, Antietam, and Gettysburg would have concluded that the South really wanted to lose. . . .

On the surface at least, it seems harder to explain what made the northern cause so compelling. Contrary to antislavery mythology, there is little evidence to sustain the view that a genuinely humanitarian opposition to black servitude ever animated a majority of the northern population. Most northerners defined their cause as the preservation of the Union, not the emancipation of the slaves. This was made explicit in a joint resolution of Congress, passed overwhelmingly in July 1861, denying any federal intention to interfere with the domestic institutions of the southern states. . . . But when considered simply as a formal ideology, Unionism seems too abstract and remote from the concrete interests of ordinary people to have sustained . . . the enthusiasm necessary for such a long and bloody conflict. In any case, the *a priori* proposition that the North had a more compelling cause, and therefore one that was bound to generate higher morale, seems questionable.

Morale in both sections fluctuated in direct response to the fortunes of war. . . . Throughout the conflict, morale seems to have been more a function of military victory and success than a cause of it. Furthermore, any comparison involving the will to win of the respective sides cannot ignore the different situations that they faced. Except for Lee's brief forays into Maryland and Pennsylvania, the northern people never had to suffer from invasion of their own territory. Whether the North's allegedly superior morale and determination would have stood up under pressures equivalent to those experienced by the South will never be known. But we do know that the resolve of the North came dangerously close to breaking in the summer of 1864, at a time when its territory was secure, its economy booming, and its ultimate victory all but assured. At exactly the same time, the South was girding for another nine months of desperate struggle despite economic collapse and the loss of much of its territory. Such a comparison hardly supports the thesis that the North excelled the South in its will to win. . . .

Some have attributed the North's success in outlasting the South to its superior leadership. One distinguished historian has even suggested that if the North and South had exchanged Presidents the outcome of the war would have been reversed. As a wartime President, Lincoln was unquestionably superior to Davis. A master politician, Lincoln was able through a combination of tact and forcefulness to hold together the bitterly antagonistic factions of the Republican party. . . . But perhaps Lincoln's greatest successes came in his role as commander in chief of the armed forces. Although lacking military training and experience, he had a good instinctive grasp of broad strategic considerations. Furthermore, he knew that he had neither the time nor the tactical ability to take direct charge of military operations and wisely refrained from interfering directly with his generals except when their excessive caution or incompetence gave him no choice. Lincoln's primary objective was to find a general who had a comprehensive view of strategic needs, a willingness to fight, and consequently the ability to take full charge of military activity. In late 1863, he found the right man and without hesitation turned the entire military effort over to General Grant, who proceeded to fight the war to a successful conclusion. In innumerable ways, Lincoln gave evidence of his common sense, flexibility, and willingness to learn from experience. Although not the popular demigod he would become after his assassination, he did provide inspiration to the North as a whole. Many who had been critical of Lincoln at the start of the war, seeing him merely as a rough, inexperienced, frontier politician, came to recognize the quality of his statesmanship. Furthermore, his eloquence at Gettysburg and in the Second Inaugural helped to give meaning and resonance to the northern cause.

The leadership of Davis was of a very different caliber. The Confederate President was a proud, remote, and quarrelsome man with a fatal passion for always being in the right and for standing by his friends, no matter how incompetent or unpopular they turned out to be. He fought constantly with his cabinet and sometimes replaced good men who had offended him with second-raters who would not question his decisions. . . . Most southern newspapers were virulently anti-Davis by the end of the war. Particularly harmful was Davis' military role. Because he had commanded forces in the Mexican war and served as Secretary of War of the United States, he thought of himself as qualified to direct all phases of operations. This belief in his own military genius, combined with a constitutional inability to delegate authority, led to excessive interference with his generals and to some very questionable strategic decisions. Unlike Lincoln, he lost touch with the political situation, and he failed to provide leadership in the critical area of economic policy. In the end, one has a picture of Davis tinkering ineffectually with the South's military machine while a whole society was crumbling around him.

It appears the North had a great war leader, and the South a weak one. Can we therefore explain the outcome of the Civil War as an historical accident, a matter of northern luck in finding someone who could do the job and southern misfortune in picking the wrong man? Before we come to this beguilingly simple conclusion, we need to take a broader look at northern and southern leadership and raise the question of whether the kind of leadership a society produces is purely accidental. If Lincoln was a great leader of men, it was at least partly because he had good material to work with. Seward was in some ways a brilliant Secretary of State; Stanton directed the War Department with great determination and efficiency; and even Chase, despite his awkward political maneuvering, was on the whole a competent Secretary of the Treasury. . . . The North, it can be argued, had not simply one great leader but was able during the war to develop competent and efficient leadership on almost all levels. Such a pattern could hardly have been accidental; more likely it reveals something about the capacity of northern society to produce men of talent and initiative who could deal with the unprecedented problems of a total war.

In the Confederacy, the situation was quite different. Among the South's generals there of course were some brilliant tactical commanders. Their successes on the battlefield were instrumental in keeping the Confederacy afloat for four years. But, in almost all other areas, the South revealed a sad lack of capable leadership. . . .

The contrast in leadership, therefore, would seem to reflect some deeper differences of a kind that would make one section more responsive than the other to the practical demands of fighting a large-scale war. Since both societies faced unprecedented challenges, success would depend to a great extent on which side had the greater ability to adjust to new situations. . . .

Lincoln himself set the pattern for precedent-breaking innovation. Whenever he felt obligated to assume extra-constitutional powers to deal with situations unforeseen by the Constitution, he did so with little hesitation. After the outbreak of the war and before Congress was in session to sanction his actions, he expanded the regular army, advanced public money to private individuals, and declared martial law on a line from Washington to Philadelphia. On September 24, 1862, again without Congressional authorization, he extended the jurisdiction of martial law and suspended the writ of habeas corpus in all cases of alleged disloyalty. The Emancipation Proclamation can also be seen as an example of extra-constitutional innovation. Acting under the amorphous concept of "the war powers" of the President, Lincoln struck at slavery primarily because "military necessity" dictated new measures to disrupt the economic and social system of the enemy. . . .

The spirit of innovation was manifested in other areas as well. In Grant and Sherman the North finally found generals who grasped the nature of modern war and were ready to jettison outworn rules of strategy and tactics. . . . In his march from Atlanta to the sea in the fall of 1864, Sherman introduced for the first time the modern strategy of striking directly at the enemy's domestic economy. The coordinated, multipronged offensive launched by Grant in 1864, of which Sherman's march was a critical component, was probably the biggest, boldest, and most complex military operation mounted anywhere before the twentieth century. Grant, like Lincoln, can be seen as embodying the North's capacity for organization and innovation. . . .

Businessmen also responded to the crisis and found that what was patriotic could also be highly profitable. There were the inevitable frauds perpetrated on the government by contractors, but more significant was the overall success of the industrial system in producing the goods required. . . . No small part of this success was due to the willingness of businessmen, farmers, and government procurement officials to "think and act anew" by organizing themselves into larger and more efficient units for the production, transportation, and allocation of goods.

It would be an understatement to say that the South demonstrated less capacity than the North for organization and innovation. In fact, the South's most glaring failures were precisely in the area of coordination and collective adaptation to new conditions. The Confederacy did of course manage to put an army in the field that was able to hold the North at bay for four years. . . . [But] Southern successes on the battlefield were in no real sense triumphs of organization or innovation. Before the rise of Grant and Sherman, most Civil War battles were fought according to the outdated tactical principles that generals on both sides had learned at West Point. In these very conventional battles, the South had the advantage because it had the most intelligent and experienced of the West Pointers. Since everyone played by the same rules, it was inevitable that those who could play the game best would win. When the rules were changed by Grant and Sherman, the essential conservatism and rigidity of southern military leadership became apparent.

Besides being conventional in their tactics, southern armies were notoriously undisciplined; insubordination was an everyday occurrence and desertion eventually became a crippling problem. There were so many men absent without leave by August 1, 1863, that a general amnesty for deserters had to be declared. For full effectiveness, southern soldiers had to be commanded by generals such as Robert E. Lee and Stonewall Jackson, charismatic leaders who could command the personal loyalty and respect of their men. The idea of obeying an officer simply because of his rank went against the southern grain.

Although the army suffered from the excessive individualism of its men and the narrow traditionalism of its officers, these defects were not fatal until very late in the war, mainly because it took the North such a long time to apply its characteristic talent for organization and innovation directly to military operations. But on the southern home front similar attitudes had disastrous consequences almost from the beginning. In its efforts to mobilize the men and resources of the South, the Confederate government was constantly hamstrung by particularistic resistance to central direction and by a general reluctance to give up traditional ideas and practices incompatible with the necessities of war.

Particularism was manifested most obviously in the refusal of state governments to respond to the needs of the Confederacy. The central government was rudely rebuffed when it sought in 1861 to get the states to give up control over the large quantity of arms in their possession. The states held back for their own defense most of the 350,000 small arms that they held. The Confederacy, initially able to muster only 190,000 weapons, was forced to turn down 200,000 volunteers in the first year of the war because it could not arm them. The states also held back men. . . .

. . . [T]he slaveholding planters, taken as a group, were no more able to rise above narrow and selfish concerns than other segments of southern society. Because of their influence, the Confederacy was unable to adopt a sound financial policy; land and slaves, the main resources of the South, remained immune from direct taxes. As a result, the government was only able to raise about one percent of its revenue from taxation; the rest came from loans and the printing of vast quantities of fiat paper money. The inevitable consequence was the catastrophic runaway inflation that made Confederate money almost worthless even before the government went out of existence. . . .

. . . What was there about the culture and social structure of the North that made possible the kinds of organizational initiatives and daring innovations that have been described? What was there about southern society and culture that explains the lack of cohesiveness and adaptability that doomed the Confederacy? Answers to such questions require some further understanding of the differences in northern and southern society on the eve of the war, especially as these differences related to war-making potential.

A fuller comprehension of what social strengths and weaknesses the two sides brought to the conflict can perhaps be gained by borrowing a well-known concept from the social sciences—the idea of modernization. Sociologists and political scientists often employ this term to describe the interrelated changes that occur when a whole society begins to move away from a traditional agrarian pattern toward an urban-industrial system. . . .

[One] theorist has provided a simple rule of thumb to gauge the extent of modernization in various societies: the higher the proportion of energy derived from inanimate sources, as opposed to the direct application of human and animal strength, the more modernized the society. Modernization therefore has its intellectual foundations in a rationalistic or scientific world view and a commitment to technological development. . . .

By any definition of this process, the North was relatively more modernized than the South in 1861. To apply one of the most important indices of modernization, thirty-six percent of the Northern population was already urban as compared to the South's nine and six-tenths percent. As we have already seen, there was an even greater gap in the extent of industrialization. Furthermore, the foundations had been laid in the northern states for a rapid increase in the pace of modernization. The antebellum "transportation revolution" had set the stage for economic integration on a national scale, and the quickening pace of industrial development foreshadowed the massive and diversified growth of the future. Because of better and cheaper transportation, new markets, and a rise in efficiency and mechanization, midwestern agriculture was in a position to begin playing its modern role as the food-producing adjunct to an urban-industrial society. Literacy was widespread and means of mass communication, such as inexpensively produced newspapers, pamphlets, and books, were available for mobilizing public opinion. . . . In short, given the necessary stimulus and opportunity, the North was ready for a "great leap forward" in the modernization process.

The South, on the other hand, had little potentiality for rapid modernization. Overwhelmingly agricultural and tied to the slave plantation as its basic unit of production, it had many of the characteristics of what today would be called "an underdeveloped society." Like such societies, the Old South had what amounted to a "dual economy": a small modern or capitalistic sector, profitably producing cotton and other commodities for export, coexisted with a vast "traditional" sector, composed of white subsistence farmers and black slaves. . . .

. . . The two main segments of the white South were united neither by a sense of common economic interests nor by a complete identity of social and political values. But the presence of millions of black slaves did make possible a perverse kind of solidarity. Fear of blacks, and more specifically of black emancipation, was the principal force holding the white South together. Without it, there could have been no broadly based struggle for independence.

The planter and the non-slaveholding farmer had one other characteristic in common besides racism; in their differing ways, they were both extreme individualists. The planter's individualism came mainly from a lifetime of commanding slaves on isolated plantations. Used to unquestioned authority in all things and prone to think of himself as an aristocrat, he commonly exhibited an indomitable sense of personal independence. The non-slaveholder, on the other hand, was basically a backwoodsman who combined the stiff-necked individualism of the frontier with the arrogance of race that provided him with an exaggerated sense of his personal worth. Southern whites in general therefore were conditioned by slavery, racism, and rural isolation to condone and even encourage quasi-anarchic patterns of behavior that could not have been tolerated in a more modernized society with a greater need for social cohesion and discipline. . . .

Such an attitude was obviously incompatible with the needs of a modernizing society for cooperation and collective innovation. Furthermore, the divorce of status from achievement made it less likely that competent leaders and organizers would emerge. Particularism, localism, and extreme individualism were the natural outgrowth of the South's economic and social system. So was resistance to any changes that posed a threat to slavery and racial domination. . . .

. . . [S]outhern politics, despite its high level of popular involvement, remained largely the disorganized competition of individual office seekers. Those who won elections usually did so either because they were already men of weight in their communities or because they came off better than their rivals in face-to-face contact with predominantly rural voters. In the North by 1861, politics was less a matter of personalities and more an impersonal struggle of well-organized parties. In urban areas, the rudiments of the modern political machine could already be perceived.

The fact that the South was economically, socially, and politically less "developed" or modernized than the North in 1861 may not by itself fully explain why war had to come, but it does provide a key to understanding why the war had to turn out the way it did. . . .

As it was, the only course open to southern leaders during the war was in effect a crash program of modernization in an attempt to neutralize the immense advantages of the North. When we consider the cultural heritage and economic resources they had to work with, their achievements went beyond what might have been expected. But the South had far too much ground to make up, and persisting rigidities, especially as manifested in the die-hard commitment to localism, racism, and plantation slavery, constituted fatal checks on the modernizing impulse.

The North, on the other hand, not only capitalized on its initial advantages during the war but was able to multiply them. In fact, the conflict itself served as a catalyst for rapid development in many areas. Modernizing trends that had begun in the prewar period came to unexpectedly rapid fruition in a way that both compounded the North's advantage in the conflict and helped set the pattern for postwar America.

> **2** | The preceding essay examines differences between Northern and Southern society. In the following selection, historian James McPherson focuses on the military turning points. Note how he attempts to disprove other interpretations about the war's outcome. Also pay particular attention to how he tries to demonstrate that individual battles affected the will to fight. What would George Fredrickson, the author of the previous selection, have said about the reasons for the outcome of crucial Civil War turning points?

Why the North Won (1988)

JAMES M. McPHERSON

. . . [A] persistent question has nagged historians and mythologists alike: if . . . Robert [E. Lee] was such a genius and his legions so invincible, why did they lose? The answers, though almost as legion as Lee's soldiers, tend to group

Source: From *Battle Cry of Freedom: The Civil War Era* by James M. McPherson. Copyright © 1988 by James M. McPherson. Used by permission of Oxford University Press.

themselves into a few main categories. One popular answer has been phrased, from the northern perspective, by quoting Napoleon's aphorism that God was on the side of the heaviest battalions. For southerners this explanation usually took some such form as these words of a Virginian: "They never whipped us, Sir, unless they were four to one. If we had had anything like a fair chance, or less disparity of numbers, we should have won our cause and established our independence." The North had a potential manpower superiority of more than three to one (counting only white men) and Union armed forces had an actual superiority of two to one during most of the war. In economic resources and logistical capacity the northern advantage was even greater. Thus, in this explanation, the Confederacy fought against overwhelming odds; its defeat was inevitable.

But this explanation has not satisfied a good many analysts. History is replete with examples of peoples who have won or defended their independence against greater odds: the Netherlands against the Spain of Philip II; Switzerland against the Hapsburg Empire; the American rebels of 1776 against mighty Britain; North Vietnam against the United States of 1970. Given the advantages of fighting on the defensive in its own territory with interior lines in which stalemate would be victory against a foe who must invade, conquer, occupy, and destroy the capacity to resist, the odds faced by the South were not formidable. Rather, as another category of interpretations has it, internal divisions fatally weakened the Confederacy: the state-rights conflict between certain governors and the Richmond government; the disaffection of non-slaveholders from a rich man's war and poor man's fight; libertarian opposition to necessary measures such as conscription and the suspension of habeas corpus; the lukewarm commitment to the Confederacy by quondam* Whigs and unionists; the disloyalty of slaves who defected to the enemy whenever they had a chance; growing doubts among slaveowners themselves about the justice of their peculiar institution and their cause. "So the Confederacy succumbed to internal rather than external causes," according to numerous historians. The South suffered from a "weakness in morale," a "loss of the will to fight." The Confederacy did not lack "the means to continue the struggle," but "the will to do so." . . .

In any case the "internal division" and "lack of will" explanations for Confederate defeat, while not implausible, are not very convincing either. The problem is that the North experienced similar internal divisions, and if the war had come out differently the Yankees' lack of unity and will to win could be cited with equal plausibility to explain that outcome. . . .

Nevertheless the existence of internal divisions on both sides seemed to neutralize this factor as an explanation for Union victory, so a number of

*Former.

historians have looked instead at the quality of leadership both military and civilian. There are several variants of an interpretation that emphasizes a gradual development of superior northern leadership. In Beauregard, Lee, the two Johnstons [Albert Sidney and Joseph Eggleston], and [Stonewall] Jackson the South enjoyed abler military commanders during the first year or two of the war, while Jefferson Davis was better qualified by training and experience than Lincoln to lead a nation at war. But Lee's strategic vision was limited to the Virginia theater, and the Confederate government neglected the West, where Union armies developed a strategic design and the generals to carry it out, while southern forces floundered under incompetent commanders who lost the war in the West. By 1863, Lincoln's remarkable abilities gave him a wide edge over Davis as a war leader, while in Grant and Sherman the North acquired commanders with a concept of total war and the necessary determination to make it succeed. At the same time, in [Secretary of War] Edwin M. Stanton and [Quartermaster General] Montgomery Meigs, aided by the entrepreneurial talent of northern businessmen, the Union developed superior managerial talent to mobilize and organize the North's greater resources for victory in the modern industrialized conflict that the Civil War became.

This interpretation comes closer than others to credibility. Yet it also commits the fallacy of reversibility—that is, if the outcome had been reversed some of the same factors could be cited to explain Confederate victory. . . .

Most attempts to explain southern defeat or northern victory lack the dimension of *contingency*—the recognition that at numerous critical points during the war things might have gone altogether differently. Four major turning points defined the eventual outcome. The first came in the summer of 1862, when the counter-offensives of Jackson and Lee in Virginia and Bragg and Kirby Smith in the West arrested the momentum of a seemingly imminent Union victory. This assured a prolongation and intensification of the conflict and created the potential for Confederate success, which appeared imminent before each of the next three turning points.

The first of these occurred in the fall of 1862, when battles at Antietam and Perryville threw back Confederate invasions, forestalled European mediation and recognition of the Confederacy, perhaps prevented a Democratic victory in the northern elections of 1862 that might have inhibited the government's ability to carry on the war, and set the stage for the Emancipation Proclamation which enlarged the scope and purpose of the conflict. The third critical point came in the summer and fall of 1863 when [Union victories at] Gettysburg, Vicksburg, and Chattanooga turned the tide toward ultimate northern victory.

One more reversal of that tide seemed possible in the summer of 1864 when appalling Union casualties and apparent lack of progress especially in Virginia brought the North to the brink of peace negotiations and the election of a

Democratic president. But [Sherman's] capture of Atlanta and Sheridan's destruction of Early's [rebel] army in the Shenandoah Valley clinched matters for the North. Only then did it become possible to speak of the inevitability of Union victory. Only then did the South experience an irretrievable "loss of the will to fight."

Of all the explanations for Confederate defeat, the loss of will thesis suffers most from its own particular fallacy of reversibility—that of putting the cart before the horse. Defeat causes demoralization and loss of will; victory pumps up morale and the will to win. Nothing illustrates this better than the radical transformation of *northern* will from defeatism in August 1864 to a "depth of determination . . . to fight to the last" that "astonished" a British journalist a month later. The southern loss of will was a mirror image of this northern determination. These changes of mood were caused mainly by events on the battlefield. Northern victory and southern defeat in the war cannot be understood apart from the contingency that hung over every campaign, every battle, every election, every decision during the war.

PRIMARY SOURCES

Northern and Southern Society

Even before the Civil War, many commentators saw differences between the North and South. Note the differences that these observers saw between the two regions. How could they have translated into advantages or disadvantages on the battlefield?

 | Helper was a white, nonslaveholding Southerner who hoped the South would throw off the peculiar institution.

The Impending Crisis (1857)
HINTON ROWAN HELPER

And now to the point. In our opinion, an opinion which has been formed from data obtained by assiduous researches, and comparisons, from laborious

Source: Hinton Rowan Helper, *The Impending Crisis of the South* (Cambridge: The Belknap Press of Harvard University Press; originally published, 1857), pp. 25, 60–61.

investigation, logical reasoning, and earnest reflection, the causes which have impeded the progress and prosperity of the South, which have dwindled our commerce, and other similar pursuits, into the most contemptible insignificance; sunk a large majority of our people in galling poverty and ignorance, rendered a small minority conceited and tyrannical, and driven the rest away from their homes; entailed upon us a humiliating dependence on the Free States; disgraced us in the recesses of our own souls, and brought us under reproach in the eyes of all civilized and enlightened nations—may all be traced to one common source, and there find solution in the most hateful and horrible word, that was ever incorporated into the vocabulary of human economy— *Slavery!* . . .

. . . To undeceive the people of the South, to bring them to a knowledge of the inferior and disreputable position which they occupy as a component part of the Union, and to give prominence and popularity to those plans which, if adopted, will elevate us to an equality, socially, morally, intellectually, industrially, politically, and financially, with the most flourishing and refined nation in the world, and, if possible, to place us in the van of even that, is the object of this work. Slaveholders, either from ignorance or from a wilful disposition to propagate error, contend that the South has nothing to be ashamed of, that slavery has proved a blessing to her, and that her superiority over the North in an agricultural point of view makes amends for all her shortcomings in other respects. On the other hand, we contend that many years of continual blushing and severe penance would not suffice to cancel or annul the shame and disgrace that justly attaches to the South in consequence of slavery—the direst evil that e'er befell the land—that the South bears nothing like even a respectable approximation to the North in navigation, commerce, or manufactures, and that, contrary to the opinion entertained by ninety-nine hundredths of her people, she is far behind the free States in the only thing of which she has ever dared to boast—agriculture. We submit the question to the arbitration of figures, which, it is said, do not lie. With regard to the bushel-measure products of the soil, of which we have already taken an inventory, we have seen that there is a balance against the South in favor of the North of *seventeen million four hundred and twenty-three thousand one hundred and fifty-two bushels,* and a difference in the value of the same, also in favor of the North, of *forty-four million seven hundred and eighty-two thousand six hundred and thirty-six dollars.* It is certainly a most novel kind of agricultural superiority that the South claims on that score!

4   Olmsted, a Northern journalist and, later, urban landscape planner, traveled widely in the South in the 1850s.

The Cotton Kingdom (1861)

FREDERICK LAW OLMSTED

The whole number of slaveholders of this large class in all the Slave States is, according to De Bow's Compendium of the Census, 7,929, among which are all the great sugar, rice, and tobacco-planters. Less than seven thousand, certainly, are cotton-planters.

A large majority of these live, when they live on their plantations at all, in districts, almost the only white population of which consists of owners and overseers of the same class of plantations with their own. The nearest other whites will be some sand-hill vagabonds, generally miles away, between whom and these planters, intercourse is neither intimate nor friendly.

It is hardly worth while to build much of a bridge for the occasional use of two families, even if they are rich. It is less worth while to go to much pains in making six miles of good road for the use of these families. . . . It is not necessary to multiply illustrations like these. In short, then, if all the wealth produced in a certain district is concentrated in the hands of a few men living remote from each other, it may possibly bring to the district comfortable houses, good servants, fine wines, food, and furniture, tutors, and governesses, horses and carriages, for these few men, but it will not bring thither good roads and bridges, it will not bring thither such means of education and of civilized comfort as are to be drawn from libraries, churches, museums, gardens, theatres, and assembly rooms; it will not bring thither local newspapers, telegraphs, and so on. . . . There is, in fact, a vast range of advantages which our civilization has made so common to us that they are hardly thought of, of which the people of the South are destitute. They chiefly come from or connect with acts of co-operation, or exchanges of service; they are therefore possessed only in communities, and in communities where a large proportion of the people have profitable employment. They grow, in fact, out of employments in which the people of the community are associated, or which they constantly give to and receive from one another, with profit. The slaves of the South, though often living in communities upon plantations, fail to give or receive these advantages because the profits of their labour are not distributed to them; the whites, from not engaging in profitable employment. The whites are not engaged in profitable employment, because the want of the advantages of capital in the application of their labour, independently of the already rich, renders the prospective result of their labour so small that it is inoperative in most, as a motive for exerting themselves further than is necessary to procure the bare means of a rude subsistence; also because common labour is so poorly

Source: Frederick Law Olmsted, *The Slave States* (New York: Capricorn Books, 1959), pp. 249–250.

rewarded in the case of the slaves as to assume in their minds, as it must in the minds of the slaves themselves, a hateful aspect.

 5 | Numerous eyewitnesses, including journalists and those serving in the Union and Confederate forces, recorded the struggles on the battlefield of Gettysburg. Franklin Haskell, an officer in the Army of the Potomac, wrote one such account several weeks after the battle. What does this selection reveal about the factors determining the outcome of these battles? Could Gettysburg have easily turned out differently?

An Account of the Battle of Gettysburg (1863)
FRANKLIN A. HASKELL

Now came the dreadful battle picture, of which we for a time could be but spectators. Upon the front and right flank of [Union general] Sickles came sweeping the infantry of [Confederate generals] Longstreet and Hill. Hitherto there had been skirmishing and artillery practice—now the battle begins; for amid the heavier smokes and longer tongues of flame of the batteries, now began to appear the countless flashes, and the long, fiery sheets of the muskets, and the rattle of the volleys mingled with the thunder of the guns. We see the long gray lines come sweeping down upon Sickles' front, and mix with the battle smoke; now the same colors emerge from the bushes and orchards upon his right, and envelop his flank in the confusion of the conflict. Oh, the din and the roar, and these thirty thousand rebel wolf-cries! What a hell is there down that valley!

These ten or twelve thousand men of the Third Corps fight well, but it soon becomes apparent that they must be swept from the field, or perish there where they are doing so well, so thick and overwhelming a storm of rebel fire involves them. But these men, such as ever escape, must come from that conflict as best they can. To move down and support them there with other troops is out of the question, for this would be to do as Sickles did, to relinquish a good position, and advance to a bad one. There is no other alternative,—the Third Corps must fight itself out of its position of destruction! Why was it ever put there?

In the meantime some other dispositions must be made to meet the enemy, in the event that Sickles is overpowered. With this corps out of the way, the enemy would be in a position to advance upon the line of the Second Corps, not in a line parallel with its front, but they would come obliquely from the

Source: Harry A. Hagen and S. Lewis B. Speare, *A History of the Class of 1854 in Dartmouth College* (Boston: Alfred Mudge and Son, 1898).

left. To meet this contingency the left of the Second Division of the Second Corps is thrown back slightly, and two regiments . . . are advanced down to the Emmitsburg road, to a favorable position nearer us than the fight has yet come, and some new batteries from the artillery reserve are posted upon the crest near the left of the Second Corps. This was all General Gibbon could do. Other dispositions were made, or were now being made, upon the field, which I shall mention presently.

The enemy is still giving Sickles fierce battle,—or rather the Third Corps, for Sickles has been borne from the field minus one of his legs, and General Birney how commands,—and we of the Second Corps, a thousand yards away, with our guns and men, are, and must be, idle spectators of the fight. The rebel, as anticipated, tries to gain the left of the Third Corps, and for this purpose is now moving into the woods at the west of Round Top. We knew what he would find there. No sooner had the enemy got a considerable force into the woods . . . than the roar of the conflict was heard there also. The Fifth Corps and the First Division of the Second were there at the right time, and promptly engaged him; and then, too, the battle soon became general and obstinate.

Now the roar of battle has become twice the volume that it was before, and it's [sic] rage extends over more than twice the space. The Third Corps has been pressed back considerably, and the wounded are streaming to the rear by hundreds, but still the battle there goes on, with no considerable abatement on our part. . . .

. . . [F]resh bodies of the rebels continued to advance out of the woods to the front of the position of the Third Corps, and to swell the numbers of the assailants of this already hard pressed command. The men there begin to show signs of exhaustion,—their ammunition must be nearly expended,— they have now been fighting more than an hour, and against greatly superior numbers. . . .

. . . The Third Corps is being overpowered—here and there its lines begin to break,—the men begin to pour back to the rear in confusion,—the enemy are close upon them and among them,—organization is lost, to a great degree,—guns and caissons are abandoned and in the hands of the enemy,—the Third Corps, after a heroic, but unfortunate fight, is being literally swept from the field. That corps gone, what is there between the Second Corps and those yelling masses of the enemy? Do you not think that by this time we began to feel a personal interest in this fight? We did, indeed. . . .

. . . Five or six hundred yards away the Third Corps was making its last opposition; and the enemy was hotly pressing his advantage there, and throwing in fresh troops whose line extended still more along our front, when Generals Hancock and Gibbon rode along the lines of their troops; and at once cheer after cheer—not rebel mongrel cries, but genuine cheers—rang out along the line, above the roar of battle, for "Hancock" and "Gibbon," and our "Generals." These were good. Had you heard their voices, you would have known these men would fight.

Just at this time we saw another thing that made us glad: we looked to our rear, and there, and all up the hillside, which was the rear of the Third Corps before it went forward, were rapidly advancing large bodies of men from the extreme right of our line of battle, coming to the support of the part now so hotly pressed. There was the whole Twelfth Corps, with the exception of about one brigade . . . and some other brigades from the same corps; and some of them were moving at the double quick. They formed lines of battle at the foot of the hill by the Taneytown road, and when the broken fragments of the Third Corps were swarming by them towards the rear, without haltering or wavering they came swiftly up, and with glorious old cheers, under fire, took their places on the crest in line of battle to the left of the Second Corps. Now Sickles' blunder is repaired. Now, rebel chief, hurl forward your howling lines and columns! Yell out your loudest and your last, for many of your host will never yell, or wave the spurious flag again!

 6 In this letter, Grant reported to the secretary of war the completion of his military assignment. What does Grant reveal about the reasons for the war's outcome?

General Ulysses S. Grant to Edwin M. Stanton (1865)

Washington D.C.
June 20th 1865

Hon. E. M. STANTON
SEC. OF WAR,

SIR:

I have the honor, very respectfully, to submit the following report of operations of the Armies of the United States, from the 9th of March 1864, the date when the command was entrusted to me, to present date. Accompanying this will also be found all reports of commanders, subordinate to me, received at these Head Quarters. To these latter I refer you for all minor details of operations and battles.

From early in the War I had been impressed with the idea that active, and continuous operations of all the troops that could be brought into the field, regardless of season and weather, were necessary to a speedy termination of the gigantic rebellion raging in the land. The resources of the enemy, and his

Source: John Y. Simon, ed., *The Papers of Ulysses S. Grant* (Carbondale: Southern Illinois University Press, 1988), XV: pp. 164–166.

numerical strength, was far inferior to ours. But as an ofset to this we had a vast territory, with a population hostile to the government, to garrison, and long lines of river and rail-road communication, tr[thr]ough territory equally hostile, to protect to secure in order that the more active Armies might be supplied.—Whilst Eastern and Western Armies were fighting independent battles, working together like a balky team where no two ever pulled together, giving Summers and Winters to almost entire inactivity, thus enabling the enemy to use to great advantage his his interior lines of communication for transporting portion of his Armies from one theatre of War to an other, and to furlough large numbers of the Armyies during these seasons of inactivity to go to their home and do the work of producing for the suport of these Armies, it was a question whether our numerical strength was not more than balanced by these [dis]advantages.

My opinion was firmly fixed long before the honor of commanding all our Armies had been confered on me that no peace could be had that would be stable, or conducive to the happiness of North or South, until the Military power of the rebellion was entirely broken. Believing us to be one people, one blood and with identical interests, I do and have felt the same interest in the welfa ultimate welfare of the South as of the North. The guilty, no matter what their offence or to what section they belong, should be punished according to their guilt. The leaders in this rebellion against the Government have been guilty of the most heinous offence known to our laws. Let them reap the reward of their offence.

Here then is the basis of all plans formed at the onset. 1st First to use the greatest number of troops practicable against the Armed force of the enemy. To prevent that enemy from using the same force, at different seasons, against first one Army and then another, and to prevent the possibility of repose for refitting and producing the necessary supplies for carrying on resistance. Second; to hammer continuously at the Armed force of the enemy, and his resources, until by mere attricion, if in no other way, there should be nothing left to him but an equal submission with the loyal section of our common country to the universal law of the land. These views have been kept constantly before me and orders given and campaigns made to carry them out. How well it has been done it is for the public, who have to mourn the loss of friends who have fallen in the execution, and to pay the expense pecuniary cost of all this, to say. All I can say is the work has been done conscienciously and to the best of my ability. It has been done in what I concieved to be the interest of the whole country, South and North. . . .

Blacks and the Civil War

During the Civil War nearly 180,000 blacks served in the Union army and navy. An estimated 500,000 to 700,000 slaves found refuge with Union forces. As you read the following sources, note what they reveal about the role blacks played in the defeat of the Confederacy.

7 | Affidavit of a Tennessee Freedman (1865)

My name is Makey Woods. I am 43 years old. I have lived with Mr. William Woods, of Hardaman County, Tennessee for about twenty years. I was his slave, about three years ago when the Union Army was in possession of Bolivar Tenn, and when nearly all the Black people were leaving their Masters and going to the Union Army Mr. Woods told me and such others as would stay with him that he would give us *one fourth* of the crop that we would raise while we stayed with him that he would clothe us and feed us and pay our doctor's bills. Since which time Mr. Wood has given *me* nothing but my clothing: about that time and soon after he made this statement to us he ran off down South into the Rebel lines *fourteen of his slaves* among whom were three of my children, Mr. Woods is now living in Memphis and refus to perform his contract or fulfil his promises to me in any respect, and when I spoke to him a few days ago about carrying out his contract he told me that he was sorry he made such a bargain with us:

There has been raised on Mr. Woods' place this year 48 bales of Cotton most of which Mr. Wood has taken to Memphis last year there were 26 bales raised which Mr. Wood sold I do not know exactly how many black people on Mr. Woods' place at present. Mr. Woods told us that any little patches we might cultivate at odd hours he would not take into the count but would let us have it besides the ¼ of the regular crop.

Source: Paul D. Escott and David R. Goldfield, eds., *Major Problems in the History of the American South* (Lexington, Mass.: D. C. Heath and Co., 1990), I, 525.

8 | Reverend Garrison Frazier on the Aspirations of His Fellow Blacks (1865)

Minutes of an interview between the colored ministers and church officers at Savannah with the Secretary of War and Major-General Sherman.

Source: Paul D. Escott and David R. Goldfield, eds., *Major Problems in the History of the American South* (Lexington, Mass.: D. C. Heath and Co., 1990), I, 525–527.

On the evening of Thursday, the 12th day of January, 1865, [twenty] persons of African descent met, by appointment, to hold an interview with Edwin M. Stanton, Secretary of War, and Major-General Sherman, to have a conference upon matters relating to the Freedmen of the State of Georgia. . . .

Garrison Frazier, being chosen by the persons present to express their common sentiments upon the matters of inquiry, makes answers to inquiries as follows:—

First. State what your understanding is in regard to the Acts of Congress, and President's [sic] Lincoln's Proclamation, touching the condition of the colored people in the rebel States.

Answer. So far as I understand President Lincoln's Proclamation to the rebellious States, it is, th[at] if they would lay down their arms and submit to the laws of the United States before the 1st of January, 1863, all should be well, but if they did not, then all the slaves in the rebel States should be free, henceforth and forever; that is what I understood.

Second. State what you understand by slavery, and the freedom that was to be given by the President's Proclamation.

Answer. Slavery is receiving by irresistible power the work of another man, and not by his consent. The freedom, as I understand it, promised by the Proclamation, is taking us from under the yoke of bondage, and placing us where we could reap the fruit of our own labor, and take care of ourselves, and assist the Government in maintaining our freedom.

Third. State in what manner you think you can take care of yourselves, and how you can best assist the Government in maintaining your freedom.

Answer. The way we can best take care of ourselves is to have land, and turn in and till it by our labor—that is, by the labor of the women, and children, and old men—and we can soon maintain ourselves, and have something to spare; and to assist the Government, the young men should enlist in the service of the Government, and serve in such manner as they may be wanted—(the rebels told us that they piled them up, and made batteries of them, and sold them to Cuba; but we don't believe that.) We want to be placed on land until we are able to buy it, and make it our own. . . .

Sixth. State what is the feeling of the black population of the South towards the Government of the United States; what is the understanding in respect to the present war, its causes and object, and their disposition to aid either side; state fully your views.

Answer. I think you will find there is thousands that are willing to make any sacrifice to assist the Government of the United States, while there is also many that are not willing to take up arms. I do not suppose there is a dozen men that is opposed to the Government. I understand, as to the war, that the South is the aggressor. President Lincoln was elected President by a majority of the United States, which guaranteed him the right of holding the office, and exercising that right over the whole United States. The South, without knowing what he would do, rebelled. The war was commenced by the rebels before he came into office. The object of the war was not, at first, to give the slaves their freedom, but the sole object of the war was, at first, to bring the rebellious States back into the Union, and their loyalty to the laws of the United States. Afterwards, knowing the value that was set on the slaves by the rebels, the President thought that his Proclamation would stimulate them to lay down their arms, reduce them to obedience, and help to bring back the rebel States; and their not doing so has now made the freedom of the slaves a part of the war. It is my opinion that there is not a man in this city that could be started to help the rebels one inch, for that would be suicide. There was two black men left with the rebels, because they had taken an active part for the rebels, and thought something might befall them if they staid behind, but there is not another man. If the prayers that have gone up for the Union army could be read out, you would not get through them these two weeks.

Seventh. State whether the sentiments you now express are those only of the colored people in the city, or do they extend to the colored population through the country, and what are your means of knowing the sentiments of those living in the country.

Answer. I think the sentiments are the same among the colored people of the State. My opinion is formed by personal communication in the course of my ministry, and also from the thousands that followed the Union army, leaving their homes and undergoing suffering. I did not think there would be so many; the number surpassed my expectation.

Eighth. If the rebel leaders were to arm the slaves, what would be its effect?

Answer. I think they would fight as long as they were before the bayonet, and just as soon as they could get away they would desert, in my opinion.

Ninth. What, in your opinion, is the feeling of the colored people about enlisting and serving as soldiers of the United States, and what kind of military service do they prefer?

Answer. A large number have gone as soldiers to Port Royal to be drilled and put in the service, and I think there is thousands of the young men that will enlist; there is something about them that, perhaps, is wrong; they have suffered so long from the rebels, that they want to meet and have a chance with them in the field.

Morale on the Home Front

Morale is a big factor in the ability of people to fight. What do these sources reveal about the problems each side had with morale, and to what extent did it appear to be influenced by events on the battlefield?

9 | By 1863, women and children in the South had streamed into cities, swelling the Confederacy's urban population. At the same time, a Union naval blockade and hoarding had helped to create shortages of basic necessities. In the face of skyrocketing inflation, bread or food riots, often carried out by women, became a common occurrence in the South. The biggest such riot occurred in April 1863 in Richmond, Virginia.

Southern Women Feeling the Effects of Rebellion and Creating Bread Riots (1863)

Source: Boston Athenaeum. From *Leslie's Illustrated Newspaper,* May 23, 1863.

10   Excerpt from Diary of Margaret Junkin Preston (1862)

April 3d, 1862: . . .

Darkness seems gathering over the Southern land; disaster follows disaster; where is it all to end? My very soul is sick of carnage. I loathe the word—*War*. It is destroying and paralyzing all before it. Our schools are closed—all the able-bodied men gone—stores shut up, or only here and there one open; goods not to be bought, or so exorbitant that we are obliged to do without. I actually dressed my baby all winter in calico dresses made out of the lining of an old dressing-gown; and G. in clothes concocted out of old castaways. As to myself, I rigidly abstained from getting a single article of dress in the entire past year, except shoes and stockings. Calico is not to be had; a few pieces had been offered at 40 cents per yard. Coarse, unbleached cottons are very occasionally to be met with, and are caught up eagerly at 40 cents per yard. Such material as we used to give ninepence for (common blue twill) is a bargain now at 40 cents, and then of a very inferior quality. Soda, if to be had at all, is 75 cents per lb. Coffee is not to be bought. We have some on hand, and for eight months have drunk a poor mixture, half wheat, half coffee. Many persons have nothing but wheat or rye.

These are some of the *very trifling* effects of this horrid and senseless war. Just now I am bound down under the apprehension of having my husband again enter the service; and if he goes, he says he will not return until the war closes, if indeed he come back alive. May God's providence interpose to prevent his going! His presence is surely needed at home; his hands are taken away by the militia draught, and he has almost despaired of having his farms cultivated this year. His overseer is draughted, and will have to go, unless the plea of sickness will avail to release him, as he has been seriously unwell. The [Virginia Military] Institute is full, two hundred and fifty cadets being in it; but they may disperse at any time, so uncertain is the tenure of everything now. The College [Washington College] has five students; boys too young to enter the army.

Source: Elizabeth Preston Allan, *The Life and Letters of Margaret Junkin Preston,* pp. 134–135. Copyright 1903 by Houghton Mifflin Company.

11 "Kate," whose first name only is known, wrote a letter to a friend in Baltimore after Robert E. Lee's army entered Frederick, Maryland.

"Kate," A Letter to a Friend (1862)

I wish, my dearest Minnie, you could have witnessed the transit of the Rebel army through our streets [of Frederick, Maryland] . . . Their coming was unheralded by any pomp and pageant whatever . . . Was this body of men, moving . . . along with no order . . . no two dresses alike, their officers hardly distinguishable from the privates—were these, I asked myself in amazement, were these dirty, lank, ugly specimens of humanity, with shocks of hair sticking through the holes in their hats, and the dust thick on their dirty faces, the men that had coped and encountered successfully and driven back again and again our splendid legions . . . ? I must confess, Minnie, that I felt humiliated at the thought that this horde of ragamuffins could set our grand army of the Union at defiance . . .

Source: The Civil War and Reconstruction: An Eyewitness History, edited by Joe Kirchberger. Reprinted with permission of Facts on File, Inc., NY. Copyright © 1991 by Joe H. Kirchberger.

12 Heyward recorded this during General William T. Sherman's march through Georgia in 1864.

Account of a Slaveholding Family During Sherman's March (1864)
PAULINE DeCARADEUC HEYWARD

May 23, 1864

I have no heart to keep this Journal or tell of the dreadful, fatal battles in Va. Oh my God! my heart is too heavy, I am entirely miserable. Many whom I know are killed & wounded. Robert Taft and Col. Shooter are killed. Capt. Barnwell killed. George Lalane wounded. Wise's Brigade was subjected to a fearful firing from the enemy at Druery's Bluff. I suppose John Cochran is wounded, from the moment I saw him I felt that his life would be given to this devouring war; and I am assured that he is dead or wounded, for I *feel it.*

Source: A Confederate Lady Comes of Age; The Journal of Pauline DeCaradeuc Heyward, 1863–1888, edited by Mary D. Robertson (University of South Carolina Press), pp. 36–37, 65–69.

CONCLUSION

The debate about the Civil War's outcome illustrates that historians are spectators in numerous arenas. In the Civil War, military leaders and events are in one amphitheater, political developments are in another, and economic and social developments are in still others. Of course, one venue is never entirely separate from another. Events on the battlefield affected in numerous ways politics and society in the North and South and vice versa. The challenge for historians is to demonstrate how they interacted.

The Civil War also illustrates the numerous ways in which historians explore the past. In searching for historical explanations, some historians look in several arenas. Others seek to understand everything about only one. Some historians conclude that leaders hold the key to understanding the past. Others insist that understanding the rank-and-file is more important. Some historians see large forces that give to events a certain inevitability. Others take a seat in the stands to witness all the unpredictable decisions and actions that took place.

Finally, the debate about the causes of the Civil War's outcome is also a reminder that the question of causation is at the heart of historical inquiry. If the Civil War's outcome was important in deciding the nation's future, then determining why the war turned out as it did is obviously crucial to our understanding of the nation's past. Yet to understand history we must know not only how the past shaped the future. As we shall see in the next chapter, it is necessary as well to appreciate how the power of interpreting past events contributes to our understanding of history.

FURTHER READING

Gabor S. Boritt, ed., *Why the Confederacy Lost* (New York: Oxford University Press, 1992).

David Donald, ed., *Why the North Won the Civil War* (Baton Rouge: Louisiana State University Press, 1960).

Joseph T. Glatthaar, *Partners in Command: The Relationship Between Leaders in the Civil War* (New York: Free Press, 1994).

James M. McPherson, *The Negro's Civil War* (New York: Ballantine Books, 1991).

Harold E. Straubing, ed., *Civil War Eyewitness Reports* (Hamden, Conn.: Archon Books, 1985).

NOTES

1. James Ford Rhodes, *History of the Civil War 1861–1865* (New York: Frederick Ungar, 1961), p. 238.

2. Ibid., p. 240.
3. Bruce Catton, *Gettysburg: The Final Fury* (Garden City, N.Y.: Doubleday, 1974), p. 88.
4. Allan Nevins, *Ordeal of Union* (New York: Macmillan, 1971), IV, 111.
5. Lee's last general order, quoted in Joe H. Kirchberger, *The Civil War and Reconstruction: An Eyewitness History* (New York: Facts on File, 1991), p. 264.

CHAPTER | 13

THE IMPORTANCE OF HISTORICAL INTERPRETATION: THE MEANING OF RECONSTRUCTION

This chapter provides two secondary sources and several primary sources on the highly controversial subject of Reconstruction.

Secondary Sources

1. Seeds of Failure in Radical Race Policy (1966), C. VANN WOODWARD
2. Negro State Legislators in South Carolina During Reconstruction (1982), THOMAS C. HOLT

Primary Sources

3. Colored Rule in a Reconstructed (?) State (1874)
4. The Ignorant Vote—Honors Are Easy (1876)
5. Black Response to a South Carolina White Taxpayer's Convention Appeal to Congress (1874)
6. Statement of Colored People's Convention in Charleston, South Carolina (1865)
7. A Republican Newspaper's Description of a Local Political Meeting (1867)
8. Testimony of Abram Colby (1872)
9. Lewis McGee to the Governor of Mississippi (1875)
10. Testimony of Emanuel Fortune (1872)
11. Testimony of Henry M. Turner (1872)

"*I* hope there will be . . . no bloody work after the war is over," declared Abraham Lincoln in April 1865, five days after Appomattox and hours before his assassination.[1] For the former Confederates whom Lincoln had in mind, there was no bloodshed; they were spared execution. However, there was much "bloody work" during Reconstruction, most of it visited upon the freedmen as Northerners and Southerners—black and white—struggled over the fate of the South and the place of African Americans in American society. And the "bloody work" did not end with the collapse of the last Reconstruction governments in 1877. The ground continued to be stained for a long time by those who challenged African-Americans' inferior position in American society.

At the same time, the passions ignited by Reconstruction have produced another kind of "bloody work" in historians' interpretations of Reconstruction. Few areas of American history have engendered more controversy and conflict than this brief period after the Civil War. And few historical periods have given rise to such conflicting lessons. For some students, Reconstruction was a tragic period of carpetbag and black rule that justified the South's redemption at the hands of conservative, white Democrats. For others, it proves just the opposite: the need for radical government action to achieve social justice. For still others, it demonstrates the depth of racism in American society. The battles over Reconstruction's meaning have been so heated that one historian declared the entire field "devastated by passion and belief." Another went so far as to call Reconstruction history itself a "dark and bloody ground."[2]

If Reconstruction is an example of the past's power to shape the future, it also clearly shows the power of historical interpretation. For generations after Reconstruction, African-Americans' second-class citizenship was maintained by law and the force of violence, and for much of that time, the historical justification for that position was found in the alleged horrors of Reconstruction. As historian Eric Foner put it, an image of these horrors "did much to freeze the mind of the white South in unalterable opposition to outside pressures for social change and to any thought of . . . eliminating segregation, or restoring the suffrage to disenfranchised blacks."[3] Thus to this historian, the idea of Reconstruction was responsible for much of the South's later attitudes toward African Americans. Historians see other consequences in Reconstruction as well. In this chapter, therefore, we cross Reconstruction's "bloody ground" by examining its lessons and meaning today.

SETTING

For several generations after the turn of the century, most scholarly accounts of Reconstruction reflected a white Southern point of view. Led by William A.

Dunning of Columbia University, most historians praised the Democratic governments established under Andrew Johnson's reconstruction plan and condemned the radicals in Congress and their "carpetbag" governments. Like the Democratic "Redeemers" who overthrew the Southern Republican governments in the 1870s, Dunning historians pictured the "black Republican" governments as a disgraceful stew of corruption, ignorance, and mismanagement. The foundation of this view was the assumption of white racial superiority. In their accounts African Americans were helpless, ignorant, disrespectful, or menacing. Not only did they have a small role in influencing events, but they were unprepared for a competitive market economy and unfit for a republican political system. The fact that they participated at all in the Republican governments was, in the words of one historian, to be "shuddered at."[4] The lesson of Reconstruction was clear. It had given too much freedom to the freedmen, and when it was over blacks had found their proper place in American society.

In the early twentieth century there were a few dissenters to the Dunning view, most notably the black historian W. E. B. Du Bois. His *Black Reconstruction in America* (1935) portrayed Reconstruction as a laudable attempt to create a more democratic and just society. Du Bois lambasted historians whose accounts ignored the role of former slaves in Reconstruction. Historians' racial bias, he said, clouded their objectivity. "I stand . . . literally aghast at what American historians have done to this field," declared Du Bois, who went on to claim that "one fact and one fact alone explains the attitude of most recent writers toward Reconstruction; they cannot conceive Negroes as men."[5] Few historians paid much attention to Du Bois's work, and the Dunning School remained historical orthodoxy for decades.

By the 1940s, however, a handful of historians began to chip away at its edifice. In 1940, for instance, Howard K. Beale called upon his colleagues to discard the notion that "their race must bar Negroes from social and economic equality."[6] Meanwhile black historian John Hope Franklin questioned the "facts" upon which Dunning historians had based their conclusions. Are these facts drawn, he asked, from "melodramatic" accounts of "wild-eyed conspirators" and "masses of barbarous freedmen"?[7] Still, the Dunning School did not come crashing down until the 1950s and 1960s. Then, as one historian put it, "Reconstruction history underwent its own reconstruction."[8]

The catalyst was changing racial attitudes and the growth of the civil rights movement. By the time such revisionist historians as Kenneth M. Stampp, Eric L. McKitrick, James McPherson, and Willie Lee Rose were finished, much of the Reconstruction story had been turned on its head. Later revisionists, in particular, demonstrated that the iniquity of "carpetbag rule" was a myth, especially when judged against political corruption elsewhere in the nation. They saw Radical Republicans as heroic champions of political and social change for the South. They contended that the great tragedy of Reconstruction was the Redeemers' assumption of power. The lesson was again clear. Reconstruction had been radical, but that had been a good thing. Those who were attempting to bring about a "second" Reconstruction with the civil rights movement could look to the first Reconstruction for inspiration.

When the demise of "Jim Crow" and the enfranchisement of blacks during the "second Reconstruction" of the 1960s failed to end the problems of racism and black poverty, some historians began again to revise their views about the first Reconstruction. By the 1970s, such postrevisionist historians as C. Vann Woodward, William Gillette, and Leon Litwack questioned just how radical Reconstruction had been. In the view of these postrevisionists, Reconstruction was limited by pervasive racism, by the conservativism of Republican leaders, and by the failure to distribute land to blacks. In other words, postrevisionists disagreed with both the Dunning and revisionist historians, who had at least agreed that Reconstruction had brought radical change. They questioned whether Reconstruction had wrought any lasting change at all. Rather than being too radical, it had actually been too conservative. Blacks had failed to achieve equality because the government had done too little and had failed to carry through on the promise of civil rights. Thus the postrevisionist interpretation taught an important lesson about the relationship between government action and social change.

Today the historical reconstruction of Reconstruction is not finished. In the late twentieth century, such historians as Eric Foner and Barbara Fields have placed the experience of former slaves rather than national political leaders and federal policy at the center of Reconstruction history. These historians have shown that African Americans were not just passive objects manipulated by whites. They have demonstrated the role that families, churches, political organizations, and other black institutions played in the quest for independence and equal citizenship. The social, economic, and political experiences of African Americans have revealed dramatic changes in the period. Once again, historians have begun to see some revolutionary aspects to Reconstruction.

INVESTIGATION

Historians need to understand how interpretations of Reconstruction reflect changing circumstances. They also must judge the validity of these interpretations and the lessons they teach. Your primary challenge, therefore, is to offer an explanation for the way Reconstruction turned out and a conclusion about its lessons for us. To do that, you must carefully evaluate two secondary selections' explanations for the outcome of Reconstruction. Both essays focus on the Republican program, but their analyses may yield different lessons about the Reconstruction experience. Primary sources relating to political developments during the period will help you evaluate these essays and reach conclusions about Reconstruction's lessons. Before you begin, read your textbook's discussion of this period, carefully noting its interpretation regarding Reconstruction's accomplishments and failures. Your analysis should address the following questions:

1. **What explanations do Sources 1 and 2 offer for the outcome of Reconstruction?** In what ways were Republican policies flawed?

2. **What do the two historians see as the most important forces affecting Republican policy?** What role do they assign to racism, as opposed to class or ideological divisions, in explaining the outcome of Reconstruction?

3. **What do the sources reveal about the problems involved in reconstructing the South?** What most important changes needed to occur for Reconstruction to have turned out differently? Is the explanation for the fate of Reconstruction to be found in the South or in the North?

4. **What were the most important changes that came about as a result of Reconstruction?** In the end, was Reconstruction too radical or too conservative?

SECONDARY SOURCES

1 │ In this analysis of the Republican's Reconstruction policy at the national level, historian C. Vann Woodward offers an explanation for the failure of Reconstruction. Who or what does Woodward blame? Note his view about the Republicans' motives and his conclusions about Reconstruction's legacy.

Seeds of Failure in Radical Race Policy (1966)
C. VANN WOODWARD

The Republican leaders were quite aware in 1865 that the issue of Negro status and rights was closely connected with the two other great issues of Reconstruction—who should reconstruct the South and who should govern the country. But while they were agreed on the two latter issues, they were not agreed on the first. They were increasingly conscious that in order to recon-

Source: C. Vann Woodward, "Seeds of Failure in Radical Race Policy," from Harold M. Hyman, ed., *New Frontiers of the American Reconstruction.* Copyright © 1966 by the Board of Trustees of the University of Illinois. Excerpted with permission of the University of Illinois Press.

struct the South along the lines they planned they would require the support and the votes of the freedmen. And it was apparent to some that once the reconstructed states were restored to the Union the Republicans would need the votes of the freedmen to retain control over the national government. While they could agree on this much, they were far from agreeing on the status, the rights, the equality, or the future of the Negro.

The fact was that the constituency on which the Republican congressmen relied in the North lived in a race-conscious, segregated society devoted to the doctrine of white supremacy and Negro inferiority. "In virtually every phase of existence," writes Leon Litwack with regard to the North in 1860, "Negroes found themselves systematically separated from whites. They were either excluded from railway cars, omnibuses, stagecoaches, and steamboats or assigned to special 'Jim Crow' sections; they sat, when permitted, in secluded and remote corners of theatres and lecture halls; they could not enter most hotels, restaurants, and resorts, except as servants; they prayed in 'Negro pews' in the white churches. . . . Moreover, they were often educated in segregated schools, punished in segregated prisons, nursed in segregated hospitals, and buried in segregated cemeteries." Ninety-three per cent of the 225,000 northern Negroes in 1860 lived in states that denied them the ballot, and 7 per cent lived in the five New England states that permitted them to vote. Ohio and New York had discriminatory qualifications that practically eliminated Negro voting. In many northern states discriminatory laws excluded Negroes from interracial marriage, from militia service, from the jury box, and from the witness stand when whites were involved. Ohio denied them poor relief, and most states of the old Northwest had laws carrying penalties against Negroes settling in those states. Everywhere in the free states the Negro met with barriers to job opportunities, and in most places he encountered severe limitations to the protection of his life, liberty, and property.

One political consequence of these racial attitudes was that the major parties vied with each other in their professions of devotion to the dogma of white supremacy. Republicans were especially sensitive on the point because of their antislavery associations. Many of them, like Senator Lyman Trumbull of Illinois, the close friend of Lincoln, found no difficulty in reconciling antislavery with anti-Negro views. "We, the Republican party," said Senator Trumbull in 1858, "are the white man's party. We are for free white men, and for making white labor respectable and honorable, which it can never be when negro slave labor is brought into competition with it." Horace Greeley the following year regretted that it was "the controlling idea" of some of his fellow Republicans "to prove themselves 'the white man's party,' or else all the mean, low, ignorant, drunken, brutish whites will go against them from horror of 'negro equality.'" Greeley called such people "the one-horse politicians," but he could hardly apply that name to Lyman Trumbull, nor for that matter to William H. Seward, who in 1860 described the American Negro as "a foreign and feeble element like the Indians, incapable of assimilation"; nor to Senator Henry Wilson of Massachusetts, who firmly disavowed any belief "in the mental or the intellectual equality of the African race with this proud and domineering white race of ours." Trumbull, Seward, and Wilson were the front rank of Republican leadership and they spoke the mind of the Middle West, the Middle Atlantic states, and New England. There is much evidence to sustain the estimate of W. E. B. Du Bois that "At the beginning of the [Civil] war probably not one white American in a hundred believed that Negroes could become an integral part of American democracy."

As the war for union began to take on the character of a war for freedom, northern attitudes toward the Negro paradoxically began to harden rather than soften. This hardening process was especially prominent in the north-western or middle western states where the old fear of Negro invasion was intensified by apprehensions that once the millions of slaves below the Ohio River were freed they would push northward—this time by the thousands and tens of thousands, perhaps in mass exodus, instead of in driblets of one or two who came furtively as fugitive slaves. The prospect of Negro immigration, Negro neighbors, and Negro competition filled the whites with alarm, and their spokesmen voiced their fears with great candor. "There is," Lyman Trumbull told the Senate, in April, 1862, "a very great aversion in the West—I know it to be so in my state—against having free negroes come among us. Our people want nothing to do with the negro." . . .

During the last two years of the war northern states began to modify or repeal some of their anti-Negro and discriminatory laws. But the party that emerged triumphant from the crusade to save the Union and free the slave was not in the best political and moral position to expand the rights and assure the equality of the freedman. There undoubtedly *did* emerge eventually an organization determined to overthrow Andrew Johnson's states' rights, white-supremacy policies and to take over the control of the South. But that was a different matter. On the issue of Negro equality the party remained divided, hesitant, and unsure of its purpose. The historic commitment to equality it eventually made was lacking in clarity, ambivalent in purpose, and capable of numerous interpretations. Needless to say, its meaning has been debated from that day to this.

The northern electorate the Republicans faced in seeking support for their program of Reconstruction had undergone no conversion in its wartime racial prejudices and dogmas. As George W. Julian, who deplored the fact himself, told his colleagues in the House in 1866, "the real trouble is that *we hate the negro*. It is not his ignorance that offends us, but his color."

In the years immediately following the war every northern state in which the electorate or the legislature was given the opportunity to express its views on issues involving the political rights of the Negro reaffirmed its earlier and conservative stand. This included the states that reconsidered—and reaf-firmed—their laws excluding Negroes from the polls. Five states with laws barring Negro testimony in court against whites repealed them, and a few acted against school segregation. Throughout these years, however, the North remained fundamentally what it was before—a society organized upon assumptions of racial privilege and segregation. . . .

This is not to suggest that there was not widespread and sincere concern in the North for the terrible condition of the freedmen in the South. There can be no doubt that many northern people were deeply moved by the reports of atrocities, peonage, brutality, lynchings, riots, and injustices that filled the press. Indignation was especially strong over the Black Codes adopted by some of the Johnsonian state legislatures, for they blatantly advertised the intention of some southerners to substitute a degrading peonage for slavery and make a mockery of the moral fruits of northern victory. What is sometimes overlooked in analyzing northern response to the Negro's plight is the continued apprehension over the threat of a massive Negro invasion of the North. The panicky fear that this might be precipitated by emancipation had been allayed in 1862 by the promises of President Lincoln and other Republican spokesmen that once slavery were abolished the freedmen would cheerfully settle down to remain in the South, that northern Negroes would be drawn back to the South, and that deportation and colonization abroad would take care of any threat of northern invasion that remained. But not only had experiments with deportation come to grief, but southern white persecution and abuse combined with the ugly Black Codes had produced new and powerful incentives for a Negro exodus while removal of the shackles of slavery cleared the way for emigration.

The response of the Republican Congress to this situation was the Civil Rights Act of 1866, later incorporated into the Fourteenth Amendment. Undoubtedly part of the motivation for this legislation was a humanitarian concern for the protection of the Negro in the South, but another part of the motivation was concerned with the protection of the white man in the North. Senator Roscoe Conkling of New York, a member of the Joint Committee of Fifteen who helped draft the Civil Rights provisions, was quite explicit on this point. "Four years ago," he said in the campaign of 1866, "mobs were raised, passions were roused, votes were given, upon the idea that emancipated negroes were to burst in hordes upon the North. We then said, give them liberty and rights at the South, and they will stay there and never come into a cold climate to die. We say so still, and we want them let alone, and that is one thing that this part of the amendment is for." . . .

The author and sponsor of the Civil Rights Act of 1866 was Senator Lyman Trumbull, the same man who had in 1858 described the Republicans as "the white man's party," and in 1862 had declared that "our people want nothing to do with the negro." He had nevertheless fought for the Freedman's Bureau and civil rights in the South. Trumbull's bill was passed and after Johnson's veto was repassed by an overwhelming majority. Limited in application, the Civil Rights Act did not confer political rights or the franchise on the freedmen.

The Fourteenth Amendment, which followed, was also equivocal on racial questions and freedmen's rights. Rejecting Senator Sumner's plea for a guarantee of Negro suffrage, Congress left that decision up to the southern states. It also left northern states free to continue the disfranchisement of Negroes, but it exempted them from the penalties inflicted on the southern states for the same decision. The real concern of the franchise provisions of the Fourteenth Amendment was not with justice to the Negro but with justice to the North. The rebel states stood to gain some twelve seats in the House if all Negroes were counted as a basis of representation and to have about eighteen fewer seats if none were counted. The amendment fixed apportionment of representation according to enfranchisement. . . .

After two years of stalling, of endless committee work and compromise, the First Reconstruction Act was finally adopted in the eleventh hour of the expiring Thirty-ninth Congress. . . .

. . . It was not primarily devised for the protection of Negro rights and the provision of Negro equality. Its primary purpose, however awkwardly and poorly implemented, was to put the southern states under the control of men loyal to the Union or men the Republicans thought they could trust to control those states for their purposes. So far as the Negro's future was concerned, the votes of the Congress that adopted the Reconstruction Act speak for themselves. Those votes had turned down Stevens' proposal to assure an economic foundation for Negro equality and Sumner's resolutions to give the Negro equal opportunity in schools and in homesteads and full civil rights. As for the Negro franchise, its provisions, like those for civil rights, were limited. The Negro franchise was devised for the passage of the Fourteenth Amendment and setting up the new southern state constitutions. But disfranchisement by educational and property qualifications was left an option, and escape from the whole scheme was left open by permitting the choice of military rule. No guarantee of proportional representation for the Negro population was contemplated and no assurance was provided for Negro officeholding. . . .

The standard southern reply to northern demands was the endlessly reiterated charge of hypocrisy. Northern radicals, as a Memphis conservative put it, were "seeking to fasten what they themselves repudiate with loathing upon the unfortunate people of the South." And he pointed to the succession of northern states that had voted on and defeated Negro suffrage. . . .

There was little in the Republican presidential campaign of 1868 to confute the southern charge of hypocrisy. The Chicago platform of May on which General Grant was nominated contained as its second section this formulation of the double standard of racial morality: "The guaranty by Congress of equal suffrage to all loyal men at the South was demanded by every consideration of public safety, of gratitude, and of justice, and must be maintained; while the question of suffrage in all the loyal [i.e., northern] States properly belongs to the people of those States." Thus Negro *dis*franchisement was assured in the North along with enfranchisement in the South. No direct mention of the Negro was made in the platform, nor was there mention of schools or homesteads for freedmen. Neither Grant nor his running mate Schuyler Colfax was known for any personal commitment to Negro rights, and Republican campaign speeches in the North generally avoided the issue of Negro suffrage.

Congress acted to readmit seven of the reconstructed states to the Union in time for them to vote in the presidential election and contribute to the Republic majority. In attaching conditions to readmission, however, Congress deliberately refrained from specifying state laws protecting Negroes against discrimination in jury duty, officeholding, education, intermarriage, and a wide range of political and civil rights. By a vote of 30 to 5 the Senate defeated a bill attaching to the admission of Arkansas the condition that "no person on account of race or color shall be excluded from the benefits of education, or be deprived of an equal share of the moneys or other funds created or used by public authority to promote education. . . ."

Not until the election of 1868 was safely behind them did the Republicans come forward with proposals of national action on Negro suffrage that was to result in the Fifteenth Amendment. They were extremely sensitive to northern opposition to enfranchisement. By 1869 only seven northern states had voluntarily acted to permit the Negro to vote, and no state with a substantial Negro population outside the South had done so. Except for Minnesota and Iowa, which had only a handful of Negroes, Nebraska, which entered the Union with Negro suffrage as a congressional requirement, and Wisconsin by decision of her Supreme Court, every postwar effort to enfranchise the Negro in northern states had gone down to defeat.

As a consequence moderates and conservatives among Republicans took over and dominated the framing of the Fifteenth Amendment and very strongly left their imprint on the measure. Even the incorrigibly radical Wendell Phillips yielded to their sway. Addressing other radicals he pled, ". . . for the first time in our lives we beseech them to be a little more politicians and a little less reformers." The issue lay between the moderates and the radicals. The former wanted a limited, negative amendment that would not confer suffrage on the freedmen, would not guarantee the franchise and take positive steps to protect it, but would merely prohibit its denial on the grounds of race and previous condition. The radicals demanded positive and firm guarantees, federal protection, and national control of suffrage. They would take away state control, North as well as South. They fully anticipated and warned of all the elaborate devices that states might resort to—and eventually did resort to—in order to disfranchise the Negro without violating the proposed amendment. These included such methods—later made famous—as the literacy and property tests, the understanding clause, the poll tax, as well as elaborate and difficult registration tricks and handicaps. But safeguards against them were all rejected by the moderates. . . .

The Fifteenth Amendment has often been read as evidence of renewed notice to the South of the North's firmness of purpose, as proof of its determination not to be cheated of its idealistic war aims, as a solemn rededication to those aims. Read more carefully, however, the Fifteenth Amendment reveals more deviousness than clarity of purpose, more partisan needs than idealistic aims, more timidity than boldness.

Signals of faltering purpose in the North such as the Fifteenth Amendment and state elections in 1867 were not lost on the South. They were carefully weighed for their implications for the strategy of resistance. The movement of counter Reconstruction was already well under way by the time the amendment was ratified in March, 1870, and in that year it took on new life in several quarters. Fundamentally it was a terroristic campaign of underground organizations, the Ku Klux Klan and several similar ones, for the intimidation of Republican voters and officials, the overthrow of their power, and the destruction of their organization. Terrorists used violence of all kinds, including murder by mob, by drowning, by torch; they whipped, they tortured, they maimed, they mutilated. It became perfectly clear that federal intervention of a determined sort was the only means of suppressing the movement and protecting the freedmen in their civil and political rights. . . .

Finally, to take a longer view, it is only fair to allow that if ambiguous and partisan motives in the writing and enforcement of Reconstruction laws proved to be the seeds of failure in American race policy for earlier generations, those same laws and constitutional amendments eventually acquired a wholly different significance for the race policy of a later generation. The laws outlasted the ambiguities of their origins. It is, in fact, impossible to account for such limited successes as the Second Reconstruction can claim without acknowledging its profound indebtedness to the First.

---

2   Unlike the previous selection, this essay examines Republican leaders in one reconstructed state. African-American historian Thomas C. Holt argues that South Carolina's black voters had clear aspirations during Reconstruction that were betrayed. How does Holt's view of the divisions among South Carolina's Republicans compare to Woodward's view of Republican divisions at the national level?

Negro State Legislators in South Carolina During Reconstruction (1982)

THOMAS C. HOLT

Reconstruction was "a frightful experiment which never could have given a real statesman who learned or knew the facts the smallest hope of success." Daniel H. Chamberlain, the last Republican governor of South Carolina, wrote this post-mortem a quarter of a century after he had been driven from office by a violent and fraudulent campaign to restore native whites to power in the fall and winter of 1876–77. Undoubtedly his view was colored by the social milieu of America at the turn of the century, when racism of the most virulent type had become the intellectual orthodoxy. On the other hand, these later reflections do not differ much from his assessment just two months after he had been forced to relinquish his office. In June 1877 he explained to William Lloyd Garrison that "defeat was inevitable under the circumstances of time and place which surrounded me. I mean here exactly that the uneducated negro was too weak, no matter what his numbers, to cope with the whites." In later years he described that weakness more explicitly: blacks were "an aggregation of ignorance and inexperience and incapacity."

The story of Reconstruction in South Carolina and elsewhere has been considerably revised since Chamberlain presented his analysis of its failure; yet, his basic premise is still shared by many revisionists. "The failure of the Radical government . . . was due not so much to its organization as to its personnel," Francis B. Simkins and Robert H. Woody wrote in 1932. Given the armed support of the federal establishment and the overwhelming black majority in South Carolina, the failure of the Republican regime could only have been caused by the venality, ignorance, and corruption of the leadership. Northern adventurers, mediocre scalawags, and uneducated, "excitable" freedmen constituted a legislature so guilty of mismanagement and fraud that the white minority rose up in justifiable wrath to put it down. Simkins and Woody were more charitable to the achievements of the Reconstruction regime than Chamberlain, but they leave little doubt that the inexperienced, undisciplined ex-slaves were the weak link in the Republican coalition.

While Simkins and Woody read the supposed incapacities of the slave into the failures of Reconstruction, a recent revisionist history of slavery reverses the process: the failures of the postemancipation political order help confirm

Source: Thomas Holt, "Negro State Legislature in South Carolina during Reconstruction," as appeared in Howard Rabinowitz, *Southern Black Leaders of the Reconstruction Era.* Copyright © 1982 University of Illinois Press.

a controversial description of the slave regime. Eugene Genovese, in *Roll, Jordan, Roll,* evokes a seminal, sometimes brilliant picture of the slave's worldview; but the essence of his argument is that that worldview was conditioned by a basically paternalistic master-slave relationship. Furthermore, the long-term consequence of that paternalism on blacks was to transform "elements of personal dependency into a sense of collective weakness." Although the slaves were able to manipulate the masters' paternalism in ways that reaffirmed their individual manhood, "they could not grasp their collective strength as a people and act like political men." This "political paralysis," this absence of "a stern collective discipline," not only accounts for their failure to mount significant slave revolts or to take advantage of their masters' strategic weakness to strike for freedom during the Civil War, but also explains their failure to "organize themselves more effectively in politics" after the war. In short, the behavior of the freedman confirms the conditioning of the slave.

But it is difficult to reconcile any of these views with events in South Carolina during Reconstruction. Certainly the cause of its failure cannot be laid to the political incapacity and inexperience of the black masses. They were uneducated. They were inexperienced. But they overcame these obstacles to forge a formidable political majority in the state that had led the South into secession. During the Reconstruction era 60 percent of South Carolina's population was black. This popular majority was turned into a functioning political majority as soon as Reconstruction legislation was put into effect with the registration for the constitutional convention in 1867. Despite violence and economic intimidation, the black electorate grew rather than declined between 1868 and 1876. The only effective political opposition before the election of 1876 came from so-called reform tickets, especially in 1870 and 1874. On these occasions, black and white Republican dissidents fused with Democrats to challenge the regular Republican party. But the strength of these challenges was generally confined to the predominantly white up-country counties and Charleston with its large white plurality and freeborn Negro bourgeoisie. Indeed, many observers condemned the unflinching, "blind" allegiance of black Republicans as evidence of their lack of political sophistication. But given the political alternatives and the records of so-called reform and fusion candidates, the black electorate could just as easily be credited with a high degree of political savvy. For South Carolina certainly, Frederick Douglass was right: the Republican party—despite its weaknesses and inadequacies—was the deck, all else the sea.

In an era when primaries were almost unknown and the nomination of party candidates was subject to manipulation by various intraparty factions, the voters had little leverage on the selection of their political leadership beyond the general election. It is difficult, therefore, to discern the political thinking and preferences of the masses of voters in any systematic fashion. However, one revealing report from an army chaplain just after the first election of Reconstruction offers some clues to the newly formed political mind of the ex-slaves. Chaplain F. K. Noble's literacy class for enlisted men of the 128th United States Colored Troop in Beaufort was polled on the advisability of immediate suffrage for illiterates. While "the more intelligent" favored a literacy qualification for voters, he observed, "those who learned less easily were in favor of immediate suffrage."

> One of the speakers—a black thick-lipped orator—commenced his speech as follows: "De chaplain say we can learn to read in short time. Now dat may be so with dem who are mo'heady. God hasn't made all of us alike. P'raps some *will* get an eddication in a little while. *I knows de next generation will.* But we'se a downtrodden people. We hasn't had no chance at all. De most uf us are slow and dull. We has bin kept down *a hundred years* and I tink it will take a *hundred years to get us back agin.* Dere fo' Mr. Chaplain, I tink we better not wait for eddication."

Despite efforts by some of their elected leaders to include literacy and poll-tax qualifications for suffrage in the new constitution, the 1868 Constitutional Convention vindicated the views of Chaplain Noble's class by bestowing the right to vote on all male citizens of the state. . . .

Thus it is difficult to see how freeborn whites could have utilized the political system to fulfill their aspirations and to satisfy their needs—given its inherent limitations—any more effectively than did the black ex-slaves. They identified and articulated their needs quite clearly and forcefully: they wanted land, economic justice, and education. They shrewdly discerned the organized political force most favorable to their objectives, the regular Republican party. They supported that party faithfully, despite the constant threat and reality of violence and economic reprisals. Whatever lessons their paternalistic masters had tried to instill did not paralyze them politically nor rob them of collective will. The black ex-slaves of South Carolina were, and acted as, political men.

Ultimately the failures of South Carolina Republicans must be laid not to their black ex-slave constituents but to the party leadership. Thus Simkins and Woody are partly right when they blame the personnel of the South Carolina government, but they are wrong to the extent that they find venality, corruption, ignorance, and inexperience as the primary causal factors. Surely there were venal men. Clearly corruption was rife. But there were corrupt Democrats before, during, and after Reconstruction, including the architects of the Democratic campaign of 1876, Martin W. Gary and M. C. Butler. Republican corruption merely offered a propagandistic advantage in the Democratic efforts to discredit the Radical regime. With the possible exception of the land-commission frauds, corruption was secondary to the major failures of that regime while in office and to its ability to sustain office. . . .

The biographical profile of the Negro leadership justifies neither the fears of white contemporaries nor the charges of many historians of that era. While the overwhelming majority of their constituents were black, illiterate, and propertyless ex-slave farmworkers, most of the political leadership was literate, a significant number had been free before the Civil War, many were owners of property, and most were employed in skilled or professional occupations after the war. At least one in four of the 255 Negroes elected to state and federal offices between 1868 and 1876 were of free origins. Indeed, counting only those for whom information is available, one finds that almost 40 percent had been free before the Civil War. Of those whose educational attainments are known, 87 percent were literate, and the 25 identifiable illiterates approximately matched the number who had college or professional training. Information on property ownership is available for little more than half the legislators. Seventy-six percent of these men possessed either real or taxable personal property, and 27 percent of them were worth $1,000 or more. Indeed, one in four held over $1,000 in real property alone. . . .

Thus, while there were differences in their respective social and economic backgrounds, neither the freeborn nor ex-slave legislators conform to the traditional stereotype of ignorant, pennyless sharecroppers rising from cotton fields to despoil the legislature and plunder the state. In truth, most of the freeborn and many of the slaveborn were a "middle" class of artisans, small farmers, and shopkeepers located on the social spectrum somewhere between the vast majority of Negro sharecroppers and the white middle and upper classes. Indeed, because of their education, class position, and general aspirations, they were more likely to embrace than reject the petty bourgeois values of their society.

Despite the obvious incentives for party unity, on "critical" roll calls the 89 Republican legislators voted with each other an average of 43.2 percent of the time as compared with 56.8 percent for the Democrats. Furthermore, the party's relative weakness does not appear to have been caused by any consistent bloc of dissidents. An examination of individual pairings of legislators reveals a lack of cohesion throughout the membership; there were hardly any strong pairs among Republicans comparable to pairings among Democrats. Twenty-eight percent of all possible Democratic pairs voted together on more than 80 percent of the roll calls, while only 3.9 percent of the Republican pairs scored as high. Furthermore, only 2 pairs of Republican members (0.06 percent) agreed on 90 percent or more of the roll calls, while there were 33 such pairs (6.6 percent) among Democrats. It is unlikely that the high turnover among the Republican membership is responsible for the difference between their political performance and that of the Democratic membership. The proportion of Democratic freshmen in the 1876 legislature was even greater than that of inexperienced Republicans, and veteran Republicans appear to have broken party ranks as frequently as did freshmen. The question remains then: Why were Republicans so fractious, especially when faced with the challenge of a reviving Democratic party?

Although no single bloc or segment of the Republican party was solely responsible for its weakness, there were political differences within the party that diminished its strength. Evidence suggests that the lack of party solidarity revealed on legislative roll calls reflected differences in aspirations and ideological orientations of various subgroups within the party. From the beginning of Reconstruction there had been conflict between white and Negro Republicans and between Negroes with roots in the freeborn mulatto bourgeoisie and the black ex-slaves. During the early meetings between 1865 and 1868, Negro aspirations for greater representation and power clashed with white efforts to maintain political control, and the demands for universal manhood suffrage and land reform articulated by black ex-slaves did not always resonate with the policy objectives and ideological orientation of their freeborn colleagues. At the end of the Reconstruction era, such differences in interests, perceptions, and orientation still undermined party unity. . . .

. . . [S]ome of the more important disagreements reflected overtones of racial and class antagonism. This was true certainly of the rather consistent deviation in the voting behavior of white and Negro Republicans. On critical roll calls a majority of the white Republicans opposed a majority of Negroes on at least one of every three votes. From 1872 to 1874 they opposed each other on an astounding 60 percent of the critical votes. Since white legislators constituted about a fifth to a third of the Republican legislative majority, such general and continuous defections could prove devastating to the party's fortunes.

It is not surprising that white Republican legislators did not see eye to eye with their black colleagues; there was ample evidence of distrust and animosity between these segments of the party. During the early years of Reconstruction, whites actively discouraged blacks from seeking their appropriate share of offices and power. On several occasions during the first two years of Republican rule, whites tried to exclude blacks from major state executive offices, congressional seats, judgeships, and even key party leadership posts. . . .

Given the nation's racial climate it is not surprising, perhaps, that tensions would develop between Negro and white Republicans or that they would often perceive policy issues differently; but there was no reason to expect that Negro legislators would be so much less cohesive among themselves than their Democratic rivals. For much of the Reconstruction period a unified Negro leadership could have dominated the legislature. Their overwhelming majority in the House together with a consistently large plurality in the Senate should have enabled Negroes, given inevitable absenteeism and defections among white Republicans and Democrats, to attain most of their major legislative objectives. But in fact Negro leaders were often at odds on legislative objectives, political policies, and ideology. Furthermore, the nature of their disunity followed a consistent pattern from the earliest political meetings and is best explained by reference to differences in their socioeconomic status and antebellum experience.

The most visible, though not necessarily most significant, divisions were between the black ex-slaves and those mulattoes who had been free before the war. The number of freeborn brown officeholders was far out of proportion to their share of the state's population, especially in the early conventions and legislative sessions, and their control of leadership positions was even more striking. In the 1868–70 House of Representatives, for example, half the committee chairmanships held by Negroes were filled by freeborn mulattoes. Between 1868 and 1876, over half the Negro state senators were drawn from this class and their average term of service was longer than that of black freedmen. Five of the seven Negroes elected to the state executive branch were freeborn brown men as well as four of the state's seven Negro congressmen.

Obviously, free brown men successfully offered themselves as prominent leaders of a predominantly black ex-slave electorate, but their very success aroused jealousy and political divisiveness within the party. In 1871 black leader Martin R. Delany complained to Frederick Douglass about mulatto dominance of patronage positions. In 1870 William H. Jones, Jr., black representative from Georgetown, publicly ridiculed Joseph H. Rainey, his mulatto rival for the state Senate because of his extremely light complexion. State Senator William B. Nash, a black ex-slave, once referred to his mulatto colleagues as "simply mongrels."

It is misleading, however, to consider these intraracial tensions as merely a consequence of differences in skin color and antebellum origins. The fact is that among South Carolina Negroes a light complexion and free origins correlated very strongly with other indicators of bourgeois class status; mulattoes and those who had been free before the war were more likely to own property and thus to enjoy higher status than black ex-slaves, who were more likely to be propertyless. These general patterns were reflected in the General Assembly, where legislators of free origins were generally better educated than the freedmen, more likely to own property, and more likely to be employed as artisans or in a profession rather than as farmworkers. These objective differences, as minor as they might have appeared to whites, generated not only consciousness of class differences but social institutions that confirmed and reinforced those differences. . . .

It appears that these differences in social background and status produced differing perspectives on public policy. During the 1868 Constitutional Convention, for example, black ex-slave delegates voted with other Negro delegates an average of 72 percent of the time, while freeborn mulatto delegates averaged 67.9 percent. The differences in voting behavior were more dramatic when sensitive issues of land reform and confiscation were debated. Robert C. De Large's resolution to halt the disfranchisement of ex-Confederates and the confiscation of their property was one early test of radical and conservative tendencies in the convention. Although De Large's motion was opposed by a majority of the Negro delegates, it drew its heaviest support from mulatto delegates who had been free before the war, about 40 percent of whom supported the resolution, and its heaviest opposition from those blacks who had been slaves, about 75 percent of whom opposed it. Debates on whether to impose literacy and poll-tax requirements for voting reveal similar divisions. Delegates from the antebellum free class argued strenuously, though unsuccessfully, that illiterates and persons failing to pay a poll tax should not be allowed to vote. . . .

Undoubtedly, for many of these men their political positions reflected specific class interest. Thomas Hamilton, for example, was a rice planter in Beaufort; his view of labor issues was, as one would expect, quite different from that of most of his constituents. During the violent strike in the summer of 1876, Hamilton lectured his workers and constituents about the common interests of employers and laborers. "You complain now that you don't get enough for your labor, but would you not have greater cause of complaint if you destroy entirely their [the planters'] ability to pay you at all? I am a rice planter, and employ a certain number of hands. Now, if my work is not permitted to go on, how can I gather my crops and pay my laborers, and how can my laborers support their families: They are dependent upon their labor for support; they are not calculated for anything else; they can't get situations in stores as clerks; they can't all write, nor are they fitted for anything else. There is but one course for you to pursue, and that is to labor industriously and live honestly." Evidently Hamilton later recognized some affinity between his interests and those of white planters; he joined the Democratic party after the election of 1876.

For most Negro leaders, however, the differences probably resulted less from specific class interests than general differences in consciousness and modes of perception. Negro and white Republicans shared generalized, though not clearly articulated, "progressive" values and orientations. Negroes were unanimous in their support for civil rights and free public education, for example. There was also general support for expanded social services, such as mental asylums and almshouses, and for state-sponsored economic developments, such as railroad construction and phosphate mining. But as we have seen, measures to regulate the new farm-labor system and to reform land ownership, both of which were critical issues for the majority of their constituents, produced no unified positions and no effective programs from the legislators.

A closer examination of two issues, education and labor legislation, suggests the political difference that social class differences made in South Carolina. The establishment of an educational system was one of the most striking successes of the Republican regime. The system did not function as well as its founders had hoped, but its creation firmly established the principle of free public education in a state that had not had such a system before the war. It also provided the infrastructure on which later systems could be based. The freedmen enthusiastically took advantage of the new opportunity, and their leaders endorsed public schooling as a major goal of the postwar period. A resolution passed at one of the early conventions declared, "Knowledge is power." Curiously, in the view of some leaders, the endorsement of education as a major objective for the new black citizens served also to set off the uneducated as degraded and unfit to participate in public life. Thus convention delegates who advocated literacy and poll-tax qualifications for suffrage, all of whom were freeborn brown men of well-to-do backgrounds, were motivated by a desire to encourage education among the masses. According to this view, uneducated adults would be encouraged to go to school to avoid disfranchisement and the poll taxes levied on registered voters would pay the costs of maintaining the school system. As we have seen, the black freedmen in the convention as well as those in Chaplain Noble's class perceived the issue differently. A literacy requirement would be political suicide for a largely illiterate black electorate, so they decided they "had better not wait for eddication."

Despite their differences, legislators were successful in passing laws establishing schools for all. But their efforts to regulate the evolving free-labor market were much less productive. Two of the scores of bills introduced on labor subjects serve to illustrate the differing perceptions among Republicans. One, introduced by James Henderson, a Negro farmer from Newberry County, on January 8, 1870, would have established labor-contract agents to directly supervise and monitor relations between planters and workers. Several days later a substitute bill was introduced by George Lee, a Negro lawyer from Charleston. Lee's bill relied on the regular court system to settle contract disputes and gave the laborer a ninety-day lien on the crop at harvest. Thus, rather than direct state intervention to resolve labor disputes, the disputants had to assume the initiative and expense of litigation themselves. Normally the planter was better situated to undertake such risks than was the worker.

Clearly, many of the legislators preferred a laissez-faire approach to regulating the labor market. John Feriter, a white native Republican, declared that the "law of supply and demand must regulate the matter"; and Reuben Tomlinson, a white northern Republican and former abolitionist, insisted, "I don't believe it is in the power of the General Assembly to do anything except to give them [farmworkers] equal rights before the law." Apparently a majority of both white and black legislators agreed with Feriter and Tomlinson; they voted for Lee's bill, which approached this laissez-faire ideal, and against Henderson's bill, which advocated state regulation. However, the minority voting for Henderson's bill included 48 percent of the ex-slaves as compared with only 11 percent of the freeborn, and 35 percent of the blacks in contrast with only 18 percent of the mulattoes. It would appear then that those whose origins were closer to the masses of the electorate saw labor problems differently than their colleagues from more privileged backgrounds. . . .

The failure of South Carolina's Reconstruction then was not caused by a weak and ignorant electorate. Despite the economic threats and physical terrors of the 1876 campaign, black freedmen turned out in force and delivered a record vote to Republican candidates. True, there was "political paralysis," an absence of "stern collective discipline," and a failure of will; but these were shortcomings of the Republican leadership, not of the masses of black voters. Divisions among the leaders—between white and black and among Negroes themselves—diminished the power these voters had entrusted to them and betrayed the aspirations they had clearly articulated. The freedmen made an amazing transformation after the Civil War; slaves became political men acting forcefully to crush the most cherished illusions of their former masters. The tragedy of Reconstruction is that they received so much less than they gave.

PRIMARY SOURCES

These sources offer additional insights into black political involvement during Reconstruction and the forces affecting Reconstruction's outcome. As you examine these sources, remember that they reflect attitudes as well as conditions.

Thomas Nast's Cartoons

Thomas Nast's cartoons appeared in *Harper's Weekly.* A Northern Republican, Nast reflected and shaped "respectable" opinion in the North. Note his view about black political activity during Reconstruction. In what ways did Northern white opinion shape the outcome of Reconstruction?

3 | Colored Rule in a Reconstructed (?) State (1874)

COLORED RULE IN A RECONSTRUCTED (?) STATE.—[See Page 242.]

Note: The female figure in the upper right corner is Columbia, the symbol of America.
Source: Boston Athenaeum. *Harper's Weekly,* March 14, 1874.

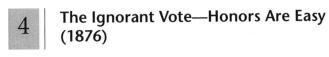

4 | The Ignorant Vote—Honors Are Easy (1876)

Note: The figure on the right is a caricature of an Irishman.
Source: Boston Anthenaeum. *Harper's Weekly,* December 9, 1876.

5 | The Associated Press wired a white Taxpayers' Convention's appeal to Congress and to newspapers across the country, but it refused to send this reply over the wires. The circulation of this response was therefore confined to the black press. What does this document reveal about obstacles blacks confronted as they asserted themselves politically during Reconstruction?

Black Response to a South Carolina White Taxpayers' Convention Appeal to Congress (1874)

Certain citizens of South Carolina, styling themselves "The Taxpayers' Convention," have memorialized your honorable bodies to grant them relief from unjust burdens and oppressions, alleged by them to have been imposed by the Republican State Government. We, the undersigned, members of the State Central Committee of the Union Republican party of South Carolina, beg leave to submit the following counter statement and reply:

The statement that "the annual expenses of the government have advanced from four hundred thousand dollars before the war to two millions and a half at the present time," is entirely incorrect, and the items of expenditures given to illustrate and prove this statement are wholly inaccurate and untrue, and skillfully selected to deceive.

We present a true statement of the appropriation of the fiscal year before the war, beginning October 1, 1859, and ending September 30, 1860, and the fiscal year beginning November 1, 1872, and ending October 31, 1873:

	1859–60	1872–73
Salaries	$81,100	$194,989
Contingents	73,000	47,600
Free schools	75,000	300,000
State Normal School	8,704	25,000
Deaf, dumb and blind	8,000	16,000
Military academies	30,000	. . . .
Military contingencies	100,000	20,000
Roper Hospital	3,000	. . . .
State Lunatic Asylum	. . . .	77,500
State Normal and High School	5,000	. . . .
Jurors and Constables	50,000	. . . .
State Orphan House (colored)	. . . .	20,000
State Penitentiary	. . . .	40,000
Sundries	184,427	444,787
	$618,231	$1,184,876

Source: The New National Era, April 16, 1874.

By the census of 1860, there were in South Carolina at that time 301,214 free population and 402,406 slaves. By the census of 1870 there were 705,606 free population. In 1860, the slave was no charge on the State Government, save when he was hung for some petty misdemeanor, and the State compelled to pay his loss.

It would be, therefore, but just and fair to divide the amount appropriated in 1859–60: $618,231 by the then free population, 301,214, and it will be found that the cost of governing each citizen was $2.05. Then divide the amount appropriated in 1872–73 by the free population now 705,606, and the cost of governing each citizen is $1.67–$2.05 during the boasted Democratic period and $1.67 under the so-called corrupt Radical rule—a difference of 38 cents *per capita* in favor of the latter. So that if the Democrats had the same number of free citizens to govern in 1859–60 that the Republicans had in 1972–73, it would have cost them $264,616 more than it has cost us.

The State organized upon a free basis necessarily created a larger number of officers, and, therefore, a larger amount of salaries. We are not ashamed of the fact that our appropriation for schools in 1872–73 is four times greater than in 1859–60. Ignorance was the corner-stone of slavery and essential to its perpetuity. Now in every hamlet and village in our state, the schoolmaster is abroad. In 1857 the number of scholars attending the free schools was only 19,356 while in 1873 the number of scholars attending the schools was 85,753.

There were no appropriations for the State Lunatic Asylum and Penitentiary in 1859–60. The Lunatic Asylum was then supported by the friends of its wealthy inmates, but in 1872–73 the State assumed its support and made liberal appropriation for its unfortunate patients. The erection of the Penitentiary was not begun until after the war and there was therefore no appropriation for it in 1859–60.

The appropriation in 1872–73 for military purposes was but $20,000. We had no occasion to appropriate $130,000 for military academies and contingencies in order to train the young to strike at the nation's life, and to purchase material for the war of secession.

There was no appropriation in 1859–60 for a colored State Orphan Home. The colored orphans that were then uncared for were free, but their parents, when living, were heavily taxed to support white orphans, while their own children, after their death, were neglected. . . .

The gentlemen who have assembled, constituting themselves representatives of the so-called taxpayers, are not what they would have the country believe. They are the prominent politicians of the old regime—the former ruling element of the State—who simply desire to regain the power they lost by their folly of secession.

The Republicans admit the existence of evils among them. They have committed errors which they deeply regret. But those errors are being daily corrected. There are enough able and good men among those who have the present charge of the government to right every existing wrong. They are determined to do so. The difficulties under which they have labored have been increased ten-fold by the hostility and the opposition of the Democratic party ever since Reconstruction. This is their third effort to regain power. First they expected it through the election of Seymour and Blair; second, through the midnight murders and assassinations of Ku Kluxism; and now, thirdly, by the distortion and misrepresentation of facts, in order to create a public sentiment in their favor and obtain relief from Congress.

Relying upon the justice of our cause we submit these facts to your impartial judgment.

> Samuel J. Lee, Chairman, *pro tem,* S. A. Swails,
> W. M. Thomas, Joseph Crews, H. H. Ellison,
> P. R. Rivers, John R. Cochran, Robert Smalls,
> E. W. M. Mackey, John Lee, H. L. Shrewsbury,
> George F. McIntyre, Wilson Cook, John H. McDevitt

Black Political Attitudes

As you read the following sources, consider what they show about black aspirations and divisions.

6 | Statement of Colored People's Convention in Charleston, South Carolina (1865)

Heretofore we have had no firesides that we could call our own. The measures which have been adopted for the development of white men's children have been denied to ours. The laws which have made white men great, have degraded us, because we were colored. But now that we are freemen, now that we have been lifted up by the providence of God to manhood, we have resolved to come forward, and, like MEN, speak and *act* for ourselves.

We have not come together in battle array to assume a boastful attitude and to talk loudly of high-sounding principles or unmeaning platforms. Although we feel keenly our wrongs, still we come together in a spirit of meekness and of patriotic good will to all the people of the state. Thus we would address you, not as enemies, but as friends and fellow countrymen who desire to dwell among you in peace.

We ask for no special privileges or favors. We ask only for *even-handed* Justice. We simply ask that we shall be recognized as men.

Source: Proceedings of the Colored People's Convention of the State of South Carolina (Charleston, 1865).

7 | A Republican Newspaper's Description of a Local Political Meeting (1867)

A meeting of colored people held at Montgomery was a remarkable one. A large room was filled with men from different parts of the state. One very intelligent, educated Negro said "I don't want the colored people to vote for five years. Here, and for twenty miles away they'll vote right, but farther off they will vote for 'Mass William' and 'Mass John' to get their good will."

Whereupon an old Negro called out, "Every creature has got an instinct—the calf goes to the cow to suck, the bee to the hive. We's a poor humble degraded people but we know our friends. We'd walk fifteen miles in wartime to find out about the battle. We can walk fifteen miles and more to find out how to vote."

Source: The Loyal Georgian, April 10, 1867.

White Violence

The following sources are accounts of violence against black Republicans during Reconstruction. What do these accounts reveal about the failure of Reconstruction policy?

 Colby was a black member of the Georgia legislature. His testimony was before a joint committee of Congress.

Testimony of Abram Colby (1872)

On the 29th of October 1869, they broke my door open, took me out of bed, took me to the woods and whipped me three hours or more and left me for dead. They said to me, "Do you think you will ever vote another damned radical ticket?" I said, "I will not tell you a lie." I supposed they would kill me anyhow. I said, "If there was an election tomorrow, I would vote the radical ticket." They set in and whipped me a thousand licks more, with sticks and straps that had buckles on the ends of them.

Q—What is the character of those men who were engaged in whipping you?

Source: Testimony Taken by the Joint Select Committee to Inquire into the Condition of Affairs in the Late Insurrectionary States (Washington, 1872).

A—Some are first-class men in our town. One is a lawyer, one a doctor, and some are farmers. They had their pistols and they took me in my night-clothes and carried me from home. They hit me five thousand blows. I told President Grant the same that I tell you now. They told me to take off my shirt. I said, "I never do that for any man." My drawers fell down about my feet and they took hold of them and tripped me up. Then they pulled my shirt up over my head. They said I had voted for Grant and had carried the Negroes against them. About two days before they whipped me they offered me $5,000 to go with them and said they would pay me $2500 in cash if I would let another man go to the legislature in my place. I told them that I would not do it if they would give me all the county was worth.

The worst thing about the whole matter was this. My mother, wife and daughter were in the room when they came. My little daughter begged them not to carry me away. They drew up a gun and actually frightened her to death. She never got over it until she died. That was the part that grieves me the most.

Q—How long before you recovered from the effects of this treatment?

A—I have never got over it yet. They broke something inside of me. I cannot do any work now, though I always made my living before in the barber-shop, hauling wood, &c.

Q—You spoke about being elected to the next legislature?

A—Yes, sir, but they run me off during the election. They swore they would kill me if I staid. The Saturday night before the election I went to church. When I got home they just peppered the house with shot and bullets.

Q—Did you make a general canvas there last fall?

A—No, sir. I was not allowed to. No man can make a free speech in my county. I do not believe it can be done anywhere in Georgia.

Q—You say no man can do it?

A—I mean no Republican, either white or colored.

9 | Lewis McGee to the Governor of Mississippi (1875)

Bolton, October 13, 1875

Gov. Ames:

I am here in Jackson and cannot leave. The white peoples is looking for me on every train and have got men on every road watching for me. They have sworn to take my life because I am president of the club at Bolton. I wish you would, if please, protect me. I am in a bad fix, with about 6 bales of cotton in

Source: Report of the Select Committee to Inquire into the Mississippi Election of 1875, Senate Report No. 527, 44th Congress, 1st Session.

the field and 150 bushel of corn to gather; no one to tend to it when I am gone. Tell me what to do, if you please.

Lewis McGee,
President of Bolton's Republican Club

Black Landowning

The limited economic opportunities that most blacks had at the end of the Civil War were realized on the land. The following testimony before a congressional committee investigating conditions in the former Confederate states in 1872 reveals something about former slaves' chances to secure land. Consider why Republican political leaders did not attempt to create more opportunities for the freedmen.

 ## Testimony of Emanuel Fortune (1872)

They will not sell our people any land. They have no disposition to do so. They will sell a lot now and then in a town, but nothing of any importance.

Q—What could you get a pretty good farm for—how much an acre?

A—Generally from $10 to $15 an acre. Very poor people cannot afford that.

Q—You can get it if you have the money?

A—They will not sell it in small quantities. I would have bought forty acres if the man would have sold me less than a whole tract. They hold it in that way so that colored people cannot buy it. The lands we cultivate generally are swamp or lowlands.

Q—Is there not plenty of other land to buy?

A—Not that is worth anything. I do not know of any Government land that will raise cotton.

Source: Testimony Taken by the Joint Select Committee to Inquire into the Condition of Affairs in the Late Insurrectionary States (Washington, D.C., 1872).

 ## Testimony of Henry M. Turner (1872)

Q—You say that colored men employed in the country have not been able to get anything for their labor. Why is that?

Source: Testimony Taken by the Joint Select Committee to Inquire into the Condition of Affairs in the Late Insurrectionary States (Washington, D.C., 1872).

A—During the year there is very little money paid to them and if they want to obtain provisions or clothing they are given an order on some store. At the end of the year these little bills are collected and however small a quantity of things have been taken, almost always the colored man is brought into debt. That is alleged as a reason why they should be bound to stay with their employers and work out what they say they owe them.

Q—A sort of practical peonage?

A—Yes, sir. Whenever there is fear that the laborer will go to work with someone else the following year, he is apt to come out $25 to $30 in debt and his employer calls upon him to work it out.

There was a bill introduced the other day to make it a penal offense for a laborer to break his contract. For instance, a white man writes out a contract. He reads the contract to the black man and, of course, reads just what he pleases. When the black man takes it to somebody else and gets him to read it, it reads quite differently. Among other things there is a provision in the contract that he must not go to any political gathering or meeting. If he does, he will lose $5 for every day that he is absent, and yet he is to receive only $50 or $75 a year. Every day that he is sick, a dollar or a dollar and a half is to be deducted. The man may want to quit and work for some person else who will pay him better wages.

Q—The effect of the legislation would be to render the laborer practically a slave during the period of his contract?

A—Or else he would be liable to punishment by imprisonment. There is no doubt that they will pass some kind of law to that effect.

Q—With a view to harmonize the relations of labor and capital?

A—Yes, sir, that is the phrase.

CONCLUSION

"In a certain sense," nineteenth-century writer Thomas Carlyle once said, "all men are historians."[9] As we saw at the beginning of this volume, all of us use history to make sense of the past. Whether trained as historians or not, we do so out of a shared assumption that the past has influenced the present. There are few clearer demonstrations of the validity of that assumption than the history of Reconstruction.

Reconstruction also shows that, as one historian put it, "To learn about the present in the light of the past is to learn about the past in the light of the present."[10] In other words, it demonstrates that all of us draw lessons from the past and that these lessons are influenced by our times and circumstances. Unlike most early twentieth-century historians, who argued that African Americans enjoyed too much freedom during Reconstruction, historians today debate how many political and economic opportunities freedmen really had. Thus, modern historians' views of Reconstruction no longer justify the need for a racial caste system. Instead, Reconstruction now yields lessons about racism's influence in American society, the power of government action to change people's circumstances, and the ability of people to control their lives under difficult conditions.

These lessons are relevant for us. Americans continue to confront the enduring problems of poverty and inequality and to debate the government's responsibility for the welfare of people. Reconstruction's "bloody ground," therefore, continues to teach lessons that may justify present-day policies. For that reason, it remains a powerful example of why all of us should care about interpretations of the past.

FURTHER READING

Richard H. Abbott, *The Republican Party and the South 1855–1877* (Chapel Hill: University of North Carolina Press, 1986).

W. E. B. Du Bois, *Black Reconstruction* (New York: Russell and Russell, 1935).

Eric Foner, *A Short History of Reconstruction, 1863–1877* (New York: Harper and Row, 1990).

Michael Perman, *Emancipation and Reconstruction 1862–1879* (Arlington Heights: Harlan Davidson, 1987).

Dorothy Sterling, ed., *The Trouble They Seen: Black People Tell the Story of Reconstruction* (Garden City, N.Y.: Doubleday, 1976).

NOTES

1. Quoted in James Truslow Adams, *America's Tragedy* (New York: Scribner's, 1934), p. 371.
2. W. E. B. Du Bois, *Black Reconstruction in America* (New York: Russell and Russell, 1935), p. 725; Bernard Weisberger, "The Dark and Bloody Ground of Reconstruction Historiography," *Journal of Southern History*, 25 (November 1959), 427–447.
3. Eric Foner, *A Short History of Reconstruction, 1863–1877* (New York: Harper and Row, 1990), pp. 258–259.
4. Quoted in Eric Foner, *Reconstruction: America's Unfinished Revolution, 1863–1877* (New York: Harper and Row, 1988), p. xx.
5. Du Bois, *Black Reconstruction,* pp. 725, 726.
6. Howard K. Beale, "On Rewriting Reconstruction History," *American Historical Review,* 45 (July 1940), 819.
7. Quoted in Eric Anderson and Alfred A. Moss, Jr., eds., *The Facts of Reconstruction: Essays in Honor of John Hope Franklin* (Baton Rouge: Louisiana State University Press, 1991), p. 219.

8. Michael Les Benedict, "Preserving the Constitution: The Conservative Basis of Radical Reconstruction," *Journal of American History,* 61 (June 1974), 65.

9. Thomas Carlyle, "On History," *The Complete Works of Thomas Carlyle* (New York: Kelmscott Society, 1869), V, Part II, 60.

10. E. H. Carr, *What Is History?* (New York: Alfred A. Knopf, 1962), p. 86.